A Confederate in the Colorado Gold Fields

A Confederate
in the Colorado Gold Fields

BY DANIEL ELLIS CONNER

Edited and with an Introduction by
DONALD J. BERTHRONG and ODESSA DAVENPORT

University of Oklahoma Press : Norman

BY DONALD J. BERTHRONG

The Southern Cheyennes (Norman, 1963)

BY ODESSA DAVENPORT

Scotsman in Buckskin (New York, 1963)

EDITED BY DONALD J. BERTHRONG AND ODESSA DAVENPORT

Daniel Ellis Conner, *Joseph Reddeford Walker and the Arizona Adventure* (Norman, 1956)

Daniel Ellis Conner, *A Confederate in the Colorado Gold Fields* (Norman, 1970)

The paper on which this book is printed bears the watermark of the University of Oklahoma Press and has an effective life of at least three hundred years.

International Standard Book Number: 0-8061-0891-6

Library of Congress Catalog Card Number: 70-88149

Copyright 1970 by the University of Oklahoma Press, Publishing Division of the University. Composed and printed at Norman, Oklahoma, U.S.A., by the University of Oklahoma Press. First edition.

Acknowledgments

Edwin W. Sandison of Wilmington, California, by keeping the original Daniel Ellis Conner manuscript secure for forty years, deserves our greatest recognition. We must again thank those who aided in the verification of events published in *Joseph Reddeford Walker and the Arizona Adventure*. Others, too, have eased our task in preparing this second volume from Conner's manuscript for publication. We especially want to thank Mrs. Alice E. Trauber, postmistress of Beulah, Colorado; Ralph C. Taylor, news director and feature writer for the Pueblo, Colorado, *Star-Journal and Chieftan;* Agnes Wright Spring, formerly assistant to the president of the State Historical Society of Colorado; Nyle H. Miller of the Kansas State Historical Society; Jay B. Wilson of Platte County, Missouri; and Mrs. Sandra Stewart of the Phillips Collection, the University of Oklahoma Library. Professors George J. Goodman, George M. Sutton, Cluff E. Hopla, and Charles C. Carpenter of the University of Oklahoma patiently led us to useful information in the natural sciences. Rhio Berthrong helped by examining the files of the Denver, Colorado, *Rocky Mountain News* and by carefully reading the final, edited draft of the manuscript.

DONALD J. BERTHRONG
ODESSA DAVENPORT

January 8, 1970

Introduction

A young Kentuckian standing on a street corner in Leavenworth, Kansas, on a fall evening in 1858, heard excited men discussing the discovery of gold near Pikes Peak. Few knew exactly where the gold had been found, but this mattered little. Daniel Ellis Conner, not quite twenty-one years of age, listened with interest and determined to make the journey to those gold fields in search of fortune and adventure.

Conner had been educated in his native city of Bardstown, Kentucky, and had also attended Hanover College, Hanover, Indiana. Employment being scarce following the panic of 1857, Conner had turned to the frontier to seek his livelihood. Failing to find work as anticipated on the western railroads, Conner had found lodging with relatives at Ridgely, Missouri, but in 1859 he joined the horde of gold-seekers swarming across the high plains to the boulder-strewn canyons and gulches of Colorado's mountains.

For gold, men starved and suffered from heat and cold while pursuing the wisp of rumor that a bonanza lay just ahead. Tantalizing reports of gold stemmed from the earliest Spanish, French, and English operations into the southern Rocky Mountains. When Americans gained control of a portion of those rugged mountains and plateaus, their explorers, like Zebulon Montgomery Pike, also hinted of extensive deposits of precious metals. So it continued: a party of mountain men found gold near Vazquez, or Clear Creek, in 1833; ten years later Rufus B. Sage also noted the existence of mineral wealth in Colorado; and Indians, it was reported, traded gold for supplies at Fort Laramie in 1857. Whatever might have been the significance of this early information, two separate incidents in the 1850's culminated in the rush to the mountains of Colorado.

A group of Cherokee Indians, on their way to California, discovered gold on Ralston's Creek on June 21, 1850. In this party was John Beck, who became the principal promoter of the Cherokee-Russell expedition of 1858. When the Cherokees returned from California to their eastern homes, Beck continued to plan and correspond, in hopes of gathering a party to search for the source of the gold found in 1850. Groups of men began organizing by the spring of 1858 in Georgia, in the Cherokee Nation, and in Missouri, and these parties merged before reaching Cherry Creek, at the site of present Denver, Colorado. In all, 104 men gathered at the mouth of Cherry Creek on June 24, 1858, but within a few weeks the greatest portion of them became discouraged and abandoned hope of finding gold. Only 13 men, led by William Greeneberry Russell (commonly called Green Russell), grimly continued panning the sands of the South Platte until productive diggings were found some eight miles above the mouth of Cherry Creek. Following the initial discovery, paying quantities of gold were located during the remainder of July and August, 1858.

Independent of these events, another circumstance led other men on a trek to the Rockies. In the autumn of 1857, Fall Leaf, a well-known Delaware Indian, who had accompanied Colonel E. V. Sumner's expedition, displayed to John Easter of Lawrence, Kansas, several gold nuggets. As the news of Fall Leaf's gold spread through the Kansas community, men made their plans. In May, 1858, the Lawrence party was ready to depart. When Fall Leaf refused to accompany the Kansans, they headed for Pikes Peak, the most prominent landmark of the supposed gold region. Unable to find gold in the vicinity of Pikes Peak, the Lawrence party proceeded to Cherry Creek, where they, too, found gold.

Although limited amounts of gold were found by these early parties, exaggerated stories buoyed up the hopes of many a man left destitute by the depression which followed in the wake of the panic of 1857. Credulous men believed the reports which stated that individuals had accumulated thousands of dollars in gold from the mines of Pikes Peak. By the winter of 1858–59, parties were organizing in the communities throughout the Missouri and Mississippi valleys. During the spring and summer of 1859 an estimated one hundred thousand persons clogged the Southern, Smoky Hill, and Platte routes to Denver or the mines beyond. Mining camps and towns arose overnight at the sites of Jackson Diggings, Gregory Diggings, or Russell Gulch. Into South Park the gold-hungry men pushed, and the sprawling shanty and tent communities of Tarryall, Fairplay, and Buckskin Joe emerged. The momentum of this human flood carried it across the continental divide where Breckenridge on the Blue River, and California Gulch, later Leadville, on the Arkansas, were the centers for thousands eagerly sifting the sands of the rivers and their tributaries for gold.

Bitter disappointment was the lot of most of the prospectors, and they sadly drifted back to their eastern homes. Those who remained became farmers or ranchers or merchants, while a few continued to believe they could still find a fortune in gold. In the 1870's, Colorado redeemed the faith of some when rich silver deposits were opened around Leadville, in the 1890's the Cripple Creek district yielded rich veins of gold. Daniel Conner found no fortune in the mountains although he prospected widely in South Park and on the Arkansas and Blue rivers.

After the Civil War disrupted the peace in 1861, Confederate forces made several attempts to wrest the Southwest from Union control. Born in Kentucky and sympathetic to the Southern cause, Conner joined an irregular Confederate band which gathered in 1862, hoping to surprise Union garrisons in Colorado and New Mexico. When their plans failed, Conner found himself among those hunted by Union troops. Seizing an opportunity to escape, our author joined the party of Joseph Reddeford Walker which was hoping to find a new gold region in New Mexico or Arizona.

This volume completes the publication of the Conner manuscript. Chronologically it precedes that portion of the narrative published under the title *Joseph Reddeford Walker and the Arizona Adven-*

ture (Norman, University of Oklahoma Press, 1956). The same procedures were used in preparing this part of the manuscript for printing as were followed in the *Arizona Adventure*. For the convenience of the reader we substituted the modern spellings of certain words, and occasionally we changed Conner's punctuation. In shortening some passages, usually those of superfluous description, we have carefully avoided distortion of Conner's meanings. Our editing changed no fact, opinion, or conclusion found in the original manuscript. Unfortunately, Conner often used initials for persons fleetingly met, and on more than one occasion he was annoyingly vague in locating the exact site of an event. It was impossible, therefore, to identify every individual encountered by Conner or to note the geographical position of every event.

Each of the volumes from the Conner manuscript makes a unique contribution to our knowledge of the Far Western frontier. In the previously published *Arizona Adventure*, Conner presents us with an eyewitness account of the brutal slaying of Mangas Coloradas, a chronicle of the opening of the mining region of central Arizona, and a full record of the last expedition of Old Joe Walker. In this volume, Conner furnishes us with a lucidly written story of the Colorado gold rush and also with the best available description of Confederate activity in Colorado. Events related to the Civil War are described more fully by Conner than in any historical literature of Colorado. Certainly, Conner's adventures from 1859 to 1867 rival anything a reader might encounter in the history of the American frontier during the nineteenth century.

Contents

	Acknowledgments	*page v*
	Introduction	*vii*
I	On the Southern Route to Pikes Peak	3
II	A Tenderfoot on the High Plains	26
III	Observations on the Habitat of the Plains	51
IV	Prospecting South Park, the Blue, and the Arkansas	62
V	Life in the Colorado Mining Camps	92
VI	News of the Civil War Reaches the Mines	109
VII	Confederates Gather at Mace's Hole	126
VIII	A Hasty Departure from Colorado	158
	Bibliography	169
	Index	181

Illustrations

Weston, Missouri   *facing page* 18
Lawrence, Kansas   19
Council Grove, Kansas   34
Ute Encampment at Hamilton, Colorado   35
Fort Lyon, Colorado   82
Pikes Peak   83
Buckskin Joe, Colorado   98
Park City, Colorado   99
Fairplay, Colorado   114
Chinese Mining Operation at Fairplay   115
Alexander ("Zan") Hicklin   130
Hicklin's Home in Rye, Colorado   131

Maps
Conner's Route to Colorado   *page* 9
Conner's Colorado Locale   66

A Confederate in the Colorado Gold Fields

CHAPTER ONE

On the Southern Route to Pikes Peak

It was in the fall of the year 1858 when the news was received at Leavenworth City in Kansas that gold had been discovered in Cherry Creek, a tributary of Platte River, and emptying into the latter at the present site of Denver City. This news created quite an excitement in Leavenworth City, and this excitement was very materially enhanced by the personal presence of some of the discoverers themselves, who had just returned from the locality to give direct confirmation to these flying reports.[1]

Just after dark on a September evening after that famous arrival, crowds of anxious citizens were seen gathering in squares on the different street corners, apparently burdened with suppressed inquiries and earnestly in search of somebody to answer interrogatories promptly. Now I was quite a schoolboy, having just been released near Mason and Dixon's line from one of those necessary evils—a public school, and had been sojourning a few months near Ridgely in Platte County, Missouri, with relatives and acquaintances.[2] I had arrived

---

[1] In July, 1858, reports began to appear in the newspapers of Kansas describing activities in the Colorado gold fields. John Cantrell and John Richards, mountain traders, C. C. Carpenter, a member of the Lawrence party, and Elmore Y. King, a member of the Cherokee party, reached the Missouri River towns in late August and early September, displaying gold brought from Colorado. James F. Willard, "Spreading the News of the Early Discoveries of Gold in Colorado," *Colorado Magazine*, Vol. VI, No. 3 (May, 1929), 98–104; LeRoy R. Hafen (ed.), *Colorado Gold Rush; Contemporary Letters and Reports, 1858–1859*, 47–49.

[2] Conner was born on December 24, 1837, at Bardstown, Kentucky. After leaving Hanover College, Hanover, Indiana, about 1858, he went to Ridgely.

on my first visit to Leavenworth City on horseback in the afternoon of the day referred to, and of course all those people were strangers to me. I sauntered down to one of the street corners, where one of these knots of men had collected, and heard many queries on the way as to what all this stir was about, without any reply. But on arriving at the corner into the crowd, I heard the query, "What's the matter?" "Gold discovered at Pike's Peak," was the hasty and impatient response. "Where is Pike's Peak?" persisted the now doubly interested interrogator. "O, Pike's Peak is in the Rocky Mountains, across the plains in Utah," growled the impatient man, without looking at the questioner.[3]

At this point I was about asking a question myself, but refrained after the assurance snatched from these two fellows, to the effect that all seemed to want information and nobody wanted to be bothered giving it. So, being afraid to do anything but listen, as of course I thought that I was the only stranger there, there was nothing else to do but settle myself into an audience and be quiet, externally at any rate.

But it was not long, however, before light was thrown upon the all-prevailing subject. A speaker mounted the rostrum and began his enthusiastic description of the new gold fields, and what might be

---

Ridgely was the second town to be incorporated in Platte County, Missouri, but its importance declined when the Rock Island Railroad bypassed it and built to Cameron, Missouri, 3½ miles away. Today Ridgely is merely a crossroads town with a general store, a church, and a few inhabitants. Daniel Ellis Conner to Miss [Sharlot M.] Hall, May 14, 1910, Conner Manuscripts, Arizona State Library, Phoenix, Arizona; Jay B. Wilson to Odessa Davenport, March 24, 1953, letter in possession of editors.

[3] Actually gold, in paying amounts, was first discovered by a small group of prospectors led by Green Russell on Cherry Creek, near Denver, July 7, 1858, which would place the activity about 60 miles north of Pikes Peak. Undoubtedly the confusion resulted from the fact that Pikes Peak was the outstanding landmark from the plains, often visible for 150 miles. It was named after Zebulon Montgomery Pike, who sighted this 14,110-foot peak on November 15, 1806. W. Eugene Hollon, *The Lost Pathfinder: Zebulon Montgomery Pike*, 124–29; Alfred B. Sanford, "The Cherokee Trail and the First Discovery of Gold on Cherry Creek," *Colorado Magazine*, Vol. VIII, No. 1 (January, 1931), 30–34; "R. J. Pierce and Jacob T. Masterson, Members of the Famous Russell Prospecting Party of 1858," *Colorado Magazine*, Vol. XXVII, No. 2 (April, 1950), 102-107.

expected of the late discovery and its results upon the whole country, and the West particularly. This soon brought a large audience and cheering became lusty and continuous. One speech followed another until nearly, or quite, midnight. One of the speakers said with great animation that "Pike's Peak was not more than eight hundred miles from the block upon which he stood and that while we had such citizens as Major, Russell, and Waddell [Russell, Majors, and Waddell] there would be no trouble to get transportation for sufficient numbers, to protect an expedition against the hostile Indians through to the uttermost limits of the earth itself." This speaker, after exhausting both the subject and his imagination, closed his lengthy speech by assurances of the safety of all who would raise an "outfit" and accompany Major, Russell, and Waddell's train of wagons, because he said that they always furnished each teamster on the plains a Bible and a rifle apiece. Another speaker, who mounted the stand during the evening, made a flaming speech upon the future prospects of Kansas, amidst frequent applause. He said that it was advisable for everyone who started to Pike's Peak to follow the example that Major, Russell, and Waddell had set on the plains: by taking with them a good rifle and a Bible and that by taking time by the forelock, Leavenworth City would be made the key to the whole Western plains and thence to the Rocky Mountains. This was all heartily agreed to by continuous and boisterous applause.[4]

Numerous speakers following detained the audience until a late hour when the picnic reluctantly broke up with happy anticipations about equally divided amongst the individuals upon which to dream and build air castles.

It is impossible to describe the generous enthusiasm which was awakened, from apathy and slumbering indifference, by this sudden and impromptu meeting. Hurrah for Pike's Peak, was shouted and repeated all about the streets long after the meeting adjourned,

[4] The great transportation firm of Russell, Majors, and Waddell dominated freighting on the plains during the late 1850's but encountered financial difficulties and was purchased by Ben Holladay on March 22, 1862. One of the projects developed by Russell, Majors, and Waddell was the Leavenworth and Pikes Peak Express which maintained daily service between eastern Kansas and Denver over a 687-mile route. J. V. Frederick, *Ben Holladay, The Stagecoach King,* 39, 54–55.

although gold was found nearly eighty miles north of Pike's Peak really; but there was so little known by the populace of that country at the time that the two localities, being both at the western extremity of the Great Plains, seemed together.[5]

I mounted my horse on the following morning and left Leavenworth early and crossed the river into Missouri at Weston. I pushed on to my headquarters in Platte County, with no other subject upon my mind than that of the mode of getting to Pike's Peak.[6]

There is but little general information as to what created the impetus to immigration to the Rocky Mountains, a region so lately unknown to nearly all of our people except the trappers, who had a knowledge of the country, but who as a class never wrote anything about it.[7]

The discovery of gold on Cherry Creek, as above stated, was what renewed the immigration for the first time since the Mormons settled the Great Salt Lake Valley.[8] This discovery was caused by about the following circumstances, in the year 1858, which resulted in the publicity given the fact, by the excitement in Leavenworth City already referred to.

---

[5] Conner overestimates the distance slightly; maps show the area of Cherry Creek approximately sixty miles north of Pikes Peak.

[6] The site of Weston, Missouri, is located a few miles above Leavenworth, Kansas, on the opposite bank of the Missouri River. It had its origins in 1837–38 and was of some importance as a crossing of the Missouri River until it was overshadowed by Leavenworth after 1854. In 1950, Weston's population was 1,067 persons. E. W. Howe, "A Bit of Weston, Missouri History," *Missouri Historical Review*, Vol. XLVII, Nos. 1 and 2 (October, 1952, and January, 1953), 29–36, 141–47.

[7] Knowledge of gold in the Rocky Mountains was common among the Indians and old trappers during the 1830's and 1840's. In 1850, John Beck, in the company of a party from the Cherokee Nation en route to California, found gold on Ralston's Creek, near Denver. Rumors of gold also circulated at Fort Laramie from 1856, but not until the spring of 1858 did systematically organized parties search for gold in present-day Colorado. LeRoy R. Hafen, *Pike's Peak Gold Rush Guidebooks of 1859*, 21 ff.

[8] The Mormons, driven from Missouri and Illinois, finally found their permanent abode in the Great Salt Lake Valley. Brigham Young led the pioneer party which arrived at their destination in July, 1847, with thousands of Mormons following later. Ray Allen Billington, *The Far Western Frontier, 1830–1860*, 198–200; Nels Anderson, *Desert Saints: The Mormon Frontier in Utah*, 60–67.

An old Georgia gold miner, who went by the familiar sobriquet of "Green Russell," was on a tour of inspection about Leavenworth City, in the winter of 1857, and like other adventurers in that place, he was looking for opportunities to better his fortune in worldly necessaries.[9]

He met, while in Kansas, a Cherokee Indian, who informed him that there was gold to be found at the foot of the Rocky Mountains, and upon application agreed to accompany a party of prospectors thither as guide.

A party of thirteen men was soon organized to make the venture, with Mr. Russell as conductor. They started in the spring of 1858 and after suffering great privations and discovering gold in Cherry Creek, the party split into divisions, each looking for their own welfare as suited them best. The consequence was that some of them found their way to Taos in New Mexico, and some of them came back to Leavenworth City that fall and raised the excitement and enthusiasm above described.[10]

[9] The full name of the individual mentioned here was William Greeneberry Russell but he was known as Green Russell by his contemporaries and companions. It is possible that Russell was in Leavenworth late in 1857. In the spring of 1857 Russell and his brother Oliver, in the company of two nephews, made their way from Georgia to Pottawatomie County, Kansas, where they purchased a farm. During the winter of 1857–58, however, they returned to Georgia and returned to Kansas again in the spring of 1858. Elma Dill Russell Spencer, *Green Russell and Gold*, 7, 40; George A. Root (ed.), "Reminiscences of William Darnell," *Collections of the Kansas State Historical Society, 1926–1928*, Vol. XVII, 503–504.

[10] A party of gold-seekers from the Cherokee Nation found gold on Ralston's Creek in June, 1850, on their way to California. This discovery was never forgotten and later in the 1850's, perhaps, formed a basis for the correspondence between Green Russell and acquaintances in the Cherokee Nation. Finally it was agreed than an exploration of the Rocky Mountains for gold would be undertaken, returning first to the area where the gold metal was first noticed. Green Russell led one party, John Beck of the Cherokee Nation led another, but before arriving at Cherry Creek two parties from Missouri joined up. In all, it is generally agreed that 104 individuals constituted these four parties, to be supplemented slightly later by an expedition from Lawrence, Kansas. The Missouri and Cherokee parties were quickly discouraged by the failure to find gold in paying quantities and departed for home on July 25, 1858. Some members of the Lawrence party, however, prospected through South Park, restocked their provisions at Fort Garland, and a few went on to Taos, New Mexico. Hafen, *Pike's Peak Gold Rush Guidebooks of 1859*, 34–37, 50–70; Muriel H. Wright (ed.), "The Journal of John Lowery

Then during the winter of 1858 and the spring of 1859, preparations were numerously made and put into execution, to visit the Rocky Mountains, resulting in a hasty and energetic building up of the city of Denver from a beginning of a trappers' cabin and the discovery of gold throughout the Rocky Mountains.

This statement of the beginning of the gold fever in these great mountain fastnesses was given to me by Mr. Young, one of the members of Mr. Russell's party, who made the discovery in Cherry Creek. I was well acquainted with Mr. Young afterward, and his account was corroborated by Mr. French, another of the party, and others.[11]

Such was the beginnings of the settlement of those great and extensive gold fields which has subsequently peopled this mountain country which so lately, it may be said, to have been unknown.

I shall return now to my arrival in Platte County, Missouri, after hearing the speeches and partaking of the enthusiasm of the Leavenworth meeting. The following spring saw my preparations for Pike's Peak under full headway.

I dreamed of sledging and prying the gold out of the hillside, like moving stone from a quarry, while restlessness and impatience seemed to lengthen a week into a month. In the meantime a number of young men in Platte [County] were rapidly discussing themselves into an organization for the long and uncertain tramp which in due time was completed.

After a sufficient number had made up their minds to go and a

---

Brown, of the Cherokee Nation en route to California in 1850," *Chronicles of Oklahoma*, Vol. XII, No. 2 (June, 1934), 177–213; William B. Parsons, "A Report on the Gold Mines of Colorado, 1858," *Colorado Magazine*, Vol. XIII, No. 6 (November, 1936), 215–18; James H. Pierce, "The First Prospecting of Colorado—Who Did It and What Led to It," *The Trail*, Vol. VII, No. 5 (October, 1914), 5–11; James H. Pierce, "With the Green Russell Party," *The Trail*, Vol. XIII, No. 12 (May, 1921), 5–14.

[11] Valorious (also Valarious) W. Young joined the Russell party just before it left Manhattan, Kansas. Adnah French was a member of the Lawrence party and later one of the organizers of the "St. Charles Town Association." Hafen, *Pike's Peak Gold Rush Guidebooks of 1859*, 63, 74, 96; LeRoy R. Hafen, "The Voorhees Diary of the Lawrence Party's Trip to Pike's Peak, 1858," *Colorado Magazine*, Vol. XII, No. 2 (March, 1935), 41–54.

8

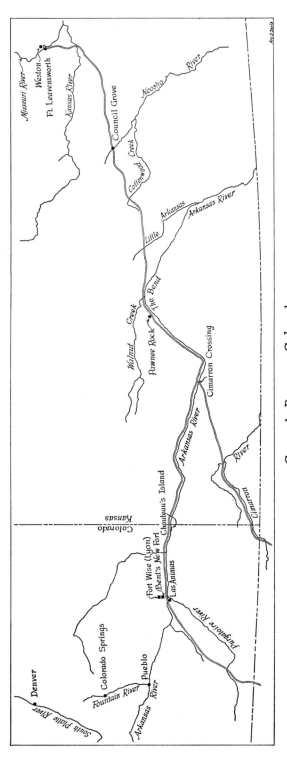

Conner's Route to Colorado

time and place of departure appointed, there was nothing to do but to proceed to final preparations and contemplate the venture and its possible results with impatience, and a little mixed with fear, and pleasure. But, however, the appointed day came at last and found us all to the number of sixteen, prepared with rough stout clothing, guns, pistols, ammunition in abundance, and so on. Our cattle were soon yoked to covered wagons (five in number) and after the indispensable good-byes were done, our little party of would-be roughs wended its way to the Missouri River opposite to Leavenworth and encamped for the night, and ate the luncheon previously prepared by kindly hands.

We arose early, breakfasted the same way, and moved on to the ferryboat, and were soon in [Leavenworth] City where I had heard such flaming speeches the fall before. It was now the seventh day of April. Our wagons were driven up in front of Henry's and Garrett's wholesale establishment and the cattle unhitched from them and taken a few squares away into the city and turned into a vacant lot and left yoked together, two and two, together.[12] Now the question was what to get and what not to provide. But the list was finally figured up and it was astonishing. It appeared to be wonderful how anybody ever got enough plunder about a house to run a family. Bacon, flour, coffee, sugar, beans, dried apples, dried peaches, rice, pepper, salt, vinegar, pickles, soap, soda, syrup, tea, fruits, and so on, with as many pots, cups, pans, and kettles, and so forth, to mix and cook them all in, and out of which to eat them when cooked. Then followed in endless progression such things as extra ox-yokes, couplings, bows, whipstocks, prospecting pans, needles, thread, physic, butcher knives, axes, shovels, picks, nails, mechanic's tools, gold scales (of largest size, of course), and many other things usually forgotten until needed, such as water kegs, canteens, etc.

In the afternoon all of these things were loaded into the wagons and our preparations for work and for war and our portable commissariat was complete, and altogether it made quite a safe-looking "outfit" for an indefinite stay in the wilderness.

[12] William Henry and Alexander Garrett ran a wholesale and retail grocery store at 59 Cherokee Street, Leavenworth, Kansas. *Leavenworth City Directory and Business Mirror*, 69, 85.

"Fall aboard" was now shouted all around in levity. The Missouri boys nearly all knew how to drive oxen under the yoke, several of whom went to fetch the cattle, to harness to the wagons. When they came down street and orderly hitched their respective pairs to the wagons, one of my mess asked me to go bring the remaining pair, which, as before stated, were several squares away in a vacant lot. Here I made my first apology by stating that I never had driven any cattle under the yoke, and expressed some fears of making a failure of getting them down to where the wagons stood.

My comrade quickly replied that I surely could drive a "yoke of cattle" loose and that if I could not I had better be learning. That argument was sufficient. I started with a huge whip, and to me very unwieldly, determined not to shirk my duty whatever might be the inconvenience, and especially on such a trip where all that could be done was reasonably expected of each member. I found the oxen and learned that they were somewhat newly broken and had been but little used. I turned them out upon the street; then they went. I don't think that they were ever before in a city.

They made up the street in the wrong direction on a full run, and although they were yoked together I found that my best speed was necessary to head them. My long eight-foot hickory whipstock was only in my way, as the long lash which was intended for a six-yoke team dragged the ground behind me.

I got ahead of them, however, when they quickly wheeled and made a desperate "bulge" for an alley nearby and entered it on the double quick. Here I checked up a little and hesitated whether to run around the square and meet them at the other end of the alley. But lest I should lose them entirely, I hastily followed and about the time I was again overtaking them, they darted into another vacant lot along the alley, through a pair of bars. They were now panting and blowing equal to myself, but still seemed determined not to go to Pike's Peak. But when I again got them to budge, they started with a rush out at those bars into the alley, thence to another street and started the wrong direction again. The alley was too narrow for me to use my mighty whip in it and I could only keep up with them, until reaching the street, where I succeeded again in heading them off. Now we all three stopped to blow, and I noticed that the people about the street were becoming amused a little, and this annoyed me some, as my cattle made another dash to pass me, whereupon I made a mighty effort with my big whip to cut them across their faces, and the long lash went in an awkward direction and cut an Irishman's mule across the face. The mule was hitched to a dray and was just passing me at some distance. That mule turned around nearly as quickly as the oxen did, and away went Paddy and the dray. It took Pat nearly half of his quick trip to regain his balance in his cart, so suddenly and unexpectedly did he change his bearings. He, however, fetched up in safety against the front of a livery stable half a square away, where some men assisted him in checking his train. Like most people, when they think they are abused, Pat got mad when the danger was all over and lit out of his dray and came walking toward me, talking fast and excitedly cutting the Irish brogue all into smithereens in a most threatening way. Here, some men who had been watching me and the cattle for pastime hurriedly and in great mirth explained to him. But Paddy could not help it; he directed his reply to their explanations to me and said, "Can't ye dthrive oxens wid out two big pisthols ahangin to ye's?" This query brought a burst of laughter from the bystanders, and upon my reply that I couldn't drive cattle with two pistols, he started back to the livery stable, apparently in good, or better, humor.

Some of my comrades appeared on the scene pretty soon and assisted to get this unruly yoke of steers under control and geared to their place in the wagon.

The order was again given to "fall aboard," and we fell aboard and proceeded to move out of the city on our road which lay westward, and bivouacked, camp-style, for the first night under shelter of the sky.

I was considerably annoyed that night in our first camp at the levity of my associates over my first attempt to drive oxen, when I learned that they had purposely sent me after the wildest yoke of cattle in the party, in order to have some fun over it at my expense; and it was still more provoking when they seemed to have so much of it.

There was nothing of interest took place in our camp that night except the most ludicrous motions made toward cooking in the several branches of that most difficult of all arts, and the arrest of one of the several visitors, who were curious to know how we would get along in camp, they said. A policeman came out from the city after night-fall, and unceremoniously marched the fellow off, after stating that he expected to find him there. The officer soon disappeared in the dark, holding the lapel of the prisoner's coat.

We awoke early, bright and cheerful on the following morning, which was the 8th day of April, and moved out in the direction of Lawrence. During our route westward through the settlements we saw a few Indians who were dressed like white people and some of them seemed thrifty, but there was not many of them to be seen.[13]

In a few days we arrived at Lawrence, where I saw (to me then) a strange sight. I saw for the first time during my life, a handsome, well-dressed white woman promenading the spacious pavement, affectionately leaning on the arm of a tall, passably dressed and very black colored man. She was apparently well entertained and seemed satisfied, and I presumed that she was both. When we look at the matter from this date, retrospectively, it does not look so queer to look upon such a spectacle. But I confess that the circumstance made a lasting impression upon my mind, which was, however, nothing strange as I was raised in a slave state amongst all of the prejudices against the social equality with slaves. I have since, frequently, seen white women in the South with black husbands, and vice versa.[14]

We took our leave of Lawrence for Council Grove, which was

[13] To pass from Leavenworth to Lawrence, Kansas, at this time, Conner undoubtedly traveled through the lands of the Delaware Indians. Thomas B. Sykes, United States Indian agent to the Delaware Indians, reported that a few of the 1,008 Delawares cultivated as many as one hundred acres of land. Paul Wallace Gates, *Fifty Million Acres: Conflicts over Kansas Land Policy, 1854–1890*, 23; *Report of the Commissioner of Indian Affairs for the Year 1860*, 102–103.

[14] Conner, born in the former slave state of Kentucky, overemphasized the prevalence of this practice. All former slave states passed statutes which prohibited the intermarriage of whites and Negroes. Most western states had comparable laws, but Kansas was among the exceptions. Pauli Murray (ed. and comp.), *States' Laws on Race and Color*, 168; Charles S. Mangum, Jr., *The Legal Status of the Negro*, 236ff.

13

at that time the extreme border of settlement in that section of Kansas.[15] Before reaching it, however, we fell in with a number of adventurers equal in number to our own party, who "outfitted" in Jackson County, Missouri, and like ourselves, bound for Pike's Peak.[16]

Here both companies agreed to unite into one for a purpose in common, and proceeded together and made our first full camp at Council Grove. Our party now assumed a more formidable appearance and looked capable of self-defense. It was at Council Grove in the fall of 1860 that a convention of citizens was held to provide for feeding the needy, and I well remember that after returning that far from the Rocky Mountains during that fall, of hearing the common remark that God had cursed Kansas with a famine and then blessed it by giving the people the Hon. Abraham Lincoln for president.[17]

This incident only serves to show what the hardy sons of the frontiers in the midst of distress will willingly undergo in emergencies and how loyal they were at the very inception of Mr. Lincoln's administration, to the favorite.

Fervently ardent in their wishes and coolly tenacious to adopted principles, these people were capable of withstanding the most cruel and distressing reverses, and of thanking God that things were no worse with an earnestness truly admirable.

The fact of Mr. Lincoln's nomination seemed for the time almost

[15] Council Grove was eighty-seven miles from Lawrence, Kansas, on the Santa Fe Trail. It received its name from a council with the Osage Indians held on August 10, 1825. A fine grove of hardwoods was also located there, and they were used to provide travelers with extra axles and replacements for wagon parts. William B. Parsons, *The New Gold Mines of Western Kansas*, in Hafen, *Pike's Peak Guidebooks*, 185; R. L. Duffus, *The Santa Fe Trail*, 89; Otis E. Young, *The First Military Escort on the Santa Fe Trail, 1829*, 76–77.

[16] The principal "Jumping-off place" in Jackson County, Missouri, was the city of Independence which was laid out in 1827. When the Missouri River flood in 1833 swept away the steamboat landing at Independence, the trade tended to concentrate at Westport Landing in present Kansas City, Missouri. Duffus, *Santa Fe Trail*, 102–105; Josiah Gregg, *Commerce of the Prairies*, 23.

[17] It was reported that from June 19, 1859, to November, 1860, general drought existed throughout Kansas and Nebraska. Everett Dick, *The Sod-House Frontier*, 212–13.

food enough for exigencies then presented; while the prevailing tri-
umph brought forcibly to mind one of my own practical adages—
that a mind well exercised will sustain the body on less than half-
rations.

Our whole party left Council Grove, the extreme outpost of
Kansas at this time, and arrived early in the day at Diamond Spring,
twelve miles distant, and pitched camp for the rest of the day and
following night.[18]

Here I had my first shooting match with an Indian "brave." He
bantered me to match one of my navy pistols against his bow and
arrows at short range, and insisted that I should wager in the contest
my knife, which was an ordinary butcherknife, against his, also a
common butcherknife. They love gambling. But I didn't want his
knife and could not afford here, just getting into the wilderness, to
lose my own; so I offered to wager a small piece of tobacco, instead
of my knife. I now saw that he wanted my knife scabbard worse than
he did the knife, for he proposed to me to stake it. But he agreed,
however, after much parrying and bartering, to accept the tobacco
stake, and the preparations for the great event began.

Neither of us could speak the other's language, so we "went" by
signs. He entered into the contest with great earnestness and caution,
with a face full of anxiety, like that of a Kentucky horse-jockey on
the eve of beginning a race. He laid off the distance several times
before it suited him, gravely eyeing at intervals his dusky, naked
comrades, who were looking on in interested silence. At last, a little
bit of paper was marked with a black spot in its center, secured in
the end of a split stick, and stuck up fifteen paces away, and all was
ready. He gave me the sign to shoot first, which I did and missed
the mark. He shot his arrow and beat me. This displaced some of
his anxious care and substituted a little confident air of dignity. A
second match, with the same result, very materially increased his

---

[18] Diamond Spring, "Diamond of the Plains," or Jones Spring, after "Old
Ben" Jones of the Joseph C. Brown surveying party, was located sixteen miles
beyond Council Grove on the Santa Fe Trail. Parsons, *New Gold Mines of Western
Kansas*, 185; Kate L. Gregg, *The Road to Santa Fe*, 46, 60; Gregg, *Commerce of
the Prairies*, 36.

self-possession and stiff dignity in the presence of his admiring associates, who were now watching with increasing interest. A third round and defeat brought down the house. Silence suppressed, now burst forth from this crowd of naked pagans, with childish and boisterous glee, intermingled with hearty shouts and triumphant yells. The now thoroughly dignified victor was the only exception to the rule. He accepted the tobacco indifferently, turned on his heel in a contemptuous mood, with grave demeanor; looked away off on to the plains like he had immediately forgotten all about it, and if he had not, he only considered the result a matter of course. He refused to notice me any more, while his companions danced, laughed, and hooted me about this "big" defeat, until I began really to be ashamed of myself, especially as my dignified naked friend tenaciously refused to laugh or notice me, while he was seriously contemplating weightier matters in the distant blank space on the distant plain.

This little recapitulation brings to mind the fleeting reminiscence, like a dream, of an execution that took place at Council Grove in the spring of 1860.

The Indians became much distressed because their medicine man permitted one sick "brave" above the legal number to die. This was fatal. I did not see the execution, but saw many of the distressed members of the tribe earnestly consulting, one with another, over the necessity of taking the life of their medicine man; but such was "so nominated in the bond" and the "brave" submitted to his fate and, with apparent willingness, lit out for his happy hunting ground, leaving an honorable vacancy for another doctor to fill at his peril.[19]

The poor savages moaned over their loss piteously, but an eyewitness testified to the firm and orderly process of putting poor "Lo" to death.

We moved in the next day to what is known as Lost Spring, about twelve more miles. This spring was really lost. It is situated in a

---

[19] Later, Conner identifies these as "Kaw" or Kansa Indians. See chapter 2 of this volume. It was common practice among the Indians to kill a medicine man if several of his patients died. He was thought to have lost his supernatural powers or to have become a sorcerer. Frederick Webb Hodge, *Handbook of American Indians North of Mexico*, Bureau of American Ethnology *Bulletin No. 30*, II, 838.

rolling prairie hidden away in a little ravine—furnishing but little water, and not sufficient to form a stream.[20]

We remained here all night and a part of the following day. Several circumstances and incidents transpired at the "Lost Spring" during this brief stay, to impress both the name and the locality upon my memory.

The first was that I had my last hearty shake of an old but protracted ague malaria during the night, while a heavy storm cloud overcast the sky, and poured down its torrents, to be swept about the dark plain with terrific force by heavy capricious winds, accompanied by thunder and lightning. Another was that all of our stock stampeded and successfully escaped the guard during this war of the elements and were not found again until late the next day.

While the guard were hunting the cattle on the following day the friendly Indians came about our camp in numbers, to trade and barter buffalo rugs, moccasins, etc.[21] The most of them carried their moccasins in their bosoms, when they were fortunate enough to boast of an old castoff frontier check-shirt, or under their blankets which they usually wore about their shoulders when visiting. One "big old brave," who was looking sour about the camp, in dogged silence, not deigning to look or speak agreeably to anyone, or for that matter to speak at all, had moccasins for barter, too proud to offer them, or maybe felt that it was useless, he stood looking off across the camp plat listlessly.

He stood thus for some time, apparently unconscious of being steadily observed. One of our party, a young boyish fellow (a Ten-

[20] Parsons places Lost Spring sixteen miles from Diamond Spring, while Josiah Gregg says it was fifteen miles from the same site on the Santa Fe Trail. Three traditions are said to have caused the name of the spring. One can choose to name the spring from the fact that it flowed intermittently, that it saved a party of travelers or hunters who were lost on the plains, or that the Indians attempted to destroy it so that it would not aid the whites when they crossed the plains. Parsons, *New Gold Mines of Western Kansas*, 185; Gregg, *Commerce of the Prairies*, 217; T. A. Cordry, *The Story of the Marking of the Santa Fe Trail*, 115–16.

[21] One cannot be certain which tribe Conner and his party encountered at this point. It might have been one of the tribes located in eastern Kansas on a buffalo hunt such as the Delaware, or the Sac and Fox. In addition, this region was within the buffalo range of the Cheyennes, Arapahoes, and Kiowas.

nessean), was also in a reverie, with a long last gaze riveted blankly upon the old "brave" as though he was a singular specimen of a warrior and needed studying. The old fellow at last chanced to notice the young man's settled attention bent upon him, and quickly turned, facing the paleface, and at the same time thrusting his hand into his bosom energetically, as though he had just taken a notion to end the burden of his reflections by prompt and decisive action. Here the disappointed old Indian stood leaning a little forward, clutching a pair of moccasins, which were now about half drawn from his bosom, looking contemptuously after the flying form of our friend, who was leaping all obstacles about the camp to get out of the way of the deadly weapon supposed lurking in poor old "Lo's" bosom, and which was now about to be used on him. But alas, a pretty pair of beaded moccasins, the handiwork of his squaw, had startled and scared out of his wits a paleface "brave," whose excitement kept up preparations for the conflict until the dusky old warrior was constrained to smile at him. The Tennessean, on reaching the far side of the camp without injury and seeing that immediate danger had passed, feelingly remarked to his friend, "John, our troubles have just begun." Our young friend was still ignorant of the old Indian's design, when thrusting his hand into his bosom, and cared not to be enlightened. The old moccasin dealer, on the contrary, saw in a moment what the matter was, and after holding out his dangerous moccasins at arm's length for a moment, quietly pushed them back into his bosom and darkly settled back into his half-contemptuous and morose mood— his natural condition. I don't think he ever offered to sell or barter the moccasins again. But after this incident, which at the time created much mirth and jollity in our careless ranks, when danger was lightly prophesied, someone would tauntingly express it by thrusting a hand into the bosom. Our Tennessee friend, of course, always enjoyed it because it was a token of the kindly generosity which is always alive in the breast of sympathy. This sympathy and humility was granted by our "boys" as a matter of right and rectitude, not to be questioned nor withheld from our Tennessee friend, because humility was taught and encouraged by the Savior of mankind; and we were now experimenting upon new speculations of doubtful results and consequently

Weston, Missouri, in 1854.
The Kansas State Historical Society, Topeka

Lawrence, Kansas, in 1858.
The Kansas State Historical Society, Topeka

needed humility somewhere. Somewhere! Doubtlessly somewhere. But where? We evidently don't want much of it at home, only in theory. Practically, we want none at our headquarters. That part of the gospel of Christ goes a begging in life and health, and draws a premium at maturity. But ready cash was the spirit of business on the plains when I crossed them, and the Tennessee holder was compelled to store away his merchandise gratuitously bestowed for a better market.

After the misunderstanding about the moccasins was rectified, our friend tried to cultivate a better acquaintance with the stolid old Indian, who now stood upon his dignity, which was of the highest order and constantly on the upgrade, and in proportion to the efforts made to conciliate the matter. But poor Lo's nature was just like the average of all other brave, intellectual, uncultivated men, who universally mistake a little attention for servility. He was inexorable.

Our Tennessee friend gave up the task of securing favor by stating that he always had depreciated aristocracy, but now he saw it in its pure nakedness and thought that it must be natural and therefore right, and that it evidently sprang from instinct, and not reason. He consequently arrived at the conclusion that it took an ignorant, uncultivated creature to make a good first-class aristocrat.

It is to be lamented that our public men had hithertofore known and cared so little about the Indian character. An Indian is as proud as anybody, and yet he has no perception whatever, of what a right, to private individual property, other than a trophy means. All the ideas of ownership to property they have is to hold it in common.

They know as little about trade and reciprocity, legally considered, as the President of the United States does about the language of a Choctaw. It is a well-known characteristic of their natures that they never think of profit or margin on a trade, but want the whole. His profit is, like the Dutchman's, 1 per cent, which is clearing a dollar on a dollar's worth of goods. Hence force or cunning is the stock in trade which they usually set off against the thing coveted.

No Indian can trade in his present condition. He can only know that he is swindled by expert and lawless agents who do know the legal import of a contract, the technicalities of which, when used against him, the Indian believes it to be equivalent, and the same as his own cunning—only that he has been outwitted. Hence he regards the contract, which defeats his expectations, as a forcible and violent taking; therefore retaliates by his own interpretation of what he regards the same law.

Our party, now of about ten wagons and over thirty men, departed from Lost Spring and for several days without incident, camped upon and crossed several small streams, tributaries to the Arkansas River—Little Cottonwood,[22] Cow Creek,[23] and others— and arrived in safety at what is known as the "Big Bend" of the Arkansas, our first approach to this river.[24]

Another storm and another stampede of cattle followed, detaining us nearly two days. Five of us overtook these domestic brutes on their way back at "Cow Creek," twenty miles from our campground. We were all afoot, as well as the cattle, and hence our return trip was slow and weary. We arrived at camp in the night, with our herd, pretty well worn out with fatigue, cattle and all. We only knew when we were about halfway back by the two celebrated "Plumb Buttes," which stand like sentinels in the plain midway between Cow Creek and the "Big Bend."[25]

We are now on the Arkansas. It has its source in the Rocky Mountains and takes its course across the great treeless plains for

[22] Parsons' distance from Lost Spring to Cottonwood Creek, called Little Cottonwood by Conner, is twenty miles, but Gregg gives twelve miles as the distance between the two sites. Parsons, *New Gold Mines of Western Kansas*, 185; Gregg, *Commerce of the Prairies*, 37, 217; Gregg, *Road to Santa Fe*, 61.

[23] Gregg gives the distance from Cottonwood Creek to Cow Creek as sixty-two miles, but Parsons' distance is fifty-three miles. Parsons, *New Gold Mines of Western Kansas*, 185; Gregg, *Commerce of the Prairies*, 40, 217.

[24] In this region the Arkansas River makes a sweeping bend along the southern boundary of Barton County, Kansas, and the party was approximately 219 miles out from Lawrence, Kansas, on the Santa Fe Trail. Parsons, *New Gold Mines of Western Kansas*, 185; Federal Writers' Project, *Kansas: A Guide to the Sunflower State*, 382.

[25] Plumb Buttes were located between Little Cow and Walnut creeks on the Santa Fe Trail just north of the Arkansas River. One viewer called them "sand mounds on which plum bushes are growing." Philip Gooch Ferguson, *Diary of Philip Gooch Ferguson, 1847–1848*, in Ralph P. Bieber (ed.), *Marching with the Army of the West*, 304.

about eight hundred miles before it plunges into the woods of Arkansas and meanders through that state, to empty into the "Father of Waters" at Napoleon in the valley. We were now to follow this stream to the mountains, across this desert.

We found ourselves at the "Big Bend" in the territory claimed by the hostile and implacable tribes of the Comanche and Kiowa Indians, and were compelled to observe greater prudence and vigilance, as all of the tribes on the plains were then at war with the paleface, except the Arapaho tribe.²⁶

We were not, however, entirely without practical assistance. Mr. N. B. [?], who had served a long apprenticeship on the plains in the capacity of wagon master for the United States freight between Kansas City, Missouri, and Santa Fe, New Mexico, was one of our party.²⁷ He knew well what prudence meant.

We proceeded up the Arkansas River and pitched our camp on Walnut Creek, another tributary; thence up the river, passing the old ford then known as the Santa Fe crossing.²⁸ Here, we departed company with the old military road, keeping on the left bank of the Arkansas, which made great bends necessitating us to make dry camps sometimes on the plain overnight, while there were many days that we were required to make long drives from one bend to another.

We were annoyed on those desert trips frequently by the feints and reckless charges of the Comanche and Kiowa Indians, who were eternally hovering [on] the distant horizon. On these occasions we would hastily "corral" the wagons and otherwise prepare for defense. To one who never witnessed the process of corralling a train of wagons on the plains, the degree of dexterity and promptness of

²⁶ There is no evidence of widespread Indian hostility on the southern plains in the spring or summer of 1859. See report of W. W. Bent in *Report of the Commissioner of Indian Affairs for the Year 1859*, 137–39.

²⁷ The editors have been unable to find the name of the person whose initials Conner gives here. Perhaps it could have been an individual named Brodwell, mentioned as a wagon master of long standing in the Kansas City *Journal of Commerce* (October 16, 1858), in Hafen, *Colorado Gold Rush*, 90.

²⁸ The mouth of Walnut Creek is about four miles east of Great Bend, in Barton County, Kansas. Parsons notes that Walnut Creek was crossed on the Santa Fe Trail five miles after reaching the Arkansas River. Parsons, *New Gold Mines of Western Kansas*, 185; Gregg, *Commerce of the Prairies*, 41n.

decision required would be amusing, except perhaps on such occasions as when the Indians would make a sudden and unexpected dash from the sand hills, bordering the river at short range. Under such circumstances the procedure of corralling would become slow, awkward, and bungling.

The train of wagons proper—used for freighting across the plains —consisted of about twenty-five in number, and traveled in orderly single file. When danger became evident, the wagon master or his assistant would order the foremost wagon to drive out of the road on the right and stop. The second he would have driven out of the road on the left side and opposite the first, leaving only the width of the road between. The third wagon is driven outside of the first wagon on the right, lodging its left-hand fore wheel just inside the right after wheel of the first wagon. The fourth wagon is driven out on the outside of the second on the left of the road, lodging its right-hand fore wheel just within the after wheel of the second wagon. Each of the wagons would thus be brought up alternately on either side until all were corralled, forming a compact row on each side of the road, widening the pen thus built as the wagons extended back.

When the cattle were unhitched from the wagons and driven into this corral, the gaps at each end of the corral would be securely closed by swinging the log chains, used for gearing the cattle to the wagons, across the road from one extreme wagon to the other, both in front and behind this corral. Some old teamsters who had been navigating for years those old prairie schooners (as the freight wagons on the plains were called those days) could manage them with more skill in the midst of danger and form their corral into an oval shape, giving more room on the inside and leaving lesser gaps at either end to be closed by chains, ox-yokes, and so forth.

Thus a pen would be built in the twinkling of an eye into which cattle, dogs, horses, teamsters, and wagon masters would crowd and tumble all together, without apparent fear of hurting one another, while the Indians, mounted on their little ponies, would go tearing and cavorting about the plain in all directions, wildly shooting, hooting, and yelling—kicking up enough dust to almost conceal themselves in it. But as soon as the besieged got their guns ready and were properly distributed amongst the wagon wheels, all around the corral ready for business, the wily savages could be seen away off on the plain, cutting up all sorts of pranks and demonstrations. Out of fair gunshot range, they would start to make a savage charge upon us and as quickly stop before getting under full headway, and end the feint with defiant yells.

It was thus that our little party was almost continuously beset from day to day in our slow progress up the Arkansas River to the Rocky Mountains on an open prairie, whose sterile seasons would not produce enough vegetation in five hundred miles from which to obtain a riding switch. It was indeed a sorry-looking prospect of ever reaching the mountains, even if let alone by the savages, as it was more than a month's jaunt under peaceable sailing.

The rain- and windstorms were frequent and severe. While I was sitting in the front of a wagon in camp looking at the cattle grazing out at the front and in the rain, a thunderbolt fell with a crash near one of the oxen, knocking him down, and keeping him there until I began to believe him to be only fit for beef. But strange to say, he staggered up again and recovered good health. The wagons being the highest objects about there, the question soon arose as to the amount of safety there might be in them, the only shelter we had; but the dark storm clouds soon dispersed, leaving everything bright and cheerful for a while.

The sandstorms were the worst, however. The sand would come with sufficient force sometimes to sting through the clothing, and the dust would come all day in such gusts as to almost blind the eyes of man and beast. The driver, who was compelled to stay out of the wagon with the team and drive all day, on arriving in camp at night, could not be recognized as a white man. He was so completely covered with dust and dirt that he, who had to drive on an unlucky day, was dubbed the gopher of the occasion. On arriving into a selected campground on the eve of such a trying day's journey, the poor old cattle would stand patiently for their yokes to be removed, with their eyelashes laden heavily with dirt and dust, lowing mournfully ever and anon, looking so pitiful and woebegone that I wished time and again that they were at home.

They were evidently cognizant of being in a confused and con-founded situation and doubtful about the end of it all, though they were only brutes. Even the wild and fractious little fellows that gave me such a race in Leavenworth City began to appear religiously in-clined to humility, if not blasphemous to say so.

When the wind was quiet some of the time it was oppressively warm. On one still warm night B. A. C[ooke]. crawled under a wagon and spread his blankets for a night's sleep. During the night he slightly poked his bedfellow and told him that this was a strange country and very changeable. He said that it rained so quietly during the night that it could not be heard, and yet it had rained hard enough to leak through the wagon, and it was still too dark to see out.

They contented themselves as best they could until daylight, wondering what sort of phenomenon that kind of rain was. They crawled out with a wonderful discovery to relate in the morning and to their surprise found that the compact and well-heated bacon sides in the bottom of the wagon bed had been leaking profusely upon them all night, while they patiently bore it, under an ever-ready impression of strange things in strange situations.

The Sioux, Kiowas, and Comanches all claimed this section of the country, and howsoever they may have settled their respective claims with each other, they were thoroughly united upon the mea-sure and mode of disposing of all white men and the latter's claims to the occupation of any part of it.[29] Consequently we had not the honor nor the privilege of having a powwow during our passage of the plains with any of the tribes except the Arapahoes. The Arapahoes seemed at the time to be a neutral tribe and at peace with all the world.[30] Just above the Santa Fe crossing of the Arkansas River we met about five hundred of them, men, women, and children. They

[29] To these Indians must be added the Southern Cheyennes and Arapahoes, who at the Treaty of Fort Laramie in 1851 were given the lands between the South Platte and Arkansas rivers as their hunting grounds. Alban W. Hoopes, *Indian Affairs and Their Administration with Special Reference to the Far West, 1849–1860*, 202–205; Charles J. Kappler, *Indian Affairs: Laws and Treaties*, II, 594–95.

[30] Here Conner is referring to the Southern Arapahoes, an Algonquian people, who lived with the Southern Cheyennes along the Arkansas River and as mentioned were among the more peaceful Indians on the southern plains. Hodge, *Handbook of American Indians*, I, 72–73.

seemed to be on a general movement of headquarters. We all, copper-clad and palefaces, came to a mutually satisfactory halt in the midst of the plains when we met, and measured opinions as to all important diplomatic affairs, and parted finally about the same way—all satisfied.

But it will take another chapter to describe this meeting and separation. So I shall therefore close this one by saying of these sincere savages that their protestations of friendship and good faith had a deeper and more earnest foundation than did the light and frivolous pretensions and nonchalant professions of our party. But for the time thereof, it was all well, as our party meant them no harm; but there is never any certainty as to where the results of careless deception will end. An act of most trifling import really may become crystallized in the tears of contrition in the course of a debate between truth and fiction. A joke is always in order where a higher language is understood, than it took to perpetrate it. Otherwise it is always doubtful.

An Indian never perpetrates nor pretends a joke. He does not understand its application. His sentences are always tendered either in genuine sincerity or unadulterated treachery. He has no middle ground, nor does he have any conception of intermediate positions of any kind. He is not a good dissembler and therefore, either lies outright or tells the truth.

CHAPTER TWO

A Tenderfoot on the High Plains

It was a beautiful and bright spring morning when our train of ten wagons were moving in single file, one after another in orderly succession on the wide plains, when we discerned in the distance a black cloud of humanity approaching from the direction of the Rocky Mountains. It was some hours before our proximity was near enough to venture a guess at what we were to expect. The dark cavalcade, however, soon drew near enough to discern a mixture of men, women, children, and the ponies of the Arapahoes.

Our train was halted there in the illimitable prairie. The wagons and teams looked small and insignificant. When we started, these wagons looked as though they were about fifteen feet high to the top of the bows that sustained the white sheets, the only shelter from the rain and sun that we had. But now they looked just what they were on these plains—a small, diminutive remnant of light and enthusiastic preparations, dwindled to real dimensions as now seen in sober reality—low, contemptible, and pretensionless.

The Arapahoes came up and halted for a friendly chat and powwow, and they got it. They possibly numbered five hundred and were on a regular and protracted visit somewhere. It was really curious to conjecture where they were going, for all this country looked alike. They were not going to spend a day with a neighbor, with their knitting also, and return after the reception was duly celebrated. No, this nomadic tribe was going to take up quarters somewhere and enjoy their own company in peace, if permitted. They were neutral in the Indian wars and at peace with the white man, but still they were Indians, with all of their native suspicions and treachery, like all other pagans.[1] This motley crew was appareled and caparisoned in many different ways, each rig having its own peculiar and independent fashion.

They were riding on ponies, singly and in pairs and triples; some were walking and others riding on their bedding piled on a funny contrivance for freighting that had no model in the patent office. This invention consisted of two limber poles about ten or twelve feet in length, with the larger ends fastened to the pony's shoulders on either side and the small ends extending back and resting on the ground, leaving a width between them of probably five or six feet, giving a similar appearance to that of the shafts of a buggy. Just behind the pony on a cross pole, from one thill to the other, was firmly tied with thongs, and still further to the rear there was another similar one similarly fastened. These two crossbars kept the shafts firmly to their places while the space between was thatched with rawhide, reeds, and grass. Buffalo rugs, tanned deerskins, and other bedding materials were piled on the platform thus made, in which papooses were secured and went swinging and bouncing along, with an undulating swing of the limber, flexible shafts, looking happy and as comfortable as children generally are. The grating sound of these poles as they drag on the ground is the most unpleasant part of this mode of traveling, but the marks they made on the ground everywhere they went gave their friends an easy trail to follow when in search of each other, which is some return for the inharmonious music produced continuously by scratching the ground on a dry desert.[2]

[1] While it was true that the "Cheyenne and Arapahoe tribes scrupulously maintain peaceful relations with the whites," in 1859 young, warlike braves of the Arapahoes often raided with Cheyennes, Kiowas, and Comanches along the frontier. Arapahoes were the traditional enemy of the Shoshoni, Ute, Navaho, and Pawnee Indians with whom they warred until finally settled on a reservation in present-day Oklahoma. *Report of the Commissioner of Indian Affairs for the Year 1859,* 137; Muriel H. Wright, *A Guide to the Indian Tribes of Oklahoma,* 42–47.

[2] This is a fair description of the travois used by Indians to transport their lodges and camp equipment, but its use was not as widespread among the southern as among the northern plains Indians. Robert R. Lowie, *Indians of the Plains,* 38–40; John C. Ewers, *The Horse in Blackfoot Culture,* Bureau of American Ethnology

But it is not all of the tribes of Indians that nestle away their little brats upon such convenient fixtures as this while moving about. Many of them in the southern section of the Rocky Mountains form out of willow and other boughs an oval, elongated contrivance of wickerwork similar in dimensions to the old-fashioned pressboard used by the country mothers of better times in the finish of the customary jeans, pantaloons, and "roundabout." The little pickaninny is laid down flat on its back on this pressboard and there made fast. The mother lays this board about anywhere convenient, with the poor little brat fastened to it with much greater indifference than is usually shown by the owner of a bird in setting the cage around and about in any convenient place out of reach of the cat. The little creature when laid down has nothing to do but patiently roll its eyes about, looking skyward, and hold still, as it is compelled to do for an indefinite length of time.[3]

I can see now an old squaw on the eve of crossing the rugged mountain on a visit for the day, or to gather lizzards and mice for supper, binding down her hopeful on its back to a platted board, preparatory to sticking it up into a crevice or cranny in the rocks, out of the way, until her return, like our careful foreparents did pumpkin seed to dry. But however, this herd of Arapahoes and our party of adventurers had met on these roomy plains. An old gentleman in our party from Jackson County, Missouri, desired to have all diplomacy with poor "Lo" conducted as becomes dignified people of different nations, and he had prepared a court suit for such occasions as this. While our self-appointed ambassador was concealed away in his wagon dressing for his debut, my attention was called to an amusing as well as a sickening incident by the remark, "Look at that d——d ole squaw settin' on that pony yonder eatin lice." The squaws ride astraddle like the men. I walked a little distance toward the squaw

---

Bulletin No. 159; George Bird Grinnell, *The Cheyenne Indians; Their History and Way of Life,* I, 96; Hodge, *Handbook of American Indians,* II, 802–803.

[3] Bark, skins, boards, mattings, and baskets were all used in the construction of devices for the carrying of young among the Indians inhabiting the southern Rocky Mountains. Hodge, *Handbook of American Indians,* II, 357–59; Grenville Goodwin, *The Social Organization of the Western Apache,* 429–38; Lowie, *Indians of the Plains,* 42–43.

and observed her closely as she sat carelessly on the pony with a child behind and a smaller one in front of her. Her pony was grazing about on the scarce tufts of grass, unnoticed by its rider, who was not at all an old squaw as the remark indicated, but rather in the zenith of life and happiness.

She was indeed attentively engaged in searching for vermin. She supported the little papoose with one hand, caught the vermin with the other, and to make sure of the game, she would bite 'em. I walked nearer to look at her dexterity in catching bugs. This drew her attention just as she had caught one and bit it, and she looked at me and smiled sweetly, displaying the blood of the victim on her front teeth. She would catch and nip another, look complaisant, and smile upon me as if to say, "Am I not a good squaw for catching and killing these chintzes that infest papoose's hair?"[4]

Now I don't make this statement to shock delicate sensibilities, but ask delicacy to hold her breath while I tell her the truth, even upon a small matter, which may sometime or other assist in finding the true position of greater ones. I offer an apology for this dusky wigwam wife, because she looked so happy in her evident conscientious rectitude here under the blue sky for her shelter and the broad plains for her home. "Where ignorance is bliss, 'tis folly to be wise."[5]

Our boys began to get impatient and restless, while our minister was arranging his toilet. Some wanted to start on again. Others were toying with a papoose of royal blood, the son of the chief, by poking hard bread crusts at him to see him snap it, like any other hungry animal. The little fellow's appetite was keen and therefore he didn't stand much upon royal merit or dignity, but ravenously disposed of all the crusts thrust at him, while the old chief looked on with great interest and glee, evidently as much amused at his little cub's voracious appetite as any of the palefaces, who were heartily laughing at the little animal.

But at last our representative crawled out of the wagon and came

---

[4] Reference is made here to the human head louse because the chinch bug is a plant-feeding insect. William B. Herms, *Medical Entomology*, 318.

[5] These are the closing lines of Thomas Gray's *An Ode on a Distant Prospect of Eton College.*

forward with stately bearing as becomes the highest dignitary of a great people and one who is the repository of such important and exalted trusts. He bolted right up to the old chief, who had not noticed him, so busy as he was watching the boy crack bread crusts. The other Indians, who had seen the red-capped, striped and spotted, ghastly-looking figure emerge from the wagon, stood in silent awe of portentious results. The general-in-chief was now in his uniform and in the presence of the other high contracting party, and to open negotiations delivered a tremendous imposing and low bow, from which he arose and settled back into a prodigiously stiff and stately attitude. The old chief just got his first glimpse of our courtier as he had settled into his attitude, from whence to observe the surprise and watch the effect. The old Indian's smiling face turned from his boy to this apparition, underwent a sudden change as he started a little backward. He was evidently startled. But when our minister saw this state of things, he quickly stepped to the front apace and repeated the bow in such a vigorous style that the old brave turned trepidatiously, to get away from there, glancing suspiciously about at the other Indians near him, to catch their thoughts about it. They, too, were looking all about for explanation as they sidled away. But now this ludicrous failure is discovered by some of the paleface portion of the spectators, who had hitherto been taking more interest in this naked crowd of barbarians than in court questions. A burst of laughter set all things right. The Indians partook of the mirth, while the old chief caught a ray of light and came back to the "big" captain, dressed in Indian buckram, and leaning a little forward and looking him sharply in the eyes, with a smile all over his face, began his bows and salutations in recognition of the grand ones, which he had just began to understand, by numerous short and rapid nods, with one foot ahead of the other, and pigeon toed, gesturing in gutterals that began to roll out in strings, in the midst of which, at intervals, a vociferous "How-How-How" (the only salutation that he knew in English) could be heard above all else. This perfect thunder-gust of continuous and hearty salutations overwhelmed our spotted and striped representative to such a degree that after many desperate efforts to be heard above the din, created by the applause of our boys, he became confused and riled into angry gesticulations only equaled by those that poor "Lo" was making.

His face became red and his conduct angry and vigorous, and this was taken by the old chief and his "braves" to be a part of the program, in which they were not to be outdone, as they had now just begun to understand it; consequently they redoubled their efforts. In this they were aided by the mischievous palefaces around them, until these gymnastic salutations became so fatiguing as to bring the perspiration from the Indians, who were all too loyal to good breeding to quit before the thing was properly ended. The old chief was much gratified at the result, while he puffed and blew like a wind-broken horse at the termination of the melee. But there could be no smile wrung from our now silent and disgusted dressy man. He was ungenerous enough to remark after all was over that he would have been glad if this devil's dance had only stampeded our stock, wagons, and all. There was great amusement in this diplomatic gathering. Even the indifferent lady on horseback quit picking bugs off of her child's head, to enjoy the great pageantry.

But it is not to be presumed that our minister plenipotentiary was to be entirely left unredressed. He came again to the breach, but in a more prudent and cautious way, for fear of again exciting the old chief's joys. After another repetition or so of how! how! in pure Anglo-Indian style, the "big brave" exclaimed with great feeling: "Nick-i-mi-pick-i-mi hick-i-mi-pi-yah."[6] This brought them to an amicable understanding, and in spite of all the levity and incredulity of the members of our party, our captain compelled them to believe at last upon the importance of the occasion by answering the chief's last remark by courteously tipping his gorgeous red cap lightly, then pointing away off toward the plain, and exclaiming "Buffalo-e-e all dead-e-e." This reply was a stunner, forcing us to the conclusion that we had mastered the situation and left nothing else for us to do but to go our way rejoicing to the Rocky Mountains.

The two great heads talked some more, but we could not comprehend them. As we moved off, we told our nude friends good-by,

[6] This is undoubtedly gibberish and only what Conner could remember approximately twenty years later.

while they heartily replied by telling us "how-how." Each commissioner seemed to be contented with this last arrangement, thus entered into for the mutual protection of each other's tribe, and we parted as peacefully as we had met, setting a worthy example for all other warlike nations by which to profit. We proceeded across Walnut Creek, a tributary to the Arkansas, and camped finally on Ash Creek[7] near Pawnee Rock.[8] As you draw near Pawnee Fork, the country changes almost imperceptibly until it merges into the arid barren wastes of an unbroken span of the width of the Great Plains.[9] The transition is marked by the occurrence of cacti and other spinose plants.[10]

This was about the beginning of the appearance of the famous buffalo grass. Cattle accustomed to be fed on grain become very weak feeding on grass alone and should never in that condition be subjected to continuous work.[11] A violation of this fact has cost many volunteers their stock and entailed trouble without end on many inexperienced travelers crossing the plains.

[7] Ash Creek is located nineteen miles from Walnut Creek by Gregg but twenty-two miles from the same point by Parsons. Gregg, *Commerce of the Prairies*, 217; Parsons, *New Gold Mines of Western Kansas*, 185.

[8] Pawnee Rock, visible for ten miles by travelers on the Santa Fe Trail, was described by Charles C. Post in his diary as "an angle of a bluff with a detached or two detached rocks about the size of the old court house in Decatur set on a small base about ten feet across. This rock seems to have been burnt or the sun has hardened and blackened the outside, which being penetrated we found nothing but soft sand stone." Many of these early travelers cut their names in the sandstone, but they are no longer visible because much of the facing of the cliff has been destroyed. LeRoy R. Hafen, *Overland Routes to the Gold Fields, 1859*, 40–41. The site is now marked by a historical monument northwest of the present town of Pawnee Rock, Pawnee County, Kansas. Gregg, *Commerce of the Prairies*, 43, 43n.

[9] Pawnee Fork or Pawnee River, as it is now named, enters the Arkansas at Larned, Kansas, about six miles from Ash Creek. Parsons, *New Gold Mines of Western Kansas*, 185; Gregg, *Commerce of the Prairies*, 43, 43n.

[10] The party was now entering the region of the short grasses of the plains. Among the grasses, various species of "small, low-growing cacti are not infrequent." J. E. Weaver and F. W. Albertson, *Grasslands of the Great Plains*, 63.

[11] Conner did not notice that the buffalo grass was mixed with equal amounts of blue grama grass, with smaller amounts of wire grass and little bluestem. F. W. Albertson, "Ecology of Mixed Prairie in West Central Kansas," *Ecological Monographs*, Vol. VII, No. 4 (October, 1937) 487; Sellers G. Archer and Clarence E. Bunch, *The American Grass Book*, 207–209.

The route we traveled from Pawnee Fork to Bent's Fort was estimated at 312 miles, and with the general direction of the river, but cutting off the meanderings; making dry camps on the dry plains, as before stated, was where the Indians were the most annoying. The river seldomly exceeded two or three hundred yards wide throughout this distance.[12] The bottom land, a few feet above the level of the water, varied in width from half a mile to two miles and was generally covered with good and nutritious grass, except when the Indians would burn it off ahead of us. On such occasions we would drive the stock loose across the river to graze during the night, which would necessitate doubling the number of herders for greater safety. The river was shallow and seldomly exceeding the depth of the waist of him who was the unlucky guardsman in the burned district. To strip and wade this river in the middle of the chilly nights appeared to many of us a serious matter; but there was no avoiding the necessity, for there was but two horses in the party.

Many times were we cheated by attempting to follow the same route back across the river to the camp when relieved by our guard mates at midnight, by the plunging into deep holes of water caused by quicksand giving away and washing off after having been stirred by the crossing of the cattle. But experience, the best of all lessons, soon taught us not to attempt to recross by the previous passage, but to avoid them. There were places where the banks were much higher than the surface of the water by more than two feet. For instance, at the Great Bend the river ran quite against the bluffs of the plains, or rather the sand hills bordering the river bottom lands on the south impinged abruptly on the course of the river itself. Pawnee Rock is nothing more than the terminus of one of the bluffs border-

---

[12] Parsons calculated the distance by the trail at 253 miles from Pawnee Fork to Bent's New Fort. Augustus Voorhees of the Lawrence party in 1858 gives an excellent description of the structure which was located on the north bank of the Arkansas River opposite the present town of Prowers, Colorado: "the fort is built on a bluff near the river is built of sand stone 100 feet wide and 200 long, with 13 rooms inside with a large yard inside, the walls are 16 feet high, the rooms are Coverd with timber and gravle, with a breast work around the top, with port holes for Cannon of which they have two pieces." Hafen (ed.), "The Voorhees Diary," *loc. cit.*, 47; Hafen, *Pike's Peak Guidebooks*, 101n.; Parsons, *New Gold Mines of Western Kansas*, 185.

ing the lowlands of the river, usually termed sand hills. Hundreds of miles were made, tediously traveled by our party without any fuel with which to prepare our food except the dried excrement of buffaloes and wild sagebrush, both of which were scarce. The soil of the plains is a granitic sand, intermixed with the exuviae of animals, with perhaps some little vegetable substance from a scanty growth.[13]

The eye wanders in vain over these immense wastes in search of landmarks, away from the trunk streams which are very limited. One exception is a vast collection of little knolls situated this side of the Rocky Mountains, between the Arkansas and Platte rivers. They are located all about the plain on a level and extensive section, a few paces from each other and from two to five feet high perhaps, and covered with grass, as is also the space between them. They look as if the earth out of which they are composed had been carried and poured into piles on a level plain, like the artificial mounds to be seen in our modern front yards, overgrown with grass. What seems to be the greatest puzzle, these little apparent, purposeless and neatly formed embankments are situated so far from any other obstacle that extends above the undeviating level country over which they are scattered, and so far from any watercourse. They are evidently a constellation of curiosities of great age, not easily accounted for.[14]

The most comprehensible description they could have is that they resemble a promiscuously scattered collection of old-fashioned burrows, in which our fathers deposited Irish potatoes to keep through the winter, only that grass grew in solid turf over them, as well as on the level space between them. It seemed impossible to

[13] The soil of the plains is of fluviatile origin, composed for the most part of unconsolidated silt mixed with smaller quantities of sand and gravel. In the valley of the Arkansas River coarse sand constitutes most of the soil. In western Kansas one finds the type of soil changing from chernozem to northern dark brown to northern brown as one passes from east to west. Nevin M. Fenneman, *Physiography of the Western United States*, 13; Weaver and Albertson, *Grasslands of the Great Plains*, 58.

[14] These are the "Tepee Buttes" which occur north of the Arkansas River and east of Pueblo, Colorado. They are formed around giant limestone concretions of "cones" some ten feet in diameter. As the surface around the cones degraded, the limestone concretions protected the surrounding shale, making some of these buttes several hundred feet high. Fenneman, *Physiography of the Western United States*, 33–34.

Council Grove, Kansas, in the 1860's.
The Kansas State Historical Society, Topeka

A Ute encampment at Hamilton, Colorado, in the 1860's.
Library, State Historical Society of Colorado

surmise the cause or purpose of this extensive cluster of miniature peaks, unless they were intended to mimic the stupendous grandeur of Pike's Peak, whose dark frowns in the distant border of the Rocky Mountains were daily photographed in the darkening landscape of his own shadow. The sun sank in the west, shooting his last evening ray toward our Lilliputian pretenders accompanied by the shade in the illimitable plain, far below and away toward the horizon. The stragglers who were off duty during a day's march frequently found written with pencil upon the animal exuviae the names of officers and privates of the U.S. Army, with date, name of company, and regiment, the length of time they had been on the *qui vive*, and what direction they were going. I found one buffalo skull which contained quite a history written upon its inside, of some of General Harney's exploits, signed by a lieutenant of cavalry and dated five years previously.[15] The skull was placed with its cavity to the ground and propped with other bones to its position, and being aided by the grass subsequently grown to keep its original position. It doubtless had never been moved since the writer placed it. The writing was in perfect preservation. I will state here that in the fall of 1860, when a portion of our party came back to Council Grove, as above stated, being the same year that the "Caw" Indians killed their "medicine" man at that place, we again passed Walnut Creek, our present locality.[16] When we arrived at this creek (there had been a private trading

[15] General William Selby Harney (1800–89) served in the Black Hawk, Seminole, and Mexican wars. During the Mexican War, in the Battle of Cerro Gordo, he distinguished himself by heroic action and was promoted to brevet brigadier general. After serving in the Mexican War, Harney returned to frontier duty, campaigning against the Plains Indians. General Harney entered the field against the Sioux in August, 1855, to punish them for attacks during the previous year. In the valley of the Little Blue River, Harney defeated the Brulé Sioux under Little Thunder on September 3, 1855. It is doubtful if Harney campaigned as far south as the Santa Fe Trail because after the fight on the Little Blue, Harney moved his troops from Fort Laramie to Fort Pierre, wintering at the latter post. Frank L. Owsley, "William Selby Harney," *Dictionary of American Biography*, Vol. VIII, 280–81; George E. Hyde, *Red Cloud's Folk: A History of the Oglala Sioux Indians*, 79ff.; Hoopes, *Indian Affairs*, 211; Eugene Bandel, *Frontier Life in the Army, 1854–1861*, 69–98.

[16] The Kaw or Kansa Indians belong to the Siouan linguistic family and lived along the Kansas River. In 1846 they were settled on a reservation at Council Grove,

post set up there since we had passed it, en route for the Rocky Mountains) we found that the deserted house (built of adobes) had been robbed. On looking about, we found three dead bodies and buried them across the road opposite of and in front of the little house. Further to the east of the road and perhaps fifty paces up Walnut Creek, we found a bottle of wine and a box of cigars, neither of which had even been opened. The bottle was closed with red sealing wax. The locality of these articles showed what directions the Indians took after the perpetration of the murder and robbery, and the loss of the articles bore evidence of their guilty haste in departing the bloody scene of their treachery, and cowardly fears of being trailed up by the United States troops. Two of those men, I afterward learned, were Allison and Boothe, strangers, who first undertook the dangerous task of establishing a settlement at the crossing of Walnut Creek. The third man's name I never knew.[17]

This little incident is responsible for this digression, for we are here just on the way to the Rocky Mountains, and have just left Walnut Creek, upon whose banks no white man, up to the fall of 1860, had ever erected a headquarters of any sort.[18] I only go a little aside of the general course to remark the above incident, thinking that

---

Morris County, Kansas, on the Neosho River; there they remained until 1873 when they were removed to Indian Territory. Hodge, *Handbook of American Indians*, I, 653–55; Wright, *Indian Tribes of Oklahoma*, 160–64.

[17] Allison and Booth, previously connected with the Santa Fe Mail and Stage, established this trading post in either 1855 or 1857, where the Santa Fe Trail crossed Walnut Creek. Another contemporary, J. R. Mead, however, presents an entirely different version of the destruction of Allison's ranch: "George Peacock was killed at Allison's ranch, also his clerk and Mexican herder, on September 9, 1860, by Satanta, war chief of the Kiowas. The 'Ranch' or trading station was built by Allison, of Independence, Mo., in 1857. It was situated on the Santa Fe trail about 100 yards from the crossing of Walnut Creek, on the east side, and on the north side of the road. Allison died suddenly of heart failure, and Peacock rented the ranch. Peacock was killed for personal reasons only." James Josiah Webb, *Adventures in the Santa Fe Trade, 1844–47*, 163–64; J. R. Mead to George W. Martin, July 11, 1908, in *Transactions of the Kansas State Historical Society, 1907–1908*, Vol. X, 664–65.

[18] Conner is in error at this point because the trading station was completed in 1855 or 1857, as noted above.

perhaps those who may inhabit and own the soil around the junction of the old road and Walnut Creek might feel some interest in a short history of the fate of those of their own race who first died in the occupancy of their present lands. Especially as this place at the present writing (1880) may be and I presume is the abode of a numerous population living in peace and plenty, and if so the transition cannot be imagined by the writer who has never been on the ground since this tragedy.[19]

The Kiowas and Comanches were the united tribes who did this mischief under the leadership of a Kiowa chief, pronounced "Tahoson." I don't know whether his name had ever been spelled or not. I know that "Old Tahoson" and "Young Tahoson" were desperate names those days. It was the young one who was in command on this occasion.[20]

We had now begun to enter the buffalo and prairie dog country, and all our camps appeared to be just alike on this level country.

[19] Several dates for the writing of this reminiscence are available. Later, when Conner was trying to interest territorial officials of Arizona in the manuscript, he wrote: "I was the only member of the Walker Party or, any one else those times to keep data, down to the fall of 1867, when I left Prescott and came to Los Angeles, spent the winter and arived [sic] home in Ky the next Spring and immediately compiled my data . . . [writing] . . . a running recital while it was fresh. . . . This was made in my own handwriting closely written to the amount of nearly one thousand pages of foolscap, cleeted [sic] into eight parts which I have kept in my possession for forty years. . . . Six of the parts are of Arizona, and two of them pertain to Colorado—as did two others which were destroyed by fire, having had them separated to make a few copies at the request of Gen. Hall for his history years ago." Daniel Ellis Conner to Hon. Jos. H. Kibbey, governor of Arizona, January 12, 1909, Conner Manuscripts, *loc. cit.*

[20] Dohasan is the spelling used by Mooney and Wright. Dohasan or Little Bluff became principal chief of the Kiowas in 1833, ruling the tribe until his death in 1866. Although he had a son possessing the same name, Satanta and Kicking Bird became the most active leaders of the Kiowas after the death of the elder Dohasan because no one in the tribe had sufficient influence to be named principal chief. In addition to the name Little Bluff, white men also called Dohasan "Little Mountain" or "Over-the-Mountain," but Nye maintains the name should be spelled "To-hauson" and correctly translated as "Overhanging Butte." James Mooney, *Calender History of the Kiowa Indians, Seventeenth Annual Report* of the Bureau of American Ethnology, 1895–1896, Pt. I, 318, 399–400; W. S. Nye, *Carbine & Lance*, 12; Rupert Norval Richardson, *The Comanche Barrier to South Plains Settlement*, 288, 289; Wright, *Indian Tribes of Oklahoma*, 171–72.

The question arose whether we could have divine services, on learning that there was in our party a young man from Iowa who professed to be a minister. I rather thought that the subject was suggested by thoughtless impiety, but it was, however, settled by the young man proposing to preach on the following night, which was heartily encouraged. Pursuant to this understanding, after arriving in camp and supper disposed of, the numerous ox yokes, water kegs, buckets, and so forth, were arranged around conveniently for seats. The young minister opened his services with prayer as usual. "Who Made Man" was his chosen text. Upon this question, or rather text, he preached a long and earnest sermon there in the dark and the silence of the plains, and listened to respectfully by the whole party, except the guard who were out with the stock.

This young preacher, whether he was an imposter or not, had the old log-cabin style to the letter, for he wound up all of his impressive long sentences with the old well-known solemn "ar-rah," in good old-time earnestness. But it was very well considered and respected, although I could not help impiously suspecting that the time, place, and surroundings were the primary causes of such decent conduct, for the most part. It was a lonesome, solemn-looking place, with a great deal of outside and distant space to stare at, without looking upward. We had services frequently afterward. Our major, captain, general of the Arapaho treaty was always present with very few suggestions. He had laid aside his court suit of calico and ribbons, red cap and blankets, and never to my personal knowledge did he ever appear in public again. Our fellows persisted in confessing his great services, now and then, but he was like most all public men: he didn't like flattery and would anger a little when it was too profuse, and modestly remind them of it, when spread on too thick. It was at last found to be more pleasant to cease expressions of admiration altogether, when the mischievous "boys" discovered that they were hurting one another's feelings.

Then besides, things began to look serious a few days after our first sermon, when a few of our party came across four men lying on their backs, side by side, a few feet apart with their feet to the road, nude, and with their hearts cut out of them, and placed upon each's forehead.[21] Evidently fresh done, or the ravens and wolves would have found them before we did. They were hastily buried just deep enough to be easily scratched out and left to their fate and the coyote wolves.

More prudence was now considered necessary, and therefore a guard of one man would go on duty around the sleeping camp. On one occasion when I was on camp guard, the night became chilly, dark, and stormy. For some minutes the rain fell in torrents, accompanied by terrific thunder and almost continuous lightning, flash after flash lightening up the now watery plain for a great distance. While this war of the elements was progressing in the midst of its best efforts I could distinctly observe apparently away off on the plain, between the rapid flashes of lightning, a horseman on the full run, darting about in a zigzag manner as though he was trying to dodge the thunder strokes. Although his course was so wild and uncertain as to point of place, he seemed to be getting nearer, very rapidly. It was difficult to watch this wild man and horse, in such blinding torrents did the rain fall; and especially so, when aided by the dense darkness between the lightning flashes. Knowing that the figure was surely, surely approaching in so strange a manner, I leveled my gun in his direction and the next instant was surprised to see the horse suddenly halt within ten paces of me, in an affrighted manner, and on its own volition. It evidently saw, by the last flash, that it was about to run against the wagons, and its rider knew not where he was going nor where he was until he was in camp and saw my gun leveled at him, and just in time to call out, "Don't shoot." He proved to be one of the herders, Mr. J. H. [?], who was trying to prevent a stampede of the stock during the storm and became lost from the stock and camp. His horse became unmanageable, ran away with him, and came to camp in spite of him. This was the heaviest rainfall I ever knew of on the plains.

It is incomprehensible why a herd of old work cattle, after traveling hard all day and until they are apparently so tired out as to be

---

[21] Plains Indians rarely practiced this form of mutilation, but the Apaches were known to cut out the hearts of their victims. John G. Bourke, *On the Border with Crook*, 26.

hardly able to put one foot before the other, will take affright, after being released from their yokes at night, and stampede like a herd of buffalo for miles before they halt. The weakest old scrub amongst them will always keep up in their wild career.

I remember one evening a bright pretty day after a long dusty drive, the wagons were corraled and the cattle turned out. Two or three of them immediately walked off twenty or thirty paces to an old dry skeleton of a buffalo. They began to paw and moan over these mortal remains until they got to bellowing. Then all the rest made a rush there to see what was the matter. They all soon succeeded in discovering a ghost and lit out from there, with their tails curled over backs as though the very devil was riding each one to market on a short line. They were soon out of sight, leaving their course marked by a train of dust in the distance, which had not settled when dark came on. It took us two days to find and to get them together again. And after getting them together after their ten-mile heat that would have run a horse down, they all seemed fresher than when turned out of their yokes.[22]

The following night we pitched camp on the dry plain out of sight of the Arkansas. Here the wagon master, who, as before stated, had had quite an experience on the plains, thought it high time that he was playing some trick upon some of the verdant specimens of the party. He was a jovial fellow and always awake to all opportunities for a frolic. It was nearly dark, and after supper was disposed of, that he was noticed to be very thoughtfully hanging the vessels that strewed the ground around his campfire, up high on his wagon. He would hang up a kettle here and pot or pan there, then look and reflect upon a good place to put some other cooking utensil—appar-

---

[22] One famous writer of the cattlemen's frontier gives his classic description of cattle stampedes as follows: "A stampede is the natural result of fear, and at night or in an uncertain light, this timidity might be imparted to an entire herd by a flash of lightening or a peal of thunder, while the stumbling of a night horse, or the scent of some wild animal, would in a moment's time, from frightening a few head, so infect a herd as to throw them into the wildest panic. . . . Frequently a herd became so [accustomed to stampeding] that they would stampede on the slightest provocation,—or no provocation at all." Andy Adams, *The Log of a Cowboy: A Narrative of the Old Trail Days*, 41.

ently wholly engaged all by himself. Someone asked, "Why, what are you hanging them things up there for?" "Why, you fool, don't you see that prairie dog town, right out yonder?" "Yes, and I saw the prairie dogs, too, but what of it?" "What of it? Just leave your camp kit on the ground overnight and you'll find 'what of it'!" "Well, why don't you put up that pot of cooked beans, there in the ashes. Won't they eat them too?" "Oh, the d——l. I am not afraid of them eating the provisions, but don't want them to carry off the cooking utensils; besides, I want them beans to keep warm to eat during the night, while I am on guard, and the prairie dogs will certainly not carry off a hot kettle. Haven't you got any sense?"

This was enough; the old wagon master picked up his gun and started off to take his place on guard. Pretty soon all the other wagons were profusely ornamented and festooned with kettles, pots, pans, cups, and camp trash of all kinds. The wagon master was much amused while he chuckled over this anticipated morning's joke, as he contemplated the result of his pretended fears of the harmless little marmot.

He ate beans at intervals until midnight when his time was out, and retired to sleep on his final chuckle for a "big" morning's laugh. All were now in the prospects of an early breakfast and an early start as well as secure in their cheap, but necessary, effects in camp life. The wagon master failed to hang up his kettle of beans when he retired after all of his prudential precautions against the nightly ravages of the little dogs.

When the relief guard of the afterpart of the night put their heads together in counsel upon the merits and demerits of the prairie dog, they soon concluded that those poor innocent little creatures would never visit any camp and rendered their verdict accordingly....

They stole the wagon master's breakfast of beans and carried them out on the plain near the cattle herd and placed the kettle by the side of a little sagebrush cluster. They, too, helped themselves from time to time during the latter part of the night, to pork and beans, which is the favorite dish in camp life on the great plains. They had made up their minds to finish the dish and return the kettle to the ashes in camp, then lay the theft upon the prairie dogs. But alas, the "best laid plans o' mice and men" often fail. When our intriguers sought the kettle at the sagebrush on the approach of daylight, behold it was gone. They searched every isolated bunch of sagebrush in the neighborhood, without success. The kettle was lost. They drove in the cattle to be yoked, feeling cheaply, to think the wagon master had at last beaten them. After the joke of hanging up the camp plunder out of reach of the prairie dogs was duly celebrated, the wagon master demanded his camp kettle. The conspirators laughed at the demand and referred him to the prairie dogs for his kettle. The wagon master, enjoying the joke a little while longer with reasonable patience, again demanded the kettle, remarking that it was carrying the joke so far as to inconvenience the whole party in starting on the journey. The guardsmen were now beginning to look incredulous and serious at the same time. They were evidently confounded by the earnest and importunate demand for the return of the missing vessel. The question arose to the dignity of a quandary, as plainly depicted on each face, and the wagon master, having the most experience, was the first to strike the key to its solution. He queried, "Did you d——n fools take that kettle of beans out to the herd with you?" "Yes, we did," was the response. "And ate the beans?" "Yes." "Well, can't you find it?" "No, it was moved from where we put it, and we thought that you had taken it while we were watching the cattle." "Yes, exactly—just what I expected. A wolf, while licking it, got his head fast in the bail and ran away with it. My kettle is gone. Why the h——ll didn't you bring it to camp and leave it? I will never joke a d——n fool again." Here it was modestly suggested that the prairie dogs had the missing piece of furniture. This brought out the impatient exclamation, "Oh, go to h——ll, it is no joke to be without a camp kettle on a trip like this."

Members of the party some time after the above incident, on arriving in the selected camp, would suggest hanging up the kettles, etc. out of the reach of prairie dogs, but the serious loss had taken all the spice out of the joke. The camp kettle was finally forgotten as well as lost amid the graver reflections now continuously imposed upon our care.

It looked very like good old genuine economy to see men jump out of their respective wagons in the evening while in motion just before camping time, to walk and gather the smallest fragments of the dried excrement of buffaloes for fuel with which to cook their suppers. Each would have a sack and would pick up the least fragment if but the size of a twenty-five cent greenback—to such limited resources were we put to fuel.

It might be interesting to those who have had no experience in cooking a meal's victuals with such fuel, and so little of it, to know how it was done. A trench four or five feet in length would be dug into the ground and about eight inches deep by about as many wide, to begin with. Such turf and grass as could be raked up would be put into this ditch, its whole length. On the arrival of each gleaner, with probably a little more than a hatful of fuel, he would pour it into the trench on top of the grass and straw until the ditch was full. Then ignite the grass at each end of the ditch and the fire is made, while the already prepared cooking vessels are set over the ditch and resting upon its edges, which serve for andirons. Sometimes the kettles would be kept supported off the ground by means of a tripod of camp hooks (so called), but even then a little hole was usually dug in which to make the fire, to prevent the wind from blowing the fuel away, before it burned to cinder, and sometimes all the fire would blow away before any heat was obtained, leaving an ashy spot to show where the fire had been made. Besides, great care had to be observed to keep from burning the plains over, so as to destroy the grass, the only food for the stock. It was astonishing how much food could be prepared with so little fuel.

We were now in the buffalo range (so called) which extends north and south and not very wide. They seemed to have contracted their territory and to have selected the middle of the Great Plains for their passage north and south, long since, judging from the well-beaten and deeply worn paths to be seen in the midst of the plains and nowhere else. Some of those narrow trails were at least a foot in depth and overgrown with grass, having the appearance of being as old as I imagine the old Roman thoroughfares look. It seems useless to suggest that the buffalo were pushed back upon the western plains from the borders of advancing states, like the Indians. It is

43

reasonable to believe that the buffalo of the plains were marching north and south in the middle of this flat grassy and treeless country and governing their speed by the changing climates, consequent to the coming of alternate winter and summer, anterior to the discovery of America.[23]

We came into the buffalo range, as before stated, and of course the characteristic prevailing disposition of such a party of men would naturally tend to incite individual enterprises in the way of sporting, with such free game. Besides buffalo this range abounded with antelope, prairie dogs, badgers, owls, rattlesnakes, lizards, and wolves of many sizes and colors—black, yellow, gray, and brindle, and in some instances they wore white spots in the breast and a white ring around the neck.[24] All of those animals, except the buffalo, were constantly in sight and also except the badger perhaps. In keeping with the natural spirit of adventure and curiosity on such an occasion, R. R. [?] and myself left the wagon train as it moved on, one morning after breakfast, to take a stroll alone quite a distance from the train. We were a long way off and kept within sight for the greater portion of the day, walking in a parallel with it. At last we discovered in the distance what we deemed a herd of buffalo, and traveled for nearly an hour in that direction before these large animals dwindled down to a number of fragments of buffalo excrement. We were strangely

[23] Carl Coke Rister notes that by 1865 the southern herd of buffalo was limited in its range between the northern boundary of Texas and the 41st parallel. Although the white man completed the destruction of the buffalo, it is estimated that Indians killed five million of these animals between 1835 and 1845. Government explorers reported, as early as 1854, that buffaloes were decreasing in numbers. Buffaloes used the same trails time after time, wearing paths a foot wide and six or seven inches deep in the prairie sod. Authorities accept the original number of buffaloes as between fifty to sixty million animals, but Frank Gilbert Roe denies any regular or general migration, thus explaining the absence of buffalo from a given area over a length of time. Carl Coke Rister, "The Significance of the Destruction of the Buffalo in the Southwest," *Southwestern Historical Quarterly*, Vol. XXXIII, No. 1 (July, 1929), 35, 41; Martin S. Garretson, *The American Bison*, 57; Frank Gilbert Roe, *The North American Buffalo*, 492–93, 594–95.

[24] For an inclusive list of mammals in Kansas, see E. Raymond Hall, *Handbook of Mammals of Kansas*. In western Kansas, the coyote, red wolf, and gray wolf existed. Many of the animals seen by Conner were undoubtedly coyotes, which were more numerous than either of the species of wolves.

puzzled thus, during the day, by any little object which, by the aid of a mirage, would be transformed into a monster. Sometimes a wolf half a mile off would appear as large as a buffalo and appear to be miles away. Prairie dogs would frequently look, as they sat bolt upright, as tall as a man, while they are not much larger than a squirrel. Perhaps the reader may think that these are hard statements. Be that as it may, I shall not claim for my precedent to cite as authority the highly colored stories hitherto the fruits of exaggerated perception, nor attempt to soften the facts so as to meet the reasoning approbation of the incredulous.

But however, we pretty soon descried in the distant horizon toward the north the front ranks of a line of real buffalo coming in single file. There was no mistaking it this time, for they could be distinctly seen to move and increase in bulk while we sat still upon the ground awaiting their approach. They looked as though they were coming out of the ground in the distant horizon, like a serpent drawing his continuous length out of his hole slowly and steadily, extending his body on the surface in a direct course without ever getting wholly out.

On and on they sturdily marched in compact single file for more than five hours and until their leader became opposite and about a quarter of a mile to the west of our position. From the large sturdy leaders, back toward the rear of this well-closed line of animals, their proportions gradually decreased until the individual animal was lost in the blended dark streak which extended and dwindled out of sight in the horizon where the line could not be seen to move at all. It was the most grand and extensive sight I ever witnessed. It seemed impossible to arrive at any conclusion as to the length of that part of this orderly string of animals which was in sight, without considering the probable number yet behind. The front and nearest ones walked steadily on as though they were going all the way before halting, and were near enough to distinctly discern the clear-cut perpendicular line or border which divides the long shaggy hair of the head, neck, and shoulders from the lighter-colored short hair of the middle and hindquarters. We didn't want any buffalo meat out of such a big herd and therefore we didn't pretend to make war upon them, but just sat and looked—"nothing more." To add to the curious conduct of this orderly procession, the whole line came gradually to a halt and each member thereof quietly changed ends and just as orderly as ever, took up their countermarch back the path which they came. And as far as we could see they were all moving back, while we still sat and looked until they were quite gone from view. We spent the most of the day looking at this wonderful and silent display and wondering how they communicated throughout this long line, without any confusion whatever, their united conclusions to go back. But they did it and that without any apparent cause or commands and without a jostle in their cumbersome ranks.

We awoke up out of our long reverie to the fact that we were now entirely alone on this expansive waste and on the moment came near losing our direction in the absence of any landmark whatever. We only saved the right direction intact by remembering the course we were going with reference to direction in which we first saw the buffalo. But on becoming confused in our sudden eagerness to start after our floating camp, which was long since out of sight, we even lost the direction in which we had last seen the retreating buffalo and differed with each other as to all directions. We had but little idea of what time of day it was, and therefore the sun had strayed from its course.

So the most prudent way we could adopt to get out of this steadily increasing dilemma was adopted in just as steadily increasing trepidation. It was plain that if we left the spot in the wrong direction the result would be calamitous. It was decided that one of us should stay to mark the place, while the other went in search of [the] freshly beaten buffalo trail, whose general course would give us the direction in which we were going when we discovered this herd coming.

I stayed and my confident friend marched off to find the buffalo trail, and sure enough he missed it and then took a great circle around me as a center until he found it. Then he thought that it was not the one upon which we had lately seen the buffalo traveling because it ran in the wrong direction, and thought that it must be some other newly made trail. But he could find but one and after following it to its end, where the buffalo turned back, he concluded that we would have to depend upon it, and took our direction accordingly and kept it for a few miles, and joyfully struck the trail of the wagon train which we vigorously followed until night came on. The darkness of night prevented rapid progress, for we were fearful of wandering from the road and therefore had determined rather to stay where we were on the trail until daylight than taking more chances without headlands to steer to. But as long as we were certain of being on the track we kept moving on, and when we lost it, the other would stop to be sure of his part of it until both got right again. But this procedure became very monotonous, and as a last effort to reach camp that night we fired off our guns in the air. Someone at camp, whose appointed duty it was to be on the quarter-deck as a lookout on such occasions, saw the flash of our guns, one after the other, and responded by a like number of shots. We saw the weak flashes, without any accompanying report, and therefore doubted whether to trust them or not. Finally we recharged our guns with powder alone and discharged them in slow succession, then closely observed our supposed direction for results. Two more flashes in about the same succession followed. We were now satisfied and walked rapidly in that direction without looking for road or trail, for perhaps half an hour. Stopping again, we repeated our signal as before. This time the flashes were plain and the reports quite distinctly heard. We took up our march again for a time and signaled again, and again, as necessity required until we reached camp in safety. We had nothing to do after reaching headquarters but to get supper and receive reproof from our old wagon master, seasoned with good-humored teasings, for not having sense enough to find the way home, etc., and finally we crawled into our blankets for the night.

How the Indians kept their even way on those plains is impossible for me to even conjecture, and should I be compelled to learn how, without a compass or timepiece, I should not know even how to begin the task. Every one place is just exactly like the other.[25]

[25] Indians in their own country followed well-known trails on their migrations. It should be realized that in their native environment, the Indians traveled and hunted over the region from youth, at first in the company of experienced warriors, and thus came to know the land forms and landmarks which to the inexperienced eye appeared unidentifiable. In strange country the Indians observed carefully the

47

The buffalo too seem to have no fear of being lost so badly as to want for water, although it is so scarce, and such great distances apart. But perhaps instinct is better than reason on those plains, and I can say from experience, if it is not more valuable than my reason in such a locality it is indeed worthless.

I will state here that a half-year later I was in this vicinity and the buffalo were crowding around a water hole in the Arkansas River. The river was dry for many miles, although I had learned that it was not usual for it to go dry. The buffalo were present and very gentle or else suffering greatly for water. It took a liberal display of firearm practice to keep them away from the cattle. It was feared that they would stampede and take the cattle with them. On this occasion one large buffalo bull left his herd—broke through the guard and came on a full run into camp amongst the oxen, while the men were sitting on the ground partaking of dinner. In this position the fellows reached for their guns, with which they sent a perfect shower of bullets at the buffalo, without killing it. There must have been fifty shots fired at the enraged animal before he made his way out on the high plains again. I will mention another incident, for the benefit of those who are inexperienced and who believe that to kill a buffalo is as easy a job as that of shooting an ox.

Before leaving these thirsty buffalo to themselves on this last occasion, three of us hid under the riverbank near the water hole referred to, while the main body of the party moved out on the journey. The coast now appearing clear, the herd of buffalo that had been huddled together in view and out on the plains for hours awaiting our departure now came marching toward the water. As they were crossing single file on the dry, sandy river bottom, we selected and fired on a calf, one of the shots breaking its spine. The rest ran off on to the plain, leaving the calf, which was reared up on its fore

---

landmarks and looked back often so they could remember the route they had taken. It should also be noted that old trappers and mountain men traveled on the plains and in the mountains without aid of maps or compasses, and by the end of the days of the fur trade, hardly a region of the West remained unexplored. Dale L. Morgan, *Jedediah Smith and the Opening of the West;* Osburne Russell, *Journal of a Trapper, or Nine Years in the Rocky Mountains, 1834–1844;* Alpheus H. Favour, *Old Bill Williams, Mountain Man.*

feet, unable to lift its hindquarters off of the ground. In this position it stood while one of my associates approached near it in front and emptied the contents of the six chambers of a United States Navy pistol into its forehead without knocking it down.[26]

The calf was finally dispatched by cutting his throat with a butcher knife. While it was being butchered I approached to within a range of sixty yards of the herd, concealed myself behind a bunch of grass flat on the ground, and fired twenty fair shots at first one and another without ever bringing one to the ground or frightening them away. The last shot I fired was after raising from my concealment and quickly dashing up to within ten paces of them and fired, and still failed to kill one. But at this juncture, the herd stampeded one direction and myself in another, resulting in all of us getting away in safety except about a dozen of the poor animals which I had uselessly and badly wounded. They alone remained, too badly hurt and too sullen to leave, and I was too sullen to go back to them, after observing how stubbornly they looked after me. The spongy skin about a buffalo's head and neck varies from about three-quarters of an inch to an inch thick, and I have measured their hump bones that stand on the top of the spine over the shoulders, and found them to be two feet in length, hence the spine in front is located about the center of the animal's bulk, especially toward the shoulders. We packed the beef thus obtained on a horse which had been kept in the distance while the game was being captured and started after the party, and was again belated and again had to resort to the firing of minute guns in the night, something after the same way as is already related. One difference, however, was that the bullets could be heard to sing from the time they left the gun until they struck the ground near us, being imprudently sent in our direction. Also, when we came nearly to camp we found them on the opposite bank of a creek, a tributary to the Arkansas, and after driving the horse, loaded with flesh, across the deep water (for the creek was not dry like the river

[26] La Bonté, Ruxton's hero, failed to kill a buffalo and it is explained: "As is generally the case with greenhorns, he had fired too high, not understanding that the only certain spot to strike a buffalo is but a few inches above the brisket, and that above this a shot is rarely fatal." George Frederick Ruxton, *Life in the Far West*, 61; Bernard DeVoto, *Across the Wide Missouri*, 39–40, 418–19.

below), the whole party began roasting the meat furnished them by the horse and laughed at our importunities to send the horse back over for us. And they were inexorable to the last. We waded over and after taking the trouble to strip to keep our clothes dry, and found after dressing again that we could have stepped over the water fifty paces above, all of which they were kind enough to tell us after it was all over. The petty wrath and petulancies of the individual members of our party were always subjects of mirth and laughter in our ranks. And it was just so on this occasion.

꙰꙰꙰꙰꙰꙰꙰꙰꙰

CHAPTER THREE

Observations on the
Habitat of the Plains

This great plain lying against the eastern foot of the Rocky Mountains for nearly two thousand miles in length and extending nearly
eight hundred in width to the frontier settlements of Kansas, Arkansas, and Texas was once called the "Great American Desert,"
because of there being no trees and but little water on it.[1] But it is
no desert. It is only a stupendous plain awaiting only for settlements
to spring up in the right places along its borders—in the right currents
of the already established circulation of the atmosphere, to be steadily
pressed into the interior by the seasonableness of one particular place
being enhanced by the proximity of another in the course of the same
current. I will venture to say that there are many particular localities
on the borders of this great plain, from whence seasonable climates
for the growth of vegetation could be lead across the plain, if those

[1] Explorers in the Trans-Mississippi West such as Zebulon Montgomery Pike,
John Bradbury, Henry M. Brackenridge, Thomas Nuttall, Stephen H. Long, Dr.
Edwin James, and Thomas Farnham contributed to the idea of the great American
desert which extended east of the Rocky Mountains across the breadth of the United
States. This idea prevailed until the 1870's, after which settlement began to creep
onto the Great Plains. Various modern authorities identified the Great Plains, called
the "Great American Desert" by early travelers, as the region west of the 1,500-
or 2,000-foot contour line, west of the 97th, 98th, or 100th meridians, or west of
the low lying, east-facing escarpment and extending to the foothills of the Rocky
Mountains. Fenneman, *Physiography of Western United States,* 1–91; Walter
Prescott Webb, *The Great Plains,* 3–46; Carl Frederick Kraenzel, *The Great Plains
in Transition,* 3–4; Ralph C. Morris, "The Notion of a Great American Desert
East of the Rockies," *Mississippi Valley Historical Review,* Vol. XIII, No. 2 (September, 1926), 190–200.

particular places could be only known. The soil is good, all over it; it only wants water to make the finest country on earth. I have noticed the regularity of the course of the clouds when passing across the same section of the Rocky Mountains year after year toward the same section of the plains, to be dissolved on approaching the dry locality as if they had approached the sun. But if the old and well-established currents from the ocean, in land, which have been turned into zigzag lines by the impediments of the mountains and trees, etc., could have at its intersection with the border of the plain, well-cultivated plantations to prevent the total dissolution of the clouds born upon it, could not the growth of vegetation be encouraged further into the plain in the line of this regular current?[2]

We made many more successive dry camps, hence our stock suffered greatly for the want of water, while they were compelled to live on the scant, dry, and stubby buffalo grass at such inconvenient localities as the Indians failed to burn over. It was only a few days after getting confounded and lost while looking at the long string of buffaloes that I was compelled to play the most important part of my whole career on the plains. It was as common as the days to see wolves of all sizes and species known on the plains collect in little bands and lazily lounge around the prairie around our camps at safe distances.

---

[2] Moist air for the interior of the United States sweeps in from the Gulf of Mexico, and precipitation results when the moist atmosphere meets the cooler air masses which originated in northern Canada. Unfortunately, the southerly air currents which pass over the Great Plains come for the most part from the arid plateaus of northern Mexico and thus bring little moisture to precipitate when they meet the colder air. When the prevailing southern winds bring the dry air from Mexico, droughts seize the Great Plains, but when the air currents manage to make their way from the Gulf of Mexico, rainfall occurs on the Great Plains. United States Department of Agriculture, *Climate and Man, Yearbook of Agriculture, 1941,* 178–79. John Wesley Powell, with the publication of his famous report, began to break down the myths of the unusable nature of the lands in the subhumid region of the Great Plains. From 1850 to 1880 the frontier was stationary at the 98th meridian, but railroads, new agricultural machines, and devices to make water available brought settlers into the area of the Great Plains. John Wesley Powell, *Report on the Lands of the Arid Region of the United States, With a More Detailed Account of the Lands of Utah;* Webb, *Great Plains,* 353ff.; Kraenzel, *Great Plains in Transition,* 125ff.; Fred A. Shannon, *The Farmer's Last Frontier,* 148ff.

There could be seen a convention of them, some standing, and some lying down, almost in any direction and almost any day. All waiting for the camp to be deserted so as to come in and fight with each other and also with the ravens, which were numerous, over the debris of the camp. A raven would alight to pick up a scrap and a wolf would savagely charge on him, while others would charge on one another in succession, until the old campground was thoroughly gleaned.[3] One morning after camping on the river's low bank, I concluded to remain under the brink until the wagon train should get well off from the place, and break up the anticipated picnic of the wolves and ravens. A wolf is monstrous cunning and cautious. The ravens, while sailing around over the campground prospecting, could see me, concealed behind the bank of the creek. And because they didn't alight the wolves were too prudent to come hastily. They kept me waiting until I became uneasy, for the wagons must have been gone an hour. I peeped cautiously over the bank and fired upon a large grey fellow and shot him through. He turned and snapped his teeth rapidly toward me after delivering a slight half-whine and half-growl in his surprise, then ran away onto the plain with the rest of them, out of reach. I was not content with one shot, but emptied one of my six-shooters after the fleeing wolves. Now there was nothing left for me to do but reflect upon my imprudence and reload my arms, both of which was soon in rapid progress. I hurried on, walking very fast to overtake the wagon train, thinking that I might not yet have been missed. I well knew that if I had not concealed myself to begin with, that I would not have been allowed to remain behind alone. But it was all over now, but overtaking safety the next most important consideration. The wolves had again gathered into their accustomed squads in the distance and quietly looking after my departing footsteps, I imagined, with pleasure, as each one had so lately delivered himself of a surprised yelp at the sudden report of the gun. The ravens promptly answered the coyote howl by all the grating and croaking tones known to their extensive language, as I left them all to their enjoyment and lonely abode. I came in sight of the wagon train about 10 o'clock A.M., but I continued my

[3] Perhaps Conner was observing coyotes during this incident.

haste until within about a half a mile or perhaps a little more from the train. I observed that the train was not in motion and this fact reassured me a little, as I presumed that some of the party had perhaps gone out a distance to shoot buffalo or other game, and the train was waiting the result. So I strolled leisurely along for a little distance, saw a little prairie dog sitting straight up a few paces off, barking at me, offering a pretty target, and I shot and wounded the little creature. I approached the dog and presented the muzzle of the gun near it, when the vicious little animal seized the iron and fought it with biting and scratching vigorously.[4] Just at this juncture, while I was busily engaged in annoying the little wounded animal, my attention was drawn by an indistinct shout in the direction of the train. On looking up and in that direction, I saw one of the party hastening from the train back toward me, waving his hat at me. He stopped and shouted, "You had better run." I misunderstood the last word and proceeded with my annoying the little dog, as I finished a soliloquy by the remark, "So do I want my gun." I have often thought since that this bit of selfishness on my part was a poor consideration for the generous efforts which were at the same instant being so earnestly made in my behalf. But seeing that I failed to move from my position, another member of the party ran back toward me, waving his hat vigorously and shouting at me to run.

This extraordinary conduct stirred up my reflections wonderfully quick. The unsafe feeling of which I had just been relieved by the sight of the wagons again flashed all over me in a moment. I scanned the horizon at a glance and observed back of the line of sand hills that bordered the river bottom and high plain, some half-mile away, a dense moving dust proceeding up a little hill range toward its terminus beyond which the wagons were standing in line upon the level

---

[4] Prairie dogs are colonial animals living in "towns" on the prairie where the grass is short and the ground fairly hard and compact. Their natural habitat in the United States coincides to a large extent with the Great Plains. These little rodents, weighing from 1¾ to 3 pounds, live in burrows, the mouths of which are surrounded by a mound which is given greater strength by dried grass which is incorporated in it. During most of the year the prairie dog found in Kansas has fur of "dark pinkish cinnamon finely lined with black and buff; underparts whitish or buffy white, terminal third of tail black." Hall, *Mammals of Kansas*, 90–92.

plain. The truth was now patent. The Indians were going to make a charge on the train, and by the aid of the sand hills of concealment they were too close to give sufficient time to corral the wagons before their proximity was discovered.

I now dashed a charge of powder in my gun and while starting the ball down I kept my eyes on the dust beyond the sand hills, which was now moving fast. In another moment I saw the Indians' heads as they dashed past a gap between the hills, one after another, in quick succession. They were riding ponies. This sight prompted me to take my gun and start for the train and trust to my strength to ram the ball down the gun as I ran. But I soon found that I could not press the ball more than halfway without stopping, to which I could not consent. I quit trying to load my gun and spent all of my time experimenting upon what amount of speed it took to compete with a Comanche pony. When the Indians completed the length of the range of sand hills, out from behind which they emerged like a set of demons plainly to view, they discovered me, in as much haste as they were, on a parallel line with the one they had been traveling. They now turned their attention to me with demoniac yells and accelerated speed, turned short around the end of the sand hills, and using every effort to cut me off from my friends; and had I been one minute later there could have been no doubt of their success. The economy of time was in this lesson forcibly impressed and spontaneously acknowledged. It would have taken all the tambourines together, according to my acute hearing, to have equaled this devil's dance in constant metallic jingle, cling, and clatter. When they found themselves disappointed, I began to feel that all the five senses were employed to detect the presence of bullets. They flew, struck, and swung all about there during the latter part of the chase, while my imagination felt a thousand wounds and saw the savages on the full run.

I came up to my associates on full speed about the time the Indians were crossing my race course in the distance behind me, and making for a position on the opposite side of the train out of reach of paleface bullets. There were about a hundred of them, all beautifully painted and rigged in numerous styles. When I came up, one of my two associates (B. A. Cooke and J[ohn] H[awkins] C[arrington]), who warned me of danger barely in time to escape, asked me reprovingly why I had not thrown away my partially loaded gun, which now laid before me on the ground with the ramrod projecting halfway out of the barrel. My answer was that I didn't think of it, and it was true, for otherwise it would surely have been left behind. Our red brethren hung around for an hour perhaps, engaged in cutting pranks and cavorting about the plain in a menacing way and disappeared, after which we proceeded on our wild-goose chase.

This was the last time I ever stopped back at old camps to shoot wolves or anything else, but I had made quite a reputation in this short time for ability to make a quarter-mile dash on the turf without previous training. I hope that I may be pardoned if I should use any-one's name improperly in this connection, but I cannot refrain from saying of John Hawkins Carrington, who was a native of Mont-gomery County, Kentucky, and who is now dead, that he was kind, generous, and brave to the last extent. The initials above indicate him as one of the persons who came back from the train to warn me and to shield me from danger by making himself a prominent target, as did also his associate, to be shot at by a hundred savages, but for which my existence would have most likely ended there and then. He was always ready, responsible, and willing for any emergency and more reckless of himself than of the safety of his friends. If I knew how to appropriately respect his character and memory I would deem it a personal privilege to do it, and all that I could say of him I could say of his associate of that occasion.

I will state here that but a little time after the above occurrence had transpired, when I saw a young man who was loitering behind his company, but not so far as I had, who was cut off by the Indians from the main party and shot, stripped, lanced, and scalped, all in the face of a continuous fire from the party. He was left at the present Fort Lyon in Colorado. I have forgotten his name but he recovered, and the last time I ever saw him was in the fall of 1860 at the above-named fort walking about, and said that he was in good health but that the reason he kept his head bandaged was because he was "bare-foot on the top of his head." This fellow's wounded head was a long while healing, but this fact is not strange to those who have seen the process of scalping and know that the scalp is rudely sawed off, the operator allowing his knife to be guided by the skull bone.

We were about this time approaching Fort Lyon. This fort was then called Fort Wise, after Governor Wise of Virginia, and on account of his disloyal proclivities it was changed to Fort Lyon after the officer who commanded at Springfield, Missouri.[5] The fort was built by old trapper Bent and was purchased of him by the United States.[6] In passing this fort our party's wagons were taken around some rolling prairie in front of it and out of sight. The soldiers were practicing at a target with Minnie muskets and accidently threw a ball through one of our wagon covers, but did no material mischief.[7] We were glad to see these cleanly well-dressed men—the first we had seen of our own race since leaving Council Grove in Kansas, a month previously. I remember of the soldiers' inquiring what the prospects were in the States for broken heads if President Lincoln

---

[5] Fort William or Old Bent's Fort, completed in 1833 or 1834, was located on the north bank of the Arkansas River between the present towns of La Junta and Las Animas, Colorado. William Bent abandoned and destroyed Old Bent's Fort in 1849, but built another post at Big Timbers some thirty-eight miles to the east in 1853. In 1860, New Bent's Fort became Fort Wise, named after Governor Henry A. Wise of Virginia, but when Virginia seceded from the Union, it was renamed Fort Lyon, in honor of Brigadier General Nathaniel P. Lyon. Lyon, commanding Union forces in Missouri at the outbreak of the Civil War, occupied Springfield, Missouri, in July, 1861, and was killed at the Battle of Wilson's Creek on August 10, 1861. Percy Stanley Fritz, *Colorado, The Centennial State*, 91–92; David Lavender, *Bent's Fort*, 386; LeRoy R. Hafen, "When Was Bent's Fort Built?" *Colorado Magazine*, Vol. XXXI, No. 2 (April, 1954), 105–19; Jay Monaghan, *Civil War on the Western Border, 1854–1865*, 170, 179; Robert D. Meade, "Henry Alexander Wise," *Dictionary of American Biography*, XX, 423–25; H. Edward Nettles, "Nathaniel Lyon," *Dictionary of American Biography*, XI, 534–35.

[6] William Bent, to whom Conner is referring, can hardly be classified as merely an "old trapper" because he with his brother Charles, in partnership with Ceran St. Vrain, dominated the trade with the southern plains Indians until its decline in the 1840's. According to the most definitive work on Bent's Fort, New Bent's Fort was not purchased but only leased or rented by the federal government from William Bent on September 9, 1860. Lavender, *Bent's Fort*, 345, 417; Hiram M. Chittenden, *The American Fur Trade of the Far West*.

[7] Before 1856 the troops on the Far Western frontier were equipped with Minié guns, rifled firearms using conical rather than round balls. These technical improvements increased the effective range of the guns from 200 to 1,000 yards. Bandel, *Frontier Life in the Army*, 102; Foster-Harris, *The Look of the Old West*, 47.

should be elected.[8] Their facilities for news were so limited in those days that it was a treat to see anyone from the States, as they expressed it. As the saying was with us, we traveled off that day and camped in the big timber. After leaving the vicinity of the fort, one of our "boys" discharged his pistol at a prairie rattlesnake of medium size. The snake pursued him, being the only instance of the kind I ever saw committed by a rattlesnake. The snake followed him around in a circle, while at intervals he fired at it several times before cutting its neck with a ball. But there were other larger snakes in the neighborhood, which will be mentioned hereafter. . . . The wild sublimity of this vast and habitless empire, as it appeared in the total absence of population all spread out there in its mere silent existence, cannot be described. There seemed nothing with which to compare it—totally without counterpart, without a model, except perhaps on a smaller scale in South America. One of our late Congressmen described the city of "Duluth" as being the center of creation with the sky coming down even all around it. This laconic description is probably the most readable one that can be given afar from the scene.

The "big timber" was a thinly scattered growth of large cottonwoods not more than a mile wide and possibly five miles long.[9] It had been reputed by old trappers as a kind of headquarters during severe winter for the Cheyennes, Arapahoes, and Kiowas to shelter and avail themselves of the scanty fuel to be obtained, and the tender twigs of the younger growth for their ponies to browse on. The old trappers say that the buffalo had been known to tarry here for a while when they seemed to have missed their latitude a little. The animals of this section and as far as the foot of the Rocky Mountains were buffalo, deer, antelope, elk, marmot, wolf, agama, cornuta, and many lesser ones.[10]

[8] Conner is not clear on his dates at this point because if this took place on his first trip to Colorado in 1859, Lincoln's nomination by the Republican party in 1860 could not have been known.

[9] Big Timbers, located in Bent County, Colorado, about twenty-five miles downstream from the mouth of the Purgatoire River on the Arkansas, was a fine grove of cottonwoods and a favorite campsite for the Southern Cheyennes and Arapahoes. Lavender, *Bent's Fort*, 133; Hafen, *Pike's Peak Guidebooks*, 178.

[10] Although agama and cornuta are given as different animals, Conner should have used the zoological term agama coronatum which is an older technical name

It was quite refreshing to see some trees again. We drove into these woods and remained long enough to take two tires off of the wheels of a wagon and reset them. This was done by tacking little strips on the fellies of the wheels, and putting the tire, after heating it, over them, which answered the purpose of cutting the tire, for the process resulted in good stout wheels again.

We moved out again and camped at the upper edge of this woodland patch on a bluff overlooking the woodland flat, which was here rather rugged, with undergrowth, dead brush, and rank fallen grass. Whilst I was lounging about this camp situated on a sandy point of the bluff in the warm evening's sun, I observed two white-headed eagles sailing in a circle above the tops of the trees in the adjacent valley, making a peculiar noise which I deemed to have been caused by our intrusion.

They were pretty fine looking birds, unlike any that I had ever seen, and I longed to capture one of them. I immediately procured a double-barrel shot gun charged with buckshot and started across the grass-entangled valley, looking upward most of the time to get a shot, as they might sail over me. I soon discovered that they had a large nest in the brushy top of a tall cottonwood. Now I thought that it was for the safety of their fledgings that cause them so much trouble apparently, and that it was a pity to kill the old ones. But I eased my conscience by the reflection that eagles always build their nests in which to hatch their young high up in cliffy, rocky promontories and not in trees. Although I felt morally certain that this was a hatchery, my silent feeble argument gained the case and I therefore proceeded with the intent to bring down one or both of the old birds.[11] While looking up and rather blundering along, I was suddenly startled by a racket in the brush and fallen grass to my right hand, and as was natural, quickly glanced that direction to divine the cause. It didn't take much observation for I had not more than turned my head before

for the crowned horned toad. Karl P. Schmidt, *A Check List of North American Amphibians and Reptiles*, 133.

[11] It is typical for the bald eagle to build its nest in high trees as described by Conner, but the golden eagle usually constructs its nesting place on cliffs. Arthur Cleveland Bent, *Life Histories of North American Birds of Prey*, United States National Museum, *Bulletin 167*, Pt. I, 294 ff., 335ff.

a huge snake, marked with black and yellow bars crosswise like a convict's breeches, glided ahead of me about fifteen or twenty feet and stopped. I guessed him to be at least ten feet in length and large in proportion.[12] He was certainly the largest serpent I ever saw at large. He raised his head, which was his farthest extremity from me, about two feet off of the ground and looked over his *shoulders*, and shot out his black, venomous-looking tongue at me with fearful rapidity.

I can see his countenance yet. His head was apparently as large as a man's closed hand and ornamented by two "big" red eyes. As soon as I got loose, for I was surely frozen to the ground, I aimed a load of buckshot with great care and caution at the monster's head, which proved effective. But to my amazement and surprise another just like him came tearing out of the brush at the report of the gun, and glided the same way out on the fallen grass and also stopped and turned to look at me and to shoot out its tongue. Another load of buckshot mangled this one's head. Each one drew itself up into a pile sufficient to fill a good-sized barrel. I was by this time so nervous that I could hardly start back to camp, but I got off at last without waiting to reload my gun. This looks like extreme trepidation, but when we consider the natural feelings of one who is afraid of snakes generally, in addition to the surprise created by the sight of such monsters, and coupled with a comparatively unknown country, such a qualm is not very unreasonable at last. But however that may be considered, it was true and I left there and left the eagles too, and left the snakes for them to feed themselves and their young with, whether they did it or not. When I arrived at the bluff at camp preparations were in progress for our departure, which took place an hour later. I proceeded to tell the old wagon master about finding and killing of two boa constrictors and desired that he should go and see them; but my explanation was soon halted by his sarcastic remark

[12] This is probably an overestimation of the size of the snake. The two species of rattlesnakes which inhabit this area do not attain the size given by Conner. No diamond rattlesnake has been captured which was larger than eight feet, and the prairie rattlesnake rarely attains a length of more than five to six feet. Further, the markings given by Conner do not correspond to either of the species. Laurence M. Klauber, *Rattlesnakes; Their Habits, Life History, and Influence on Mankind,* I, 144, 147–48.

that he supposed that I had discovered a mare's nest. I held my tongue, supposing that such serpents about the streams of the plains were very common and that perhaps that he knew it. But I have since learned from quite an experience of my own that they were not very common and that they were the largest serpents I ever saw out of doors, to this day.

We passed on up the river toward the mountains without any particular incident worthy of note, save a few little misunderstandings with the Kiowas and Comanches from time to time; but we managed to keep a respectful distance from each other except upon one occasion when about half a dozen of them came up to three or four or us who chanced to be straggling behind. They rode up to us on their ponies, all painted up and on the warpath. In order to pass themselves for Arapahoes, they inquired if we had seen any "Kiowas and Comanches." When hand-shaking began we drew out pistols and offered them the left hand, at which they affected to be amused, but their sour venom could not be so effectively concealed as to allay our doubts. Those were rough and suspicious salutations, but they were justified, for soon after our departure and theirs, we met quite a cavalcade of friendly Arapahoes in pursuit of them. Actions speak louder than words, says an old adage. The art of dissembling is a science. It is not natural. We had no doubts nor fears when we met the Arapahoes. Their appearance, their conduct, and bearing was ample and satisfactory proof of their genuine good will. No pistols were drawn to aid a safe salutation, although there were five to one of the Kiowas and Comanches that we had so lately met. . . . Yet all of them were painted alike.

CHAPTER FOUR

Prospecting South Park, the Blue, and the Arkansas

We passed the dilapidated remains of Bent's old fort. There was nothing left of it but a portion of the adobe walls, the highest part of which were not probably more than seven feet. Some parts of those old weather-beaten walls were crumbled quite to the foundation. We guessed its locality at about forty miles above the present site of Fort Lyon, on the Arkansas River.[1] Early one morning attention was drawn by the interesting remark that the long-sought Rocky Mountains were in sight.

Cooking and all other camp duties were quickly suspended amidst the stirring about after good positions to look for the mountains. "Where are they?" and "I don't see them" and so on were heard impatiently expressed all about the camp. But the dim outlines of Pike's Peak, like a cloud so much higher than expected at that distance was plainly visible and equally deceptive. I saw a supposed cloud, but failed to notice it until I was told to look at the cloud. Then I believed that it was a cloud until time enough had transpired for a cloud to change its shape at least enough to detect.

But it proved indeed to be a cloud that never changed. As the sun arose gradually, the fixed and dim outlines of this grand old sentinel of the Rocky Mountains also gradually went out before we left the

---

[1] Old Bent's Fort was destroyed by William Bent on August 21, 1849, after a cholera epidemic struck the Southern Cheyennes. As noted previously, Fort Lyon was located at New Bent's Fort, some thirty-seven or thirty-eight miles east of the older establishment. Lavender, *Bent's Fort*, 313ff., 413–14.

camp. Nor did we see it again during that day, nor did its outlines after a day's travel toward it appear more plainly marked on the following morning than when we first saw it. And indeed could we see it only in the early morning for many days' travel after its first appearance.

The distance to this peak was estimated at 170 miles.[2] But whatever may have been its true distance it was evidently a long way off, plainly evidenced by the little change that a week's travel made in its appearance. The whole body or outline of the Rocky Mountains came in sight slowly and as gradually as did the peak. My impatience gradually subsided, as I became accustomed to the elephant, long before reaching it.[3]

We drove up near the riverbank just after a long dry stretch and determined to refresh the stock while near the water and therefore pitched camp at noon. Nearly all of the party wandered off from the camp except the herders who took the stock across the river to graze, because of the grass being burned on our side, and except also one of each mess, who are supposed to attend camp duty in the absence of those who chose to go in quest of fresh meat for the replenishing of the common larder.

I refused to go hunting for game and therefore represented my mess. Being ordered by our steward before he left to cook a kettle of beans for supper, I proceeded to work off the task as soon as the hunters departed. It was my first attempt at cooking of any kind, for I had always exchanged my cooking services until this effort. I proceeded to fill a four-gallon sheet-iron camp kettle with those small, dry, white navy beans, which are always used on the plains by the army, and by the way a splendid prairie dish when properly seasoned. After the kettle was filled and a sufficiency of water poured on to cover them, they were hung on the camp hooks over the fire, and I considered my work done. I therefore laid down on a blanket to read. It was not long, however, before the kettle began to overflow.

---

[2] As the crow flies, Pikes Peak was about one hundred miles northwest of Old Bent's Fort.

[3] Conner's phrase "accustomed to the elephant" is merely an expression of the time meaning to see the sights or to see a curiosity. Mitford M. Mathews, *A Dictionary of Americanisms on Historical Principles*, I, 550.

Yes, I discovered that I had put a little too many beans in the kettle and therefore dipped out a quart tin-cup full and again settled myself on the blanket. Pretty soon the kettle overflowed again. I took out another quart cup full. It ran over again and I obtained a larger vessel and filled it. I soon discovered that all the vessels in our branch of this department would fail in point of capacity, and I crawled into the wagon and searched for and finally found a prospecting pan, brought it out, and filled it. And still the orginal kettle was full and on the increase. I here stepped over to the campfires and proposed to furnish the respective messes with beans partially cooked, as it would save fuel. No, they didn't want any, as their kettles were as full as they would hold and quite sufficient for supper and breakfast, and they had no way of carrying them in a soft state. They appeared ignorant of the dilemma, but when the "boys" came in at night, these cooks knew more about my bean-cooking than I did.

Although we were a long distance from a supply depot and couldn't afford waste, I went back to my kettle and dipped beans out of that kettle and sowed them broadcast on the prairie, and continued the process until I finally got the bulk of the beans to conform to the capacity of the kettle. But I had one consolation: that there was plenty for the whole mess. I was thenceforth excused from the culinary department, but it was a long while before I heard the last of that miserable pot of beans. One of the members of the party who was particularly complimentary of my thoughtfulness in cooking the beans to different degrees—from half raw to well-done, in order to suit the different tastes—began to get loud, and from thence loudest, on the subject of cooking beans.

But revenge came at last, as it always does. He was in the wagon a short time after this incident, throughout the whole day, while we were on a long dusty and dry stretch without water. Toward evening, he awoke from his stupor very hungry. For the want of something to do he reached for a sack of dried apples upon which he munched until arriving in camp at night. He stupidly crawled out of the wagon and instead of going at his camp duties he took a seat, complaining that he didn't feel well. Pretty soon supper was ready, but our friend couldn't eat his supper, but concluded to take a cup of coffee and retire for the night. His complaints increased rapidly. It was now evident to him that hot coffee and dried apples either agreed too well together, or didn't agree at all. Each member of the party were alternately engaged during the night, to keep him from either choking or bursting. He recovered, however, but was still weak when morning came. He was still in his blankets after daylight, and I went close to him and ventured to say to him that it was a pretty day, and that Pike's Peak appeared so close that the snow on it was plainly visible. He remarked, "D——n Pike's Peak. I am not well yet." I further ventured to ask how he would have his beans cooked. He quickly replied that "D——n ruffians would rather annoy a sick man than a well one."

I now asked him how he would have his dried apples for breakfast, with or without coffee. I was already fixed to leave after this question, and didn't wait a moment after he reached for his belt of six-shooters, to see what he would do. After he got entirely well, he never seemed as pleasant as he had been before this circumstance, nor did he ever say "beans" to me again.

As we drew nearer the mountains, the Spanish Peaks and Long's Peak began to claim attention.[4] They too first put on a morning garb for display and retired from view during the bright and sunny days, to come out again on the following early mornings. But when we had become close enough to see them and their surroundings plainly and constantly, what a picture was presented from this vast plain.

These old peaks seems to stand up above their neighbors like the shattered segments of another world, fearfully frowning upon all irreverent levity and sternly holding all who are accountable to an awful consciousness of the necessity of respectful obedience to the wonderful laws that created them. I cannot describe the Rocky Mountains. They must be seen to be appreciated. History teaches us that

[4] Spanish Peaks, called "Huajatolla" or "Breasts of the World" by Indians and Spaniards, are located in Huerfano County, Colorado. Long's Peak, named after Major Stephen H. Long, was also called "Les Deux Oreilles" or "Two Ears" because the peak appears as twin cones from the direction of the South Platte. It is doubtful if Conner could distinguish Long's Peak for it is located in Boulder County, Colorado. Federal Writers' Project, *Colorado*, 374–75, 446; Hafen, *Pike's Peak Guidebooks*, 143.

Corner's Colorado Locale

N

NORTH PARK

MIDDLE PARK

SOUTH PARK

South Platte River

Fort Morgan

Platte River

Denver

South Platte

Cherry Creek

Colorado City

Pikes Peak

Fountain

Fountain River

Cañon City

Arkansas River

Big Sandy Creek

Fort Wise (Lyon)
Bent's New Fort

Arkansa River

Rule River

Two Butte Creek

Los Animas

Purgatoire River

Pueblo (Dotson's Station)
Boone

Greenhorn R.

Apishapa River

Huerfano River

Walsenburg

Apishapa

Trinidad

Mace's Hole (Beulah)
Greenhorn Station
Greenhorn

Fort Garland

Salida

San Luis Creek

Rio Grande

Alamosa Cy

Conejos Creek

Durango

Gunnison

Gunnison River

Continental Divide

Divide

SOUTH PARK

Georgetown

Swan Cr.

Tarryall
Jefferson
Como
Fairplay Tarryall Cr.

Breckenridge
Hamilton
Buckskin
California Gulch (Leadville)

Blue River

Continental Divide

Steamboat Springs

Yampa River

White River

Colorado River

Little Snake R.

Vermillion Creek

Green R.

MILES
0 10 20 30 40 50

they constitute the greatest range of mountains in the world and my observation confirms the fact, without seeing all the rest, so far as my verdict is concerned.[5]

It is no easy stretch of the imagination, for it to grasp the extent of this wild and weird land, extending as it does throughout the length of the United States possessions and the continent for that matter, shooting forth its long lateral ranges with their interminable number of dips, spurs, and angles that multiply to infinity. All of this confused mass of creation is spread out everywhere for from two to five hundred miles through in width, drained by numerous streams, rivulets, and creeks, aided by their tens of thousands of ravines and gulches and gorges throughout.[6] He who can contemplate this chaos, and then give a rational guess at what it means, is indeed an ingenuous philosopher.

The student who studies this landscape thoroughly will become amazed at the trifling character of his metaphysics. He will desert all theories, lose all orders and dismiss all calculations about fixed plans, and finally confess in sheer helplessness the futility of investigation. I wondered in silent contemplation what in the distant future would be the name of this hill, or that peak, among the thousands of others in plain view, yet to be named—perhaps by some herder or miner, whose little territory will be bounded by the local names that he may choose for each of his pet hills.

We kept up the Arkansas on its north bank to the mouth of the Fontaine-qui-bouille, a small stream flowing out of the Rocky Mountains by the foot of Pike's Peak and emptied into the Arkansas at the point where Pueblo now stands.[7] This stream has since been named

[5] If one considers the Rocky Mountains as a portion of the cordillera which extends through South and North America, they are truly the longest chain of mountains in the world. The Rockies, however, do not rival the Himalaya Range in height.

[6] The southern Rocky Mountain province, in which Conner traveled, extends two hundred miles in width and five hundred miles in length. Fenneman, *Physiography of Western United States*, 94.

[7] Fountain or Fontaine qui Bouille Creek, which received its name from the boiling fountain of Manitou located just west of present Colorado Springs, Colorado, heads near Pikes Peak and flows south into the Arkansas River at Pueblo, Colorado. Zebulon M. Pike, as early as 1806, built a rude log shelter on the modern

Río Grande. The first building ever erected at Pueblo was a little low log cabin made for a trading post and for the sale of ardent spirits and occupied, when I last saw it, by one Jack Allen.[8] We proceeded thence up the Fontaine-qui-bouille on its north side, thus taking our final leave of the Arkansas on this trip, and passed the present locality of Colorado City as we proceeded on into the mountains and camped at what we called Soda Springs, about two miles into the hills.[9]

Colorado City is located on this creek on the extreme western border of the Great Plains near the foot of Pike's Peak, and the springs were on the south side of the creek and about twenty feet from it.[10] We now bid farewell to the plains as we saluted the monstrous mountain regions ahead of us. The Soda Springs boil up on

---

site of Pueblo as did Jacob Fowler in 1822. Several decades later traders constructed an adobe building and occupied it until the Utes massacred the occupants and destroyed the building on December 25, 1854. Josiah Smith and others in the fall of 1858 settled Fountain City, but during the following winter a rival townsite was developed just to the west, called Independence at the outset and shortly afterwards known as Pueblo. In 1859, Fountain City, which merged into Pueblo, contained forty or fifty log or mud cabins. Pueblo received most of its population from New Mexico, growing slowly until it was reached by a railroad in 1872, and during the next year it was organized as a city. Parsons, *New Gold Mines of Western Kansas*, 178–79; Hafen, *Colorado Gold Rush*, 78, 210–11, 239, 243; Federal Writers' Project, *Colorado*, 185–86; LeRoy R. Hafen, "Colorado Cities—Their Founding and the Origin of Their Names," *Colorado Magazine*, Vol. IX, No. 5 (September, 1932), 170–83.

[8] Several buildings had already been built in Fountain City by the winter of 1859–60 when Jack Allen established what was called by some a "drug store" but was described by Allen as a "Taos lightning factory." Wilbur F. Stone, "Early Pueblo and the Men Who Made It," *Colorado Magazine*, Vol. VI, No. 6 (November, 1929), 199–210.

[9] These great springs were a sanctuary for Indians and a neutral ground where violence did not occur. They are also called Manitou Springs and are located near present Colorado Springs. Federal Writers' Project, *Colorado*, 228–29.

[10] Two previous townsite developments, El Paso and El Dorado City, failed where Colorado City was successfully launched on Fountain Creek, in present El Paso County, Colorado, in August, 1859. The name of Colorado City was derived from the fact that it was astride a practical route to the mines on the Colorado River. Known as "Old Town," Colorado City was absorbed by Colorado Springs in 1917 and subsequently has been called West Colorado Springs. Federal Writers' Project, *Colorado*, 113–16; Hafen, "Colorado Cities," *loc. cit.*, 173; *Handbook of Colorado for Citizen and Traveler*, 113.

the Pike's Peak side of the creek, out of what would be supposed, upon casual observation, a light-colored flat stone about eight feet or more in diameter.

But on close observation it is found to be formed by the strong soda water which boils out of an opening in the center, probably two feet in diameter. The water boiled up vigorously but escaped along a natural groove to the creek very weakly, where it pitched off of the supposed stone surface, into the rapid and swift current of the creek.

The water was very strongly impregnated with soda, but clear. We would put a little vinegar in a quart cup, sweeten it with sugar, and pour in soda water until it would foam and sparkle to exceed any experiment I ever saw with like materials, and thus mixed it made a fine refreshing drink. But perhaps our long and weary jaunts gave a keener relish for such a treat and enhanced and exaggerated its merits.

When used for making bread, this water is perhaps superior to any invention in the way of yeast. The dough could be made entirely with this water without the detection of soda, by the color and smell.[11] We waited on three of our "boys" to ascend Pike's Peak. They were gone nearly three days. When they returned grand stories were related of the scenery about the summit, but after they became tired of dwelling on their imaginations in the sky, they confessed that they had failed to reach the top for want of pluck and wandered back to camp. We passed on into the mountains, following the Fountaine-qui-bouille over and through a roadless country, picking low gaps with prudence and for several days at a stretch worked and toiled, rolling rocks, digging passways, and mending harness continuously. From this on, the usual monotony was continually broken by long pulls and hard tugs, never to be forgotten. This state of perpetual annoyance lasted until we came to South Park, a high rolling country lying between Pike's Peak and the main cordillera or backbone of

[11] Other travelers also used the waters of Soda Springs to make bread. They noted that it tasted like soda water or "Congress (Saratoga) water." Undoubtedly the leavening action came from the sodium bicarbonate content of the water. Hafen, *Colorado Gold Rush*, 340; Denver, Colorado, *Rocky Mountain News* (September 22, 1859).

the continent.[12] The common name of this divide in that section is Snowy Range.[13] This park was a fine, grassy, grazing country in the summer and perhaps forty miles across it. In the winter the snow falls two or three feet deep and remains until May. It is rolling country, interspersed with clumps of trees and small open parks, and at that time a great range for wild game and Ute Indians in the summer.[14]

I found here in some of my lonely walks a pair of elkhorns more than six feet in length. They were still attached to the skull. I leaned

[12] South Park, Bayou Salado to the old mountain men, is drained by the South Platte River and its tributaries. Situated in present Park County, Colorado, it is surrounded by the Rampart Range, the Arkansas Hills, the Mosquito Range, and the Tarryall Mountains. James Purcell told Zebulon M. Pike that he found gold there in 1803. More than fifty years later prospectors moving south from the overworked Gilpin County mines founded the mining camps of Hamilton, Tarryall, and Fairplay in 1859. Placer mining quickly played out in South Park, and within a few years only the deserted camps remained. Today the region is used mostly by large cattle ranches. George Ruxton has written one of the finest descriptions of South Park: "The Bayou Salade, or Salt Valley, is the most southern of three extensive valleys, forming a series of table-lands in the very centre of the main chain of the Rocky Mountains, known to the trappers by the name of the 'Parks.' . . . The Bayou Salade especially, owing to the salitrose nature of the soils and springs, is the favourite resort of all the larger animals common to the mountains; and, in the sheltered prairies of the Bayou, the buffalo, forsaking the barren and inclement regions of the exposed plains, frequent these upland valleys in the winter months; and feeding upon the rich and nutritious buffalo grass which, on the bare prairies, at that season, is either dry and rotten or entirely exhausted, not only are enabled to sustain life, but retain a great portion of the 'condition' that the abundant fall and summer pasture of the lowlands has laid upon their bones. Therefore is this valley sought by the Indians as a wintering ground; and the occupancy has been disputed by most of the mountain tribes, and long and bloody wars have been waged to make good the claims set forth by Yuta, Rapaho, Sioux, and Shians." Ruxton, *Life in the Far West*, 32–33; Rufus B. Sage, *Scenes in the Rocky Mountains*, II, 188; Federal Writers' Project, *Colorado*, 393–94; Fenneman, *Physiography of Western United States*, 103; DeVoto, *Across the Wide Missouri*, 161.

[13] If Conner followed the usual route to South Park from Colorado City, he would have used Ute Pass and crossed the Rampart Range. Snowy Mountains, as named today, are north of South Park and west of Denver. Also, the continental divide is west of South Park in this region.

[14] The Ute Indians are members of the Shoshonean linguistic family and formerly occupied the entire central and western portions of Colorado and the eastern portion of Utah. At one time their lands extended into New Mexico throughout the upper drainage area of the San Juan. Hodge, *Handbook of American Indians*, II, 874–75.

them upright against a tree and stood on the skull between them so as to guess their height.[15] I have seen elk standing about amongst the clumps of trees in the shade here as lazily and as much annoyed by flies as the horses and other cattle of our woodland pasture during the summer months.

After the usual trials and hardships attendant on sleepless nights and constant care, the result mostly of standing guard every alternate night for a period of twelve hours, we arrived at the foot of the cordillera or Snowy Range. This dividing ridge of the Atlantic and Pacific oceans bounds on the western border of South Park.[16] We pitched camp on the spot where the town of Hamilton was since built, after a continuous journey of forty-five days from Leavenworth City.[17] We arrived here about the last of May. The mountains presented the most terribly bleak aspect.

A grand confusion of mountain crags, peaks, and ranges of the most imposing proportions all covered with snow. They seemed illimitable in extent and quantities. Many fearful gorges and attritioned fissures lay hidden far beneath the surface of the drifted snow here and there, and everywhere. The innumerable and distant white-snow-crested peaks, with their bases hidden behind others as they arose higher and higher and further away toward the top of the main divide, presenting a magnificent picture of gloom and starvation. But the morning's sun relieved the scene materially by the bright sparkling smile apparently given in derision of the dark chilly frown assumed during the night.

The "untrodden snow," as it lay in long continuous sweeps from

[15] Antlers of the Rocky Mountain elk rarely exceed a spread of a little more than five feet. Edward Royal Warren, *The Mammals of Colorado: Their Habits and Distribution*, 277.

[16] Conner, looking west from South Park, observed the Mosquito Range which also contains the continental divide.

[17] The mining town of Hamilton was probably named after E. Hamilton who was among the first group of prospectors in South Park during June, 1859. The town itself sprang up in 1860, occupied until 1879, and was located on Tarryall Creek in present-day Park County, Colorado. LeRoy R. Hafen, "Ghost Towns— Tarryall and Hamilton," *Colorado Magazine*, Vol. X, No. 4 (July, 1933), 137– 43; Irving Howbert, *Memories of a Lifetime in the Pike's Peak Region*, 23–24; Muriel Sibell Wolle, *Stampede to Timberline*, 100–101.

the summits to the fatigued-looking swagging gaps and thence up the ever-increasing grade to the summit of another, only to descend and repeat again and again away in the distance, offered a wonderful picture "engraven" on the sky. These contemplations brought to mind the historical paintings of the countless tents of Xerxes spread out upon the plain on the occasion of and during his unsuccessful invasion of Greece. These too were spread out as far as obstacles would permit them to be seen, and far beyond.

We were now eighty miles westerly of Pike's Peak and near where it was purported that gold had been found. It was on the other side of the cordillera a distance of sixteen miles.[18] On the following morning of our arrival at the great range we began our ascent of Snowy Range. But we only took one wagon, the lightest in the party, loaded with about five hundred pounds of provisions, bedding, etc., to which was hitched six pairs of work steers. We left only one man to each wagon in camp behind, as there were no Indians seen as yet, to become dangerous. The redskins must have been confused or surprised at our sudden invasion of this portion of their territory, or else it was too early yet for them to come up to these snowy highlands.

At any rate they were not there nor any sign of them. We started up a ravine in which a small creek flowed and emptied out upon the park just above where Hamilton is now.

We soon came to where the snow was too deep to proceed without tedious difficulties. On the ridges the snow was comparatively solid, with a stout crust on top, but in the innumerable ravines where the snow was drifted the crust would break and let us down. Across those places we begun to cut grades with long-handled shovels, of which we were supplied to the extent of one to the man. Thus we cut a railroad grade in appearance, wherever it was absolutely necessary. Continuously at work all day long, as we ascended the Snowy Range until within half-mile of the summit, we were compelled to cut a grade of three hundred paces in length. It became so deep that we couldn't throw the snow out, consequently had to carry it out at

[18] Contemporary estimates place the Tarryall diggings fifty-seven miles from Canon City and seventy-three miles from Denver. Denver, *Rocky Mountain News* (April 18, 25, 1860).

each end. We wanted to reach the summit by dark and camp there. It being nearly night enhanced our efforts, and while a number of us were digging away in the lowest place about midway in the grade, the bottom gave away and precipitated us into a wide hidden creek up to our waists in the water. We crawled out, however, and brought the wagon and cattle. The cattle were unyoked from the wagon and had to be pushed into this creek here, having the appearance of a dangerous hole of water. We next rolled the wagon into it by hand. And those of us who were already wet rolled it across until the cattle could be hitched to the tongue, to pull it out. Before reaching the top we came to another heavy, bad place, but not so steep. We here discovered that to cut a grade would delay us until after night, and as the crust on the snow was hardening, as also was the snow itself, we fell upon a speedier plan to cross a hundred yards or so by first tramping a solid path across the snow and unyoking the cattle and driving them across it single file, all of which proved a success. We next went back after the wagon and helped it up on the snow crust and rolled it over by hand. But every now and then a wheel would break in as deep as the hub, but no farther. We also would break in occasionally, but not deeper than the hips. We arrived on the summit just after dark and pitched camp, after one of the most continuously laborious day's work of taking a wagon and team over the greatest obstacles that I ever knew or heard of one passing, before or since. Many times during the day this wagon and team looked strangely, perched upon some precarious place, on this tedious route. We set fire to some old dead pine logs and soon had a cheerful-looking camp located amongst the clouds. But the poor, lonely old oxen did without food that night while they appeared to be wondering where they were to go next.

I do think that a discouraged work ox is the most sorrowful-looking brute on earth. He can moan the lowest, look the saddest, and give up the ghost the most completely of any other animal.

On the following day we passed down the other side of Snowy Range over about the same character of obstacles as were encountered coming up, except that a down grade gave us better speed, and as a consequence we arrived on the headwaters of Blue River earlier in

73

the evening than we did on top of the mountain the previous day.[19] We were now in the boundaries of the new "Eldorado," our pre-destination. This section was then in Utah Territory, but soon after became Colorado Territory, whose subsequent legislature named our locality Summit County, whose kindly folds spread over mining districts and gave us civil government in less than two years from our arrival in this wilderness.[20]

The first mining district ever organized in Summit County was called Miner's District, and laid across the waters of Blue River, which was its central line or cone (as it were). We remained here for the time as a headquarters and busily prospected the surrounding country for a distance of twenty miles. But we never did bring over the remaining wagons which we had left on the other side of the Snowy Range. I never did see them again after our departure shoveling snow, but some of the party conveyed the provisions, etc., over on pack animals. During this summer good wagons with their covers, yokes, chains, and all could be bought for ten dollars apiece in numbers or by retail. The owners having used cattle to draw them and on arrival killed the cattle for beef. Then a disease called the black tongue broke out among the cattle, choking them to death by numbers during and at the beginning of the first settlements of Colorado.[21]

[19] The party could have used Breckenridge or Hoosier Pass to reach Blue River, a tributary of Colorado River. From the Tarryall diggings, Blue River was some fourteen miles over the present-day Mosquito Range, which was called at that time the Snowy Range. Denver, *Rocky Mountain News* (May 16, 1860).

[20] Utah Territory, as established in 1850, extended to the continental divide in present-day Colorado. Jefferson Territory from 1859 to 1861 claimed all lands bounded by the 37th and 43rd parallels and the 102nd and 110th meridians. When Colorado Territory was organized in 1861, the present Colorado boundaries were drawn, consisting of the 37th and 41st parallels and approximately the 102nd and 109th meridians. Summit County in 1861 consisted of the whole northwest corner of Colorado Territory, but the original county has now been carved into six counties. LeRoy R. Hafen, "Claims and Jurisdictions Over the Territory of Colorado Prior to 1861," *Colorado Magazine*, Vol. IX, No. 3 (May, 1932), 95–102; LeRoy R. Hafen, "The Counties of Colorado: A History of Their Creation and the Origin of Their Names," *Colorado Magazine*, Vol. VII, No. 2 (March, 1931), 48–60.

[21] Black tongue, caused by a deficiency of vitamin B in animals, is considered to be an analog of pellagra. Lore A. Rogers, *Fundamentals of Dairy Science*, 498.

Frémont made one of his paths across this mountain but he didn't take a wagon with him. It appears that he was in search of a guide and came across Captain Walker, who had charge of a corps of trappers in the interests of the American Fur Company. The great pathfinder offered Walker five thousand dollars to pilot him and his party to California. Walker asked eight thousand dollars and Frémont refused to give it, and was given directions by Walker where to find Kit Carson, who was also in charge of a company of trappers and encamped on Green River, a stream to which Blue River is a tributary.[22] Frémont found Carson, who accepted the task for five thousand.[23]

The reader knows the rest. Kit Carson was published into the greatest mountaineer of the American continent. These two men, Walker and Carson, went together to California in 1832, from whence they roamed the Rocky Mountains at pleasure long before this region was noticed by the outside world. These little jottings are put here not as my own information, for it was obtained from Captain Walker himself after I had traveled with him a year in these mountains and became well acquainted with him.[24]

He told me many other things connected with the different expeditions made in the Rocky Mountains, including those of General Frémont, but as the latter has given his own account of them, I shall

[22] Blue River is not a tributary of Green River but rather forms a juncture with the Colorado River near Kremmling, Grant County, Colorado.

[23] This account of the meeting of Joseph Reddeford Walker and John C. Frémont does not correspond with available information. Joe Walker left the employ of the American Fur Company before 1842, and was engaged, perhaps, in the California–Santa Fe trade. Kit Carson met Frémont for the first time in May or June, 1842, while traveling by steamboat between St. Louis and Chouteau's Landing, now Kansas City, Missouri, before Frémont's first expedition. It was agreed that Carson would receive $100 a month for guiding the party to the Wind River Mountains. Allan Nevins, *Frémont: Pathmarker of the West*, 94; Edwin L. Sabin, *Kit Carson Days, 1809–1868*, I, 317; Christopher Carson, *Kit Carson's Own Story of His Life*, 51; M. Morgan Estergreen, *Kit Carson: A Portrait in Courage*, 87–89; Daniel Ellis Conner, *Joseph Reddeford Walker and the Arizona Adventure*, xviii.

[24] Kit Carson did not accompany Joe Walker on the California expedition which took place between the summers of 1833 and 1834. For the most complete account of Walker's experiences during this journey, see Zenas Leonard, *Narrative of the Adventures of Zenas Leonard*, 101 ff.

leave the subject.[25] Immigration now began to crowd Miner's District with an unruly population, the individual number of which were nearly all unacquainted with each other; and in truth, there were but very few acquaintances there, because of the continuous influx of strangers, who immediately became savage on the questions of the ownership of mining claims. A miner could hardly leave his pit long enough to get his dinner without finding someone in it at work with all the tools left there when he returned. This was called jumping claims. The result of this sort of conduct was that neighboring claim holders united their protests on such occasions by visiting the "jumped" claim in an armed body, and invited the intruder to leave, without standing upon the manner of going. This gradually got up a fashion of prepared resistance, again resulting unfavorable to mine-owners. Lives were lost and conflicts inaugurated without limit. A body of tramps would unite and "jump" the whole district, drive out the original owners and pass new laws, and work until they would be served the same way. But somebody always had possession.[26]

[25] Joe Walker did travel with Frémont from Mountain Meadows, Utah, to Old Bent's Fort on the latter's second expedition. When Frémont went to California on his third expedition, Walker joined the party at Old Bent's Fort in August, 1845, and remained with Frémont until February, 1846. Douglas S. Watson, *West Wind: The Life Story of Joseph Reddeford Walker*, 90–97; Conner, *Joseph Reddeford Walker and the Arizona Adventure*, xviii–xix; John Charles Frémont, *A Report on an Exploration of the Country Lying between the Missouri River and the Rocky Mountains, on the Line of the Kansas and Great Platte Rivers;* John Charles Frémont, *Report of the Exploring Expedition to the Rocky Mountains in the Year 1842, and to Oregon and North California in the Years 1843–'44.*

[26] Late-comers to the diggings often demanded reductions in the size of original claims. Some waited until an original claim expired when it was not worked and then appropriated it over the protest of the original claimant. Shootings, stabbings, and occasional murders were reported in early Colorado newspapers, indicating a lack of order. Henry Villard, however, reported: "The utter absence of all laws during the spring, summer and fall of 1859, together with the large number of desperadoes that always infest border and especially gold countries, caused a good deal of lawlessness. It was, however, confined to the towns in which many individuals, that relied on their wits more than their muscles and sinews for a living, flourished. The mines were nearly free from it, thereby proving that remunerative employment is the best preventative of crime." "People's courts" sprang up in many communities and dispensed summary justice. Henry Villard, *The Past and Present of the Pike's Peak Gold Regions*, 129; Howbert, *Pike's Peak Region*, 20; Ovando J. Hollister, *The Mines of Colorado*, 76.

While this character of citizenship was being enjoyed in Miner's District, my friend B. A. C[ooke] and myself took a tramp down the river seven or eight miles and camped in the edge of the woods at the foothills bordering the river about one mile below the mouth of Swan River.[27] The latter flows into the Blue from the right-hand side or section. There was an old unused Indian trail meandering along the edge of the woods. We spread our blankets within a few feet of this trail and retired to sleep after dark. Our heads were about three feet from the path as we lay at right angles with it, and feet toward the river, which was some three hundred paces away. We slept comfortably during the night and until after the sun arose. A light snow fell during the night. The first observation made, on crawling out of the blankets, was directed toward a herd of deer on the opposite side of the river near the edge of the woods. They were playing and capering about upon their native heath in the early morning's sun, at once the picture of peace and innocent happiness, surrounded with an illimitable territory of woodland mountains and grassy valleys, all their own. How I envied those noble animals, away in this their peaceful mountain home, perhaps where they had never yet heard the crack of a murderous rifle.

But however, peace to them. We now turned our attention to things nearer home. I was surprised to observe the steady footprints of a huge Rocky Mountain lion marked regularly along this old trail.[28] When he came opposite to our heads, he lifted a forepaw and placed it within a foot and a half of our heads and examined us, then gently raised it again and marched off up the trail with as steady a step as those of his approach. He evidently was dignified and proud of his cool deportment, or else he considered us rather small game for him to bother with, so concluded to journey on in quest of better prospects. We were not in the least frightened but on the contrary slept soundly all the while. But then we only saw his tracks. These animals are numerous in the northerly section of the Rocky Moun-

[27] Swan River is a tributary of Blue River, forming a juncture about five miles north of Breckenridge, Colorado.

[28] The mountain lion or Rocky Mountain cougar has been reported weighing as much as 276 pounds partially dressed and exceeding eight feet seven inches in length. Warren, *Mammals of Colorado*, 101–104.

tains. On another occasion I left the camp to hunt deer and came across one of these animals that seemed more stubborn than any I had yet seen. They will generally flee unless they are hungry or wounded. But this one had every opportunity to leave me, but he stood thirty or forty yards off, curling and twisting his monstrous tail around and about over his back, thence to the ground again after the fashion of an elephant's movement of his trunk. He was evidently considering what was best to do. That he saw me was certain, for I could see him notice me now and then. I knew it would be dangerous to show the white feather in the least; therefore to start away would precipitate a battle to a certainty.

I raised my gun just as he looked toward me again and fired. His proud look left him immediately as he ran backward to a sitting posture like that of a dog and dropped his ears. Thus he sat and looked at me all the while with his big flat head and eyes directed toward me like he was taking sight. He kept perfectly still. When my gun was recharged I took careful aim at his head and fired again. He never flinched or moved, but contented himself with simply holding up his lips to show me his splendid teeth. I fired at his head again and he smiled at me again. I then reloaded and directed a half-ounce ball at his breast, which proved fatal. He laid over on his side and scuffled about a little and surrendered.

On examination I found that my first shot had broken his shoulder, which caused him to take a sitting position. And that was a lucky shot and [it took] the war spirit out of him.

Before leaving our temporary camp on Blue River, myself and friend concluded to cross the river where we saw the contented herd of blacktail deer and see how many there were over there.[29] We crossed the shallow water and were soon on the side of the mountain beyond the river. I never saw sheep paths more numerous in a stock pasture than appeared here. We quickly had a deer and took it to camp. It would be useless to kill them for no purpose, we thought, and therefore didn't pretend to kill more than we could use. During the second day in this camp we had company in the persons of other

[29] Conner's "blacktail deer" is more properly called the mule deer. Warren, *Mammals of Colorado*, 281–83.

prospectors who camped with us. On the following day I left the camp alone, passed the river, and climbed the opposite mountain to the top, where I found an extensive tableland extending back from the river farther than I went. The woods on this level mountaintop was open and withal rather pretty. On my return late in the evening I discovered that I was belated and walked rapidly as dark began to hover over these woods. When within probably a mile of the river I was startled by a sudden racket proceeding from my left, like the surprised start of an animal, and its succeeding leaps, thence to a sudden halt. I was not acquainted with the different sounds made by different animals when in motion, and I thought this one was a deer. It was now quite dark. After I heard it stop and just as I began to peer about through the darkness to catch a glimpse of its outlines, the thing uttered a piercing scream that entered my very soul. It resounded hideously through the dark woods. I knew now that it was one of those insidious panthers.[30] I never did hear him move again and knew that if he was moving, that he was skulking, and it is their nature to skulk for a purpose. I walked off, the only action left for me. After going ten paces I stopped, listened, and looked. All was as still as death, except my heart—I could hear that thumping away.

I took another walk and another look and listen, and still all was silent. The third time I continued until I reached the front overlooking the river and fired my gun to learn where I was. Like the Indian chief, I was not lost but my wigwam was, which amounted to all the same.

I was gratified, however, to hear my signal answered by a shot just opposite at my camp on the other side of the river, where I soon landed and found all of its inmates happy and contented as well as myself. We struck camp and returned to Miner's District and found different quarrels going on about the ownership of different claims, as usual.

But a cessation of hostilities pretty soon enlarged to a permanent peace in Miner's District on the reception of the news that a rich

---

[30] Again this is the mountain lion or Rocky Mountain cougar. There is some debate concerning whether the animal screams, but the consensus of opinion seems to be in the affirmative. Warren, *Mammals of Colorado,* 103.

gulch had been discovered across the rugged country north, some eight miles distant. It had been secretly worked with rockers for some time before outsiders knew of it. It was called Gold Run and it did prove very rich.[31] I stampeded to the object of this new excitement with the rest of the ambitious, and found the gulch looking like it had been worked for months. I didn't wonder at it having been so long a secret, for it was well hidden away up in the side of a dark, brushy gorge, not easily found.

Gold Run was soon overrun with men who desired to make new laws and cut the claims down to half their original size, because one claim, as it stood, was too much for one to claim and work.

One morning while I was there, a North Carolinian started out after a deer that he had killed late the evening before and hung up on a tree. It seemed to be upon a high tableland near the head of a steep gulch where he had left it. He came back to his camp at Gold Run without the deer and gave his reasons for not bringing it. He said that on going out of the head of the gulch he came within ten paces of the deer before he came in sight of it. And that when he did arrive upon the level he found himself too close to the grizzly bear which was feeding on its carcass to retreat. The bear saw him and acted just like all grizzlies do when hungry, and made an assault instead [of] fleeing.

According to his own story, the North Carolinian lost no time in walking up a tree, as he expressed it. The bear reared up against the tree and fretted piteously because he refused to come down, and scratched the tree with savage ferocity, refusing to be quieted for a time. North Carolina said that as his gun was on the ground he had nothing to offer in the way of a compromise. But the bear walked back about halfway to where the deer lay, stopped, looked back and up the tree and growled, as much as to say, "Keep quiet up there," then proceeded to the deer. Here he smelled a little and looked up the tree and growled. Again he examined the meat cautiously, found a good hold and seized it, then vigorously slapped his huge foot upon

---

[31] Gold Run, located near Breckenridge, was heavily worked during the spring of 1860, and by summer was being mined "from one extremity to the other." Denver, *Rocky Mountain News* (April 11, June 13, 1860).

it and snatched out flesh, bones, and all, accompanying the act with a vicious hoarse growl, and started for the tree chewing, walking, and growling—meow, meow, meow, until reaching the tree, where he would look up until his mouthful was disposed of, then start for another. North Carolina said that this old grizzly repeated this way of eating his breakfast, again and again, until he nearly finished the deer. He said, "The old d——l liked to have choked once, while trying to look up the tree, growl, and swallow, all at the same time." After bruin got his meal, according to the North Carolinian, he moved off slowly a little distance, stopped and looked back up the tree, and growled a threat "as much as to say keep quiet up thar." Thence on a little further and repeated his growl, louder. He continued this cautious way of working off until reaching the brow of the mountain, when he gave a "big" snort like a scared hog and struck out on a "lope" over the hill out of sight. The North Carolinian gave a pretty true story as to the natural actions of the grizzly. Press him too closely and he will not flee, although he wants to go. Give him time to work himself off and he will growl threateningly one minute and whine anxiously the next, and continue to indicate war and anxious impatience alternately until he is far enough off to feel safe in fleeing, which he will begin by a sudden and frightful impetuosity.

He always leaps with first one foot forward for a while, then changes by putting the other forward for a while, thus resting both forelegs, alternately, as either gets tired.

Our party, now, as winter set in, went to the valley and spent the winter and returned to Miner's District, and remained but a short time before we were scattered through the mountains, prospecting for gold diggings. It must be remembered, in new mining camps in this section, that July, August, and September about constitute the mining season on top of the ground in placer and surface diggings. By this time there was a large log house or two built in Miner's District, and they took the name of "fort." The Indians began to threaten the paleface's safety. About the first of July, 1861, my friend W. B. [?] and myself left the fort on a prospecting tour down Blue River, about ten miles. After camping in the woods and brush for three days we concluded to return to the fort on the next morning because our bed of grass, the night before, had been shot into while we were out of it. We had accidentally set the woods on fire and were compelled to leave our quarters on account of it, but were not far off in a dark nook when the shot was fired and we knew not whether it was done by an Indian or a white man. My first impulse was, when the report was heard so close, that one of us had dropped a pistol in our escape from our bed and that when the fire approached it, exploded it and thus caused the report. But upon examination we had our pistols. We therefore hid ourselves for that night, and it was in the evening of the following day when we resolved to return to the fort. But about the time we were preparing a lunch for supper, we discovered in the distance, coming down the river, forty or fifty Ute Indians, all riding ponies in single file.[32]

We again concealed ourselves in the brush. They passed within thirty paces of us and kept down the river on our side as long as we could see them. The whole line of them passed us without uttering a word. They were fearfully painted, and evidently on business, for there were no squaws with them. We lay concealed until after dark, when we could dimly see the outlines of a man walking slowly about the edge of the woods near where the Indians had passed. We could not conceive what any white man could be doing here alone. Therefore, the verdict was that this was an Indian spying out our locality, if they had seen us, when they passed. We could come to no other conclusion. We boldly arose from our concealment and fired upon the straggler with our rifles and missed him. He ran toward the river and we pursued him until he plunged into it, and then we began to fire on him with our six-shooters as he ran through the water knee deep. We were fearful of his getting away to report us to his tribe, and he did make good his escape unhurt. We now took up our march in the dark and continued it until we came in the neighborhood of the fort—crawled into some brush and slept soundly until noon the next day. When we arrived at the fort during that evening we learned

[32] No widespread Indian hostility was reported in the mining region in 1859, 1860, or 1861, but some "murders" were attributed to the Utes in newspaper stories. Denver, *Rocky Mountain News* (September 3, November 3, 1859); *Report of the Commissioner of Indian Affairs for the Year 1861*, 102.

Fort Lyon, Colorado. New Bent's Fort is in the background.
From an oil painting by Robert Lindneux
Library, State Historical Society of Colorado

The majesty of Pikes Peak, in Colorado.

that a man came in during the night and reported that the Indians had attacked him in the dark—ran him across the river and fired at him as long as he was in sight. He showed some bullet holes in his coat to confirm his story. His auditors said that he reported that there was at least twenty of them and that they had fired as many as fifty shots at him. He didn't tarry long, but passed on over Snowy Range, declaring that he would leave the country instantly. That man is ignorant to this day of the fact that white men of his own race and not poor "Lo" did the shooting on that occasion. It was only a few days after this incident that a man was sitting on a rock in a little ravine prospecting for gold when a hunter shot and killed him for a bear because the unfortunate fellow wore a brown jeans coat. Many accidents of this character transpired in all the districts during this season.

Another rush was made from Miner's District to the newly discovered "Georgia Gulch," a tributary to Swan River, some twelve miles away toward the north. This was about the first of June, 1860.[33] On arriving there it was all claimed up, tributaries and all. It proved to be the richest diggings ever found in this section of the Rocky Mountains. It was found by a little party under the leadership of Mr. Highfield, a Georgia gold miner, hence the name of Georgia Gulch.[34] Humbug Gulch, a tributary to it, proved very rich.[35] Four of our party bought a claim and worked it two seasons. In this gulch a miner's meeting declared one hundred feet square, lying across the ravine, should constitute a mining claim. Bleak winter came on be-

[33] The first prospectors made their way from South Park into the valley of the Blue in July, 1859. Later in August and September other prospecting parties discovered placer gold in the gulches on the headwaters of the Blue and Swan rivers. Georgia Gulch is located on the west side of Swan River about five miles east of Breckenridge. Charles W. Henderson, *Mining in Colorado: A History of Discovery, Development, and Production,* United States Geological Survey *Professional Paper No. 138,* 9; Hollister, *The Mines of Colorado,* 72–74.

[34] Highfield is not mentioned in the available historical literature.

[35] Humbug Gulch belonged to the Breckenridge District, and like Georgia Gulch was located about five miles east of Breckenridge. Humbug Gulch, however, is not marked on the maps given in Frederick Leslie Ransome, *Geology and Ore Deposits of Breckenridge District, Colorado,* United States Geological Survey *Professional Paper, No. 75.*

fore we had time to open the mines in this gulch. So we left the gulch covered with snow and five of our old party made our way out of the mountains by way of Pike's Peak toward New Mexico and spent the winter along the foot of the Rocky Mountains south of the Arkansas, bordering the Great Plains.

Our party, now consisting of five in number, filled our little wagon, drawn by two oxen, full of necessaries and encamped on all the creeks which flow out of the mountains into the plains between the Arkansas River and the border of New Mexico. These streams, when there was enough water, flowed into the Arkansas, except in some instances, where some of them united before reaching the Arkansas.

When the party made the last day's circular drive to reach Pike's Peak, on coming out of the mountains, I took a direct course across the hills to the Peak from the high country behind it. I was not on the top of it, but I came across level land on the side of that stupendous hill, sufficient in extent for a large plantation. I became lost and the sight of the level plains, which seemed to rise higher as they receded in the distance like the ocean seen from a high elevation, lent no assistance to dispel my confusion. Instead of passing across the foot as I intended, I was keeping around it and got higher all the while. At last I concluded to follow a gorge directly down to Fountaine-qui-bouille, which flowed to the Arkansas at the point where Pueblo now stands. I seemed to be traveling sheer downward for a half-mile at a stretch. I sometimes had to drop my gun end foremost quite a distance and climb after it. I came to a narrow place in this steep descending hollow about eight feet in width, with a solid troughlike bottom, worn deep into the stone and swept clean. The sides ran up hundreds of feet perpendicular.

There was a great boulder from eight to ten feet in diameter that had worked down this steep and precipitous gulch and lodged above and against this narrow gatelike place, resting on the trough and leaving space enough for me to walk down the incline trough beneath the boulder without difficulty. When nearing the foot of Pike's Peak and consequently the mouth of this hollow, there was, for considerable distances, continuous shelving rock projecting out

84

of either side under which there were large beds of leaves, undoubtedly the property of the grizzly bear. I was in constant dread of discovering one in that narrow contracted place. However, I came at last out on open ground and soon found the wagon tracks and followed them to the Soda Spring, now called "Colorado Spring."[36] But when I had gone a half-mile down this creek I looked back to see if I could find any landmark by which I could again know this gorge, and I noticed on the far side from me, high up toward the brow of the hill overlooking this terrible rugged hollow, a good imitation of stonework like an old wall, high up in the side of the mountain. I am told that there is now a topographical station on the summit of Pike's Peak, and I presume this gorge has been since explored.[37] I remark the existence of my "big" boulder at the tollgate midway of this semi-perpendicular gulch, and the stone wall overlooking it, to direct some of the officers by my route to the top of Pike's Peak, if they should ever see this landmark.

We left the spring and passed out of the mountains on the plains, crossed the Arkansas, and encamped on the creek called St. Charles and killed a wild turkey for supper the evening we arrived there.[38] We camped from time to time on the numerous little streams that flowed out of the Rocky Mountains toward the Arkansas River. The border of the mountains and plains here for many miles southerly extended in nearly a parallel line with the Arkansas River. Perhaps they diverged a little as they extended southeasterly, leaving a strip of comparatively level plains between, probably twenty miles or less. This strip lies opposite to Pueblo, which is about its middle. In the fall of 1861, being the same time of our arrival, as stated above, I saw no less than one thousand antelope at one sight on this narrow plain between the present site of Pueblo and Mace's Hole, and we were unable to get near enough to shoot a single one, after a day's

[36] Again Conner is referring to the Manitou Springs near Colorado Springs, Colorado.

[37] The United States Army Signal Corps operated a station on the summit of Pikes Peak from 1873 to 1889. Harvey L. Carter (ed.), *The Pike's Peak Region: A Sesquicentennial History*, 21.

[38] St. Charles River, a tributary of the Arkansas River, joins the latter from the south below present-day Pueblo.

trial.[39] At the same time we encamped in the pine woods along the foothills of the front mountains opposite, and nearly twenty miles from Pueblo, where we found the ground amongst the trees profusely marked by the footprints of elk, on every hand, looking like recent presence of a large herd of yearling cattle. But they seemed to have immigrated in a body, as we failed to find them after diligent search. Up higher on the mountain we would see one occasionally dash away with leaps almost equal to those of a deer.

We were encamped on a creek called Muddy on one of those occasions, which is below an opposite point to Pueblo.[40] One morning while I was out in the woods alone and seated against a tree on the ground I heard the familiar gobble of a wild turkey. I had been sitting thus in a lazy thoughtful mood for a long while when my attention was aroused by this turkey, and I began to imitate their usual language as best I could on this my first occasion. But I soon got tired of this nonsensical attempt at mocking a turkey and had nearly forgotten the event in my reverie, when all of a sudden the old gobbler came up to me on a keen run and stopped within six feet of me in surprised attitude—looked puzzled a moment—said "quit-quit," and darted off on foot, running with an amazing speed preparatory to mounting on his wings, which he did as I fired after him without effect. All of this transaction was begun and over in less than the quarter of a minute, leaving me sitting in the same position with an empty gun.

We moved on from our camp on the "Muddy" and halted on the Greenhorn for a few weeks.[41] There was only one road in this section of country, and the Civil War, then going on in the States, necessitated quite a continued use of this road. It was a military route located on the plains, beginning at the then chrysalis-town of Denver and conforming its course to the contour of the Rocky Mountain

[39] Mace's Hole was named after a Mexican outlaw, Juan Mace, who made the valley his hiding place. Later the valley was renamed Beulah and is in Pueblo County, Colorado. Colorado Writers' Program, "Place Names in Colorado (B)," *Colorado Magazine*, Vol. XVII, No. 3 (May 1940), 85.

[40] Muddy Creek flows into the Greenhorn at Greenhorn, Pueblo County, Colorado.

[41] Greenhorn River is a tributary of St. Charles River, joining it in Pueblo County, Colorado.

front, all the way around to Ft. Union in New Mexico.[42] There were way stations established at intervals of about forty miles along this road of probably five hundred miles in length, for the accommodation of the escorts for the United States military mail. One of those stations was built between Muddy and the Greenhorn creeks and not far from the later well-known Mace's Hole.

Around Greenhorn and Mace's Hole was the scene of some lively transactions a year later, which will be explained further along. We left the Greenhorn and proceeded southerly to Huerfano and followed this stream to a point not far distant from Ft. Garland in New Mexico, which was then an outpost, a great way from the New Mexico settlements, and was in the command of Major [Charles] Whiting, who had with him only thirty or forty soldiers.[43] But the fort contained quite a supply of arms and ammunition. This fort being connected with the lively transactions aforesaid, I will dismiss it also for the present and allude to it again—in the proper connection. We remained up this creek for a month alone and obtained all the wild meat we could use. Bear, deer, antelope, beaver, squirrels of several different species and sizes—black, white, and gray. There was a tiny gray squirrel in those mountains at that time in all respects like our gray squirrel in the States, except that it was so remarkably diminutive as to require a dozen of them to make a dainty meal for an adult, and they lived in the ground during the night and played in the trees during the day. The large gray squirrel was about the size of the fox squirrel known in our States, except that the hair of its tail grew from the side, forming a flat-shaped tail like that of a beaver and bordered around the edges with a white fringe. And lastly, on the question of squirrels, the black species chattered like a bird or

[42] Fort Union was established by Colonel E. V. Sumner in 1851, one hundred miles northeast of Santa Fe, New Mexico, to check raids by Apaches and Utes. A. B. Bender, "Government Explorations in the Territory of New Mexico, 1846–1859," *New Mexico Historical Review*, Vol. IX, No. 1 (January, 1934), 1–32.

[43] Fort Garland was built in 1858 about eighty-five miles north of Taos, New Mexico, in present Costilla County, Colorado. It replaced Fort Massachusetts, built only six years previously, as a deterrent to Apache and Ute raids and was abandoned in 1883. Bender, "Government Explorations in the Territory of New Mexico," *loc. cit.*, 28; Colorado Writers' Program, "Place Names in Colorado (G)," *Colorado Magazine*, Vol. XVIII, No. 1 (January, 1941), 29.

tree frog, and the white one had pink eyes similar to those of the "pine top" moonshining animals in the mountains of Kentucky. I neglected to say, as pine trees are rarely found to be hollow, these squirrels built their nests in the trees like birds.[44]

While passing down Huerfano alone in quest of my repeatedly lost camp one evening when the "sun was low," I descried, in a little abrupt gorge choked up with boulders, a reddish-looking object, which I immediately agreed to be a sleeping Rocky Mountain lion.[45] The more I stealthily walked around and changed positions to investigate, the better his outlines came to view. I continued hunting better positions until his outlines gradually became perfect from any point I viewed him. But my object was to make a fatal shot and therefore wanted to be certain to have a good view of his head. After this necessary precaution took possession of my mind I saw his head, eyes, and ears plainly. I took a long and prudent aim and fired and made a white spot on the animal's head. Standing still now and wondering why the brute didn't move, I could distinctly see the animal form gradually fade away into a reddish, shapeless, granite rock with the spot on it made by the rifle ball. I now saw the rock so plainly I began to question the soundness of either my eyes or my mind, but after concluding that they were both all right, I resolved to keep my imagination under proper restraint thereafter. I found the camp at last, but forgot to tell the "boys" about shooting this lion.

We came on back toward our old camps on the Greenhorn, but spent a little while on Apishapa.[46] This is another of those little streams which flow across this narrow plain from the mountains to the Arkansas. On this stream we killed several white-tail deer in less than an hour after pitching camp.[47] I was sitting down in the tall

[44] Both the mimic and Frémont's squirrels have whitish fringes on their tails. Twenty-three different species of squirrels are listed as natives of Colorado. The mimic, the plain-backed, and Frémont's squirrels nest in trees or in hollows of the larger pines. Warren, *Mammals of Colorado,* 152–56.

[45] The Huerfano River is a tributary of the Arkansas, converging with the latter opposite Boone, Colorado, in Pueblo County.

[46] Apishapa River, taken from an Indian word meaning "stagnant water," enters the Arkansas River from the south about twelve miles west of Rocky Ford, Colorado.

[47] The western white-tailed deer, once numerous in the woods, brushy, and swampy places, are now virtually exterminated in Colorado. Warren, *Mammals of Colorado,* 284.

weeds to rest, when some of the party ran a deer directly toward me and in trying to get out of his way, so sudden was his approach, that I had not time to get upon my feet before the animal made a frightful leap, passing over me as easily as the rebounding of a football.

In this little valley there were numerous little diminutive deer called towheads.[48] They had a tuft of wool in the forehead and could travel with a speed calculated to amaze even a jack rabbit, and no one who had ever seen a jack rabbit on the plains lay back his tremendous ears and go in earnest will ever doubt his judgment on a mere matter of speed. We moved from here over on the Huerfano and camped by that very singular freak of nature, the Huerfano Butte.[49] It is a little peak standing on level ground near the creek, capped with dark-colored rocks. Its sides are very steep and regular like a sugarloaf, running to a sharp point, and having never climbed it I can give but little idea of its height, which may be fifty or an hundred feet. I know it can be seen for thirty or forty miles distant. The antelope here became wild, and we resorted to watching their watering places, where we would lay in wait for them in the evening. On one occasion I was surprised, while butchering an antelope, to see its horn so easily pulled off. I had been repeatedly informed that these animals never shed their horns, but I learned by my own experience that it was a mistake. In the spring of this winter I observed several with their horns off and several horns pulled off, this being about their shedding time. They don't shed their horns like a deer, but the horn simply pulls off from over a gristly pith that increases and grows and hardens into another horn.[50]

The species of antelope that inhabit the great Western Plains do not wear the shaped horn that Webster's dictionary illustrates, or anything like it. During our hunting excursion of seven months

[48] Perhaps Conner is describing a Sonora or fantail deer. Bucks of this specie do not exceed one hundred pounds and does, seventy-five pounds. Since they are "extremely pale in color," Conner might have called them "tow-heads." Glover M. Allen, *Extinct and Vanishing Mammals of the Western Hemisphere*, 294–96.

[49] Huerfano Butte, from the Spanish word for "orphan," is located in the valley of the Huerfano River about nine miles north of Walsenburg, Huerfano County, Colorado. Hafen, *Pike's Peak Guidebooks*, 102–103.

[50] Antelope do shed their horns annually, but this occurs in the autumn or early winter. Warren, *Mammals of Colorado*, 293.

throughout this, the winter of 1861, there came a tall, fine-looking and well-dressed man to our camp with half dozen mules. He was accompanied by a boy to take care of the mules, and they both encamped with us for a week. We all moved up into the mountainside on one occasion when it was cold. He showed, from his handy way of deporting himself in camp life, that he was accustomed to it. He would burn great log fires just at dark and remove the ashes and embers and spread his blankets on the spot and sleep there. He would take a deer's head, or two or three of them, and place them undressed as they were in a deep hole lined with embers, then cover them with fire coals and then build a fire on them, and retire to bed. In the morning he would have the best-cooked venison I ever ate. I learned that this man had been selling some bogus or forged United States vouchers of some sort for mules to take to Texas with him, but he sold the mules in New Mexico and escaped through the Confederate lines into Texas.

While we were upon this mountainside the snow fell to a depth of two feet, and we could see the edge of it on the plains from the camp, apparently not over three miles away. But spring was on us again and we determined to retrace our steps to Miner's District in the mountains forthwith. As we started over the dry plain between two of those streams and nearly opposite to the site of the present town of Pueblo, the tire came off one of the wagon wheels and the wheel broke to pieces. We went on to the next water, encamped, and on the following morning cut a pole and dragged it back to the wagon some five miles and helped our crippled vehicle to the camp. While our amateur workman was cutting and making spokes from a little brittle post oak, the rest of us went on a raid with some friendly Arapahoes to corral some antelope in a nook along the mountainside. We all took a position in a semicircle and while contracting our semicircle around the crag-bound nook, the Indians became afraid of our big guns and consequently left too large a gap between their ranks and ours through which the antelope made their escape. We went back to camp and found our wagon wheel just about finished and proceeded on our route to the mines, which was about 150 miles. We went by way of Canon City and was offered a large house there which was built by Kitchen and Co. of Leavenworth for a wholesale establishment, for our one pair of cattle and rickety wagon.[51] We declined the proposition and proceeded to South Park again and found it covered with snow, and consequently waited a while before going over the range to Miner's District.

[51] Canon City, laid out in 1859, is the present county seat of Fremont County, Colorado. It was so named because its site was near the Grand Canyon of the Arkansas River. C. W. Kitchen was in 1860 a well-known merchant and freighting contractor in Canon City, but his name is not listed in the early Leavenworth, Kansas, city directories. Colorado Writers' Program, "Colorado Place Names (C)," *Colorado Magazine,* Vol. XVII, No. 4 (July, 1940), 128; Hafen, "Colorado Cities," *loc. cit.,* 172–73; Hafen, *Colorado Gold Rush,* 90; Denver, *Rocky Mountain News* (October 31, 1860).

CHAPTER FIVE

Life in the Colorado Mining Camps

Our little party of five were again in the vicinity of our old original camp where we crossed Snowy Range by shoveling snow. The snow had nearly all gone off and another winter had replaced it. We were now at this place earlier than we were more than a year previously, because we had a much shorter distance to come than we had when we originally came from the States. So we were at Hamilton, which had been built since we first came.

There had been also two other towns built to quite respectable dimensions, five or six miles down the range south of our original bisection with the Snowy Range on the Atlantic side and in the direction of California Gulch, the present site of Leadville.[1] These

---

[1] California Gulch is a tributary of the Arkansas River, just south of present Leadville, Lake County, Colorado. A contemporary observer stated that the gulch was six to eight miles long and had an average width of 150 feet. Gold was discovered in California Gulch early in 1860, and Oro City sprang into existence by the summer of that year. In 1860, five thousand miners worked their claims but during the next season their numbers doubled. Gold, however, in the surface deposits was worked out by the end of 1861 and the miners moved to other fields. Silver ore was found in the same vicinity by W. H. Stevens in 1876, followed by other discoveries in 1877. New Oro City and Slabtown merged into Leadville on January 14, 1878, with Horace A. W. Tabor becoming its first mayor. Near its peak, Leadville had a population of about thirty-five thousand. Federal Writers' Project, *Colorado*, 168–81; Colorado Writers' Program, "Place Names in Colorado (L)," *Colorado Magazine*, Vol. XVIII, No. 6 (November, 1941), 232–33; Hafen, "Colorado Cities," *loc. cit.*, 179; Wolle, *Stampede to Timberline*, 41ff.; Samuel F. Emmons, J. D. Irving, and G. F. Loughlin, *Geology and Ore Deposits of the Leadville District*, United States Geological Survey *Professional Paper No. 148*; Denver,

two mining towns were "Buckskin Joe" and "Fairplay."[2] We went first to Buckskin Joe and found quite a mining camp there and a number of stores. There was one lady in this place from Kentucky, whose husband was a merchant. Our little party were quite snow blind on arriving there. We were without goggles, and this lady was kind enough to make a pair for me out of a remnant of a black silk dress, which beat no goggles considerably. This whole land and the imposing mountains of the main divide were all covered with snow and offered a terribly bleak-looking aspect. One who has never seen it has but a slight idea of its dazzling brightness in the sun, and its powerful effect on the eyes.

I saw an amusing incident in the way of a trade while at this place. Buckskin Joe was located on the woodless foothills of the cordillera where the snow would naturally drift deep. The warm sun had formed a crust on the snow sufficient to bear the weight of a man without difficulty. The trade referred to was the sale of six large freight wagons which had been left the fall previously, standing out a few hundred yards toward the main divide, with their beds and bows to hold the covers, all on, ready for traveling.

The owner and purchaser walked out to the locality on the snow to find the wagons. The owner would take a survey of the different mountains near by and mark the snow by kicking with his boot heel and say, "I think they are about here." He would survey a little more, change his position and kick another mark on the snow crust, and remark that "Possibly they are nearer this point." Look a while

Rocky Mountain News (July 25, 1860); Golden, *The Western Mountaineer* (July, 26, 1860).

[2] Buckskin Joe, near Alma on Buckskin Creek, Park County, Colorado, arose in 1859 and was named after Joseph "Buckskin Joe" Higginbottom (also spelled Higganbottom). The camp was renamed Laurette in 1860, for two sisters, Laura and Jeanette Dodge. By 1865 the town was deserted and the county seat was moved to Fairplay. Fairplay received its name when a group of prospectors driven from their claims around Tarryall founded their new camp. Jim Reynolds, later a notorious bandit, demanded "fairplay" for everyone. After the placer mines played out, Fairplay remained the trading center of the surrounding region. Federal Writers' Project, *Colorado*, 405–406; Roy A. Davison, "Some Early Manuscript Records of Park County, Colorado," *Colorado Magazine*, Vol. XVIII, No. 5 (September, 1941), 168–83; Wolle, *Stampede to Timberline*, 92–94; Thomas F. Dawson (ed.), "The Old Time Prospector," *Colorado Magazine*, Vol. I, No. 2 (January, 1924), 64.

longer, and "I guess they will be found to be about here as near as I can come at it." The delivery was considered satisfactory and on assurances being given by residents that the wagons were there, the bargain was finally closed and June came on and the wagons were found to be as represented. They had been completely snowed in, out of sight.

As we left Buckskin Joe for Hamilton at our old camp, we became too blind to make the whole trip at once and consequently stopped at Fairplay. There was a large rude house built of logs there, and fitted up for one of those earliest of all institutions necessary to completing mining camps, to wit: a drinking saloon or more properly speaking, in miner's parlance, a deadfall. The proprietor had received by some accident an illustrated newspaper. Its most imposing cut represented the president of the Southern Confederacy and his troup of theatrical performers on the back of a huge turtle. The turtle was represented as swimming away vigorously. The picture had written under it in large letters, "We will perform at Alexandra next." The landlord had this picture stuck up on the wall in a conspicuous place in this large room. The people had just heard of the battle of Bull Run and there was quite a crowd assembled there after supper to carouse and play cards, and this picture was creating quite an amount of mirth.[3] It was evidently a loyal crowd from the witty remarks and hearty laughs indulged on the occasion.

One fellow read slowly, "We will perform at Alexandra next," and wound up his sentence by a hearty "Ha, ha, ha. I wonder where he performed at last." "Bull Run" was the ready response of a voice from the crowd near the door. "Who was that?" came from different parts of the house, but no one could be found to acknowledge the remark. The more this crowd failed to find who the traitor was, the louder they became, until they concluded to wash away the stain by a general treat on the overjoyful, after which they settled quietly around the gaming tables to business.

This establishment had a hotel connected with it and an old bowlegged gentleman whose real name I never knew, and who went by

[3] The Battle of Bull Run was fought on July 21, 1861. James G. Randall, *The Civil War and Reconstruction*, 274–75.

the sobriquet of "Ole Mack." He could neither read nor write, but was considered sharp and was successful in his undertakings. He was regarded as a very clever old gentleman and was quick and nervous in his motions, and always had an eye to business. He had a broad face, little keen gray eyes set back under shaggy brows; of low stature, broad shouldered, and bald headed. I was in the saloon referred to on the following morning when Ole Mack was without custom and apparently very busy behind his rude counter. His house was quite roomy, but was rather intended more for shelter and protection from the weather than for providing food and bedding for his customers; but still he professed to do the latter two things, minus the bedding on such occasions, as when he had a large run of customers. When the whisky gave out, the common remark was, "Don't be uneasy. Ole Mack will churn tonight and there will be plenty in the morning." And the prophecy was always correct. He made his whisky from drugs and rain water, or rather snow water. One evening, while the snow lay heavy and damp on the face of the country, a stranger came into Ole Mack's barroom and promptly queried, "Is this a hotel?" "Yes, sir," quickly answered old bowlegs, as he walked around behind the rough counter with a businesslike air, eyeing his customer steadily as he walked. The stranger advanced and continued, "I wish to stay all night. Can you keep me?" "Certainly I kin, what's to hinder me?" "What do you charge for a night's lodging here?" "We-al, I hardly know what is jist right—hev you any blankets with you?" "No, sir, I am just from the States and came on a man's wagon to this place, except when I had to walk." "Ah, jist from the States. Ah-ha-yes, jist from the States. Will you take a drink?" "Well—yes, sir, being as I am cold and ———." "Jist help yourself, sir; jist help yourself to some of this old bourbon—this bottle, sir, this bottle. It is like yourself, sir—jist from the States." The stranger poured a moment and hesitated. "Fill her up, fill her up, stranger, you look chilly and cold—it won't hurt you, it's the best of old bourbon, jist from the States. I hev plenty of good old rye on hand, too; but it's all good this sloppy weather."

Here the stranger set the glass down while Old Mack rattled away about the purity of his liquors without a halt, until the stranger smacked his lips and remarked that "It tastes only a little new, but very strong ———." "Yes, yes, oh yes, you see it's above proof; it's made above proof accordin' to orders; so as to bear shipping so far, you know, and it does taste new after crossing the plains into this fresh light air, you know. I venture to say you feel yourself fresh like a new man in this light and healthy air, don't you? Oh, I know you do—you can't help but feel like a new man." The stranger did of course feel like a new man, and asked to be shown his room, as he was very tired. Ole Mack, with a prompt "Yes, sir," turned hurriedly toward a shelf behind the counter, from which he pulled down an old greasy and well-used pack of cards. He deftly ran them off, one hand to the other, like a man experienced in handling them, and quickly drew the trey of clubs and pitched it on the counter toward the stranger with the remark, "That's your room, I'll show it to you." The stranger picked up the card and with an incredulous look remarked, "You are mistaken this time, sir, for I am no gambler, and don't understand your signs—you will have to talk plainly to me." "Who said you're a gambler? That's your own business, but if you want to play, you can easily git a game." The stranger responded, "I don't want any game, but want to go to my room to rest." "Well that's your room." "What is my room?" Ole Mack here impatiently snatched up the card off of the counter and thrust it into the stranger's hand with the remark, "Why that is it. Can't you hold it a moment?" The stranger, who all the time seemed confounded, at last struck light and smiled and proceeded. "Oh yes, I see you mean this for a little bill; I will pay for the drinks." "Ah, no; no, I gave you the drinks. I don't want you to pay for any drinks—it was my treat—you see, when a stranger comes to put up with me I always treat and give him credit for his blankets, if he has any, and always give him credit for his deer meat, if he brings any, and ———." "Well," broke in the stranger, "take my name on your ledger and give me a room." "Oh, I care nothing about your name, I ain't afraid of any of my customers, going off without ———." "Well," again says the stranger (now badly puzzled), "give me a room and show it to me." "D——l take it, hain't you got your room in yer hands, and come on and I'll show it to you." Ole Mack made his way rapidly to the door of the room, followed closely by the stranger. He arrived at the door, turned, and unceremoniously took the card from the fellow's hand and compared it to the trey of spades, which was tacked on the door, and exclaimed, "Don't the trey of clubs and the trey of spades make a pair?"

He earnestly waited for an answer and finished by saying, "I don't think you *are* a gambler if you can't understand that much." Now the stranger fully comprehended the situation and greeted Ole Mack with a hearty laugh as he entered the room and took back the trey of clubs, as a check to his quarters.

But he soon recovered from his mirth when he looked around the room, whose only furniture was, in the Rocky Mountain parlance of the day, termed a bunk. This bunk consisted of a crazy rectangular frame two feet in height bottomed with poles and covered on top by small pine boughs, to serve as a mattress. This sleeping apparatus was completed by a couple of old blankets; but even this protection was a grateful relief to the weather-beaten adventurers of those days, when it was a very common practice to thatch the top of the snow with pine boughs to sleep on, in the open air amongst the sterile and bleak mountains and amid the constant music of the chilly requiems of gloomy wrath.

In contemplating this vast mountain region, formed as it is from such materials as it would take to build a multitude of specimen "Alps," one cannot but feel as totally lost as he would be if plunged into the infinite labyrinth of plans conformably to the construction of the world itself.

But let us look at this region covered with snow—yea, from three to forty feet deep and in the absence of shelter, food, or population. View it from a position within its own limits and hundreds of miles from its external boundaries. Then let the timorous heart or the stoutest answer whether the weird and mute despair embraced within the merciless arms of lawless Jove is a myth. While facing this bleak snowy world of reality, the very name of reindeer bears thrilling impulses of awe, tempered with sympathy because of his nature and of his bleak home.

Embraced in the chilling reflections of cold reality and in such catastrophes as result naturally to each victim, hope may shed the tears of contrition in vain for mortal considerations, whether her sister Faith ever dries them up in celestial realms or not. The throbbing, anxious heart, whether in the reindeer or in the human casket, moves both fast and slow by an involuntary power, all the same whithersoever may be its source. But these beautiful and majestic animals, whether in Lapland or the Rocky Mountains, are always found ready and wide awake to any emergencies, sleek and lithe as nature intended them.[4] It seems wonderful that they can and do find food to keep them in such splendid condition in a land more than half of the time under snow and where there is no fruit tree—not even of forbidden fruit—in the whole country.

But I shall leave Fairplay and bid farewell to all of its citizens, including Ole Mack, whom the stranger guest dubbed as "Ole Jack of Clubs" before we left. I never was again in his town and never heard from him since I left, but I have ever since hoped and trusted that Ole Mack to this day has never found a worse place than his hotel.

We returned to our camp near Hamilton and found that another little town was in course of becoming a city, up the range about six miles toward the north. It was called Jefferson.[5] We proceeded to Jefferson, where I afterward saw the ugliest woman I ever saw, dressed in man's clothing, including the plug hat, and herding sheep for some ranchmen. We arrived at Jefferson on the 27th day of April, 1862.

I bundled up some blankets before daylight on the following morning and started afoot over the Snowy Range for Georgia Gulch, a distance of sixteen miles.[6] I started this early so as to get the most

[4] Certainly Conner did not see reindeer in the Rockies but refers to them only as a fanciful illusion.

[5] Jefferson, located at the foot of Kenosha Pass, Park County, Colorado, emerged from two settlements, Palestine and Jefferson, about 1861. Today it is a very small village serving as a shipping point for cattle and timber. Colorado Writers' Program, "Place Names in Colorado (I, J, and K)," *Colorado Magazine*, Vol. XVIII, No. 5 (September, 1941), 190; Wolle, *Stampede to Timberline*, 88; Federal Writres' Project, *Colorado*, 394.

[6] Georgia Gulch is located on the north side of Farncomb Hill about five miles east of Breckenridge, Summit County, Colorado. Ransome, *Geology and Ore*

Buckskin Joe, Colorado, in 1864.
Library, State Historical Society of Colorado

Park City, in Stray Horse Gulch, two miles east of Leadville.
Library, State Historical Society of Colorado

of the way before the sun softened the crust of the snow enough to break through easily. Before I arrived at the top of the mountain I met a man from Georgia Gulch, who had been traveling most of the night and was carrying a sack of one hundred pounds of flour. The miners had kept a pack train of horses, mules, and burrows for half the winter and had carried their provisions over during the latter part of the winter on snowshoes.

These snowshoes consisted of a slat four inches in width and about eight feet in length with a piece of leather or old shoe tacked across the middle in which to thrust the front part of the foot. I arrived in the gulch that day and was surprised to hear the number of horses and mules that had been lost on the trail across the range over which I had just come. During the winter, when a pack train would come over to the gulch, some of the animals were sure to miss the beaten trail, which was constantly hidden by the constantly drifting snow from the action of the winds, and when once off of the trail the poor creature was lost. The pack of provisions would be taken off and the animal left to work deeper into the snow as he struggled, until he was finally left to be drifted over by the ever-changing snow. A little burro could be lifted upon the beaten trail again when he was unlucky enough to wander off of it, but the larger mules and horses were promptly deserted when they made the fatal misstep.

I found the little park at the foot of Georgia Gulch pretty well covered over with cabins and the cabins pretty will covered over with snow. In some instances along the foothills a black sooty hole in the snow indicated a chimney to some miner's cabin that had a slanting hole in front down into it, which they would follow to get into the door of their cabin. There had been a tenpin alley built there the fall previously, and I had left a large freight wagon with high bows on it standing near this alley. It had been left in my care and I naturally remembered to look after it. In the following morning, April 28th, I found the hindermost bow projecting out of the snow about six inches and thought that the bed had been set on the ground

Deposits of the Breckenridge District, Colorado, Plate II; Henderson, *Mining in Colorado*, 9.

and the wagon itself taken away. But in this I was mistaken, for when June came and the snow went off the whole concern was there just as I had left it.

The American Gulch, a half-mile away, had been discovered to have gold in it and a mining camp established there.[7] During this summer I saw an old fallen tree moved out of the way of a mining pit, and there was frozen ground directly under it for several feet deep in the ground. This was in the month of August. But we had frost there every month in the year. A miner planted a considerable garden on the mountainside, and the seeds never sprouted.

Prospecting was now carried on to an extraordinary extent. Some party or other was continually out and on the go, like the old forty-niners of California. This season there were about five hundred men in Georgia Gulch at work either as owners of mines or hired laborers.[8] The first lumber out of which to make Long Toms was cut with a whipsaw.[9] But a number of us left the operations here and went in quest of mines of our own and frequently turned prospecting into hunting for game. Some of those short expeditions were toward Montana, Dakota, etc., and others were away in the direction of Great Salt Lake City. On one of those occasions fourteen of us, after having been out for several weeks, came across a grizzly bear in a currant patch. It was an extensive growth of really what we call in

[7] American Gulch is just south of Georgia Gulch on the north side of Farncomb Hill. Ransome, *Geology and Ore Deposits of the Breckenridge District, Colorado,* Plate II.

[8] It was estimated by William P. Pollock, county clerk and recorder of Summit County, that Georgia Gulch produced $3,000,000 in gold from its discovery in 1859 to the close of the season in 1862. Henderson, *Mining in Colorado,* 227.

[9] One Colorado historian describes the "Tom" or "Long Tom" as " a trough six to twelve feet long, eight inches deep, about fifteen inches wide at the head and thirty inches wide at the foot. It has a pitch of one inch in twelve. The bottom of the tom at its foot or wide end is a riddle of sheet iron punched with holes half an inch in diameter or a grill of iron bars separated about one-half inch.

The gravel enters the tom at the head or narrow end from a trough containing enough running water to wash the debris down the slope. The fine particles filter through the riddle on to a flat box with cleats to catch the gold. The coarse gravel is forked out and discarded." Fritz, *Colorado,* 158–59; John Walton Caughey, *Gold Is the Cornerstone,* 164–65, describes the Long Toms used in California.

the States gooseberries.[10] And they were large fine berries. The bushes were over waist high to a man, with a scattering growth of little limber trees amongst them. It was all spread out on a level creek bottom with well-beaten roads through it in all directions. We were about passing by this little thicket when a grizzly bear arose upon his hind feet to look at us. He stood up as erect as a man, giving us a hideous object to contemplate. But he didn't stand long thus before one of the party fired on him, which act was promptly imitated by all of the party. The bear tumbled over backward into the brush with a loud whine of pain and surprise, which he changed into a prolonged hoarse growl. The top of his back could be seen as he traveled along one of the meandering trails in this thicket toward deeper brush, where he concealed himself. We now distributed ourselves into a circle at a safe distance around the bushes. David Rader rode into the brush to discover the bruin's exact location and found him and fired on him with a pistol. Old bruin arose suddenly and started for him with a made-up mind, and this frightened the horse so badly that it ran away with the rider. But R. R. [?], who was stationed across the creek, fired at the bear as it was pacing along the trail toward him with its head down like a hog, and wounded one of its forefeet with a very large bullet and thus disabled the bear materially. But bruin started immediately for the would-be murderer and received another shot from another direction, and turned after this breaker of the peace, only to receive additional wounds from different directions. The bear continued thus to turn upon the last one who shot in rapid succession and continuously, without ever prosecuting any one determination further than a good start, until his wounds began to weaken him. He began to look for a concealment again and quietly kept in the brush without selecting any particular place to hide himself. We had seen bruin's propensity to dash after the last man who shot, and we took advantage of it and shot regularly and in the right time to turn him from his intended

---

[10] Gooseberries are found between the 8,000- to 12,000-foot level in Colorado and belong to the same family as the currant bush, also noted by Conner. William A. Weber, *Handbook of Plants of the Colorado Front Range*, 117; P. A. Rydberg, *Flora of Colorado*, 176–77.

victim. But we lost him again and O[liver] Sweeny from Platte City, Mo., thinking that bruin was dead, ventured into one of the crooked paths in the brush. He turned from one cross path to another amongst the dense bushes, when behold the bear had come into his trail behind him by another crossroad and turned his direction.

Oliver Sweeny, finding himself in this predicament so suddenly and unexpectedly that he became confused and reached for one of those little limber trees by which he expected to pull himself out of the trail through the stubborn, unyielding brush. But the provoking tree gave way and our friend contented himself by pressing against the brush as closely as he could, holding the little tree with one hand and holding out his pistol toward the bear as it passed him (without knowing it) with the other hand, as though he would push bruin away from him. He was much relieved to see the bear pace loosely along by him, with its head down and within arm's length, without any knowledge of his presence. O[liver] S[weeny] came out of those brush with a heartier activity than he was ever guilty of before, and exclaimed, "By the Holy Moses, s'pose that old d——l had just seen me—whew—by thunder, let's go, we can't kill 'im." But we did kill "im," for pretty soon after this he gave up the ghost and laid down and refused to rise again. It was not long before his flesh was divided and packed upon the different pack mules and going over the hills never to return again to his wild nativity. This animal must have weighed nearly or quite a thousand pounds and was perforated with heavy rifle balls nearly fifty times before it gave up, and had there not been so many to shoot and confuse the animal therefore he could not have been killed in those brushes.[11]

After butchering this animal, it was plain that he could never have been killed by stabbing, for the longest butcher knife in the party would not reach the cavity of its body.

[11] A wounded grizzly bear was undoubtedly the most feared animal in the mountains. Many a veteran trapper and mountain man fled before the enraged rush of the grizzly bear. Conner overestimates the size of these animals because the range of weights of grizzly bears actually recorded in Colorado was 350 to 500 pounds. Warren, *Mammals of Colorado*, 37; DeVoto, *Across the Wide Missouri*, 113–14; Stanley Vestal [Walter F. Campbell], *Joe Meek, The Merry Mountain Man*, 195–96.

In two or three days we pitched camp on a tributary to Green River without further incident worth noticing except when hungry we thought to capture an elk, deer, or an antelope might be of some consideration, but when we were happy we didn't count them more than shooting a beef.[12]

We found no more luxuries equal to the gooseberries that we had left, but feasted upon whortleberries at pleasure.[13] In some places one could lie flat on the ground and reach as many whortleberries as desired. On one occasion I saw same pheasants walking about, quietly picking these berries as gently as domestic chickens would have done, and came [so] close to me while lying down that I shot the neck of one off with a pistol, and yet the rest of the covey refused to be frightened off any considerable distance.[14] We found some gold and quantities of quartz, which is said to be the mother of gold; but if that be true, the parent was not prolific, for gold was as scarce as quartz was plenty. An amusing incident occurred while our party was encamped at the foot and side of a long, low ridge. I mean that the ridge was low with reference to the distance from its base to the top.

This ridge began by a small treeless hill and extended a little, descending for about three hundred paces to and into a deep, dark, and heavily wooded country. The little hill and ridge were bare of trees until near to the woods where a lone tree, here and there, studded its topmost line. Two of our "boys," like many others of the party, had been exploring the adjacent country and had found a grizzly bear and wounded it. They trailed bruin to the chaparral on the little hill in sight of the encampment, but became too cautious to enter the low brush and came on to camp and informed all whom it might concern of the sure proximity of a wounded grizzly. F. G.

[12] The Green River touches Colorado only once. It makes a bend through the Utah-Colorado line in Moffat County, Colorado. The Little Snake, Yampa, and White rivers, tributaries of the Green, drain much of the northwestern corner of Colorado.

[13] The whortleberry belongs to the genus *Vaccinium* and is also called the blueberry. H. D. Harrington, *Manual of the Plants of Colorado*, 418.

[14] The bird here described is probably a ptarmigan, a member of the grouse family. W. W. Cooke, *The Birds of Colorado*, 202.

Gillilan[d], who was regarded the fleetest of foot of any of the party, put down his frying pan and remarked that he would "rather catch a grizzly any time than make flapjacks."[15] He caught up his gun and bid his informer to come and show him where the wounded grizzly was concealed. His informer led the way to a position near the summit of the little hill and pointed out the locality where the bear entered the brush. F. G[illiland] immediately begun his circle around the edge of the chaparral and beat the brush vigorously now and then, exclaiming in loud indifferent demands, "Git out of here and skedaddle—git out, I say, and ske——." A crash in the brush, accompanied by a vicious growl and a sudden leap out of the chaparral, commingled with the crack of the gun, all constituted the beginning of a quickening melee. The bear gave him so little time that he was compelled to shoot without aim, drop the gun and run, closely pursued by the bear, down that ridge until he got his eye on one of those lone trees to which he steered at the top of his speed, followed by the bear, not over three lengths behind him. When at the proper distance of the tree he made an extraordinary leap and as it was down the descent, he struck the tree pretty high up and was just able to hold to it long enough for the bear to pass under him at full speed and go on into the woods without halting.

All the camp had turned out to his assistance, but if he had failed to cling to the tree a moment there would have been no hope for him. He fell off of the tree to the ground badly hurt, and his breath was entirely jolted out of him by the shock created by coming in contact with the tree. After he recovered so as to talk he remarked that he was killed, but he finally recovered and was about as fast on foot as ever, but more prudent. "Git out of here and skedaddle" were the usual commands given to F. Gilli[land] by the guard to arise from his bed for some time after this incident. I have remarked this incident as being about the usual result of a singlehanded contest with a grizzly bear. There has been so much written about old trap-

15 Francis G. Gilliland, a native of Kentucky, was about twenty-three years of age at this time and was one of the members of the party led by Joseph Reddeford Walker into New Mexico and Arizona in 1862–63. Conner to Miss [Sharlot] Hall, May 1, 1910, Conner Manuscripts, *loc. cit.*

pers attacking these animals with impunity and slaying them without difficulty that if I had never seen any such contests, I should have believed the exaggerated stories. I have no doubt that many of these animals have been killed by a single shot, but such instances are rare exceptions. They will not die fast; no way they can be killed, unless perhaps by being shot with a cannon ball. I have seen a deer run over one hundred paces after having been shot directly through the heart with a half-ounce ball, and I once saw a buffalo travel at least five hundred yards after having been shot directly through the heart with a large bullet.

I noticed at and about this camp many beautiful flowers. There were no verbenas here; palladium-esculentiums and carnations &c; the pets of the hothouses, and botanical monstrosities so much appreciated, loved, and cared for by the ladies because of the variety of hues and of kinds. And we may truthfully say, because of the various sickly tints caused by disease and decay which are mistaken for variety. A splendid flower may be put into the hothouse until it gets the yellow jaundice, and the different stages of the disease distort it into a singular and rare specimen, not to be found outside of a greenhouse. But the prettiest things I ever saw in those wilds and amongst the flowers just referred to were the tiny old-fashioned pinks and lilies away in those wild woods, looking just as innocent, modest, and sweet as they did during my boyish days. But they did indeed look as though they were "wasting their sweetness on the desert air," and still as sweetly proud as any of their kinsmen amongst the most prominent places in our floral gardens, admired, petted, and loved in a land where the foot of the red man has ceased to tread forever.

We took a northerly course from this encampment as soon as our friend F. G[illiland] was able to travel, and after a few days scaling mountains and traversing gorges, encamped again on a little creek where the heavy woodland occupied one side and an undergrowth of pines eight or ten feet high covered probably a thousand-acre mountainside upon the other side of the creek. These young pines stood so dense as to obstruct the view of a distance of twenty feet. I thought it was a magnificent-looking locality to investigate, until I was in it. At some previous period a fire had swept this country and killed all of the trees at the same time, and their roots had decayed sufficiently regular for the trees to fall and become entangled with each other in the same generation. The undergrowth of young pines had sprung up almost as regularly as wheat in the field and was now tall enough to conceal the old trunks, which lay thick and in all directions amongst them. Apparently ten feet was about the average distance which we could travel without crawling under or over the old trunk or limbs of a dead pine.

I took to the opposite side of the creek where the old timber was comparatively open. It was nearly noon when I heard at a short distance the lazy, undecided, half-howl of an animal. I knew it was no little brute from the tone of his bass notes. I cautiously took a course toward the sound and crept upon a clump of granite boulders that had some trees amongst them. I had to tiptoe to see over the topmost boulder. But when I did see over, the first thing observable was a mountain lion. He was not over thirty paces from me, standing looking about from one direction to another, with his ears pricked up and tail winding slowly and curling around and about like we see cats do sometimes. The motions of his head were quick, but when he looked in a direction he seemed to observe closely and steadily, while in the meantime he would now and then continue a lazy grunt into a low, lonesome, indecisive whine and thence finally to a hoarse growl. Sometimes he would wind it all up with a peevish sneeze and then look impatiently in another direction. In attempting to shift my position a little, I broke the least twig, and its weak snap was heard sufficiently plain by the lion to cause a quick, involuntary depression of his back and head, as though a ball had passed over him. His ears and tail were pendent as he quickly rounded an old tree-lap and started into a trot and thence to a run, and when my gun went off he looked back and saw the smoke of the powder and began to check his speed, as though he was not afraid after discovering the exact locality of danger. He now stopped entirely—raised his brush and ears again and demeaned himself like he didn't intend to be frightened off in a hurry. But he finally walked on until he was lost to view by the woodland obstacles surrounding him, and I saw him no more.

We started for Georgia Gulch and hunted game and prospected various gulches all the way, and of course we were several days on the move. One morning we came over a low mountain and stirred up a large herd of deer, which scattered in all directions as they received volley after volley from the whole party. One of the party gave pursuit to one of them, which ran down a long smooth ridge.

He was riding a mule and the girth broke and the rider sailed over the mule's head like a flying squirrel and lit in a sitting position fronting down the ridge. The mule, being unable to stop, now took his "turn" at leapfrog and jumped over the rider and fell headlong down the hill. The sitting one of the two confusedly exclaimed to his sprawling mule, "Look here! What in the h——l is the matter with us?" The mule replied with a labored grunt as it staggered to its feet, when its master continued, "Yes, d——n you, you ought to grunt after nearly killing me." Our friend gathered himself up amid the frolic of the crowd, who had now come up to inquire if he was hurt, &c, and mended his girth and mounted again. As we moved on he began to complain some. Pretty soon he says, "I feel mighty stoved up, don't I look lower and shorter in the saddle than usual?" "Yes," says one of the party, "you look like a long-legged, short-backed boy." This was followed by a jolly laugh at the unlucky fellow's expense. But he consoled himself by believing that if the last remark was true, he would thereby become a better rider. We missed our route to Georgia Gulch and found ourselves a little out of the right course and on Blue River. Here we came up to some prospectors who had two dogs that had treed a porcupine about the size of an opossum. The animal was clubbed out of the little bush and fell to the ground, all drawn into a round ball of thorns. It was amusing to see the dogs dart at it and stick their noses with the little animal's quills, yelp and fall back alternately. One dog concluded to lay down against the porcupine and feel for a hold, but to no purpose; they had to quit, the worst-puzzled dogs in Utah. It was right hard for anybody to find that little animal's head or any other part of him. He looked plainly defined while on the tree, but he surely had an easy and cunning way of hiding himself within himself, after he

107

struck the ground. But these fellows succeeded at last and killed and ate the little animal.

We went on to Georgia Gulch and found an extraordinary increase of population and all at work. The gulch was exceeding all expectations in richness. It was common for three or four men to take out from $300 to $500 per day of good-quality of gold-dust.[16]

[16] Individual claims produced as much as $10,000 in a single season when placers were at their peak in Georgia Gulch. Henderson, *Mining in Colorado*, 227.

CHAPTER SIX

News of the Civil War
Reaches the Mines

A party of us again departed Georgia Gulch toward the head of Swan River to explore what we supposed to be one of the tributaries called Bald River.[1] I don't know how the former came to take the name of Swan River, for I never heard of any swans being seen there, nor indeed anywhere in those western territories, except on the Arkansas River. I have seen quite a number of white swan here when crossing the plains.[2] Bald River flows through terribly mountainous country heavily timbered with pine, fir, and other resinous wood. When we came near to this creek, which is possibly twenty miles from Georgia Gulch, one of the party shot and killed a beautiful "silver" fox.[3]

These animals are curiosities. Their fur sparkles like dewdrops, and their pelts were said to be very valuable, but our party were not hunting foxes and therefore set no value whatever upon its fur. We arrived on the highest ridge in the land apparently, and such another torn up country as was presented did not seem possible to exist, all in the same world.

[1] No Bald River is given on the maps in this region. Perhaps Conner meant to write the Blue River, which heads in the area described.

[2] Either the trumpeter or whistling swan could have been present in this region. The trumpeter swan is still found in the Yellowstone Park, and its numbers are increasing.

[3] The silver or black phase of the western red fox is the "silver" fox described by Conner. The white tips of the hair give the silver-gray effect to the pelt. Warren, *Mammals of Colorado*, 88.

But however, we descended to the creek and camped before night. On the following morning after the final arrangement of our camp and stock, each member of the party took his own course as suited him best, either to prospect for gold or to explore the country at pleasure. I directed my course to the top of an adjoining mountain to take another view of this country of numberless peaks and ridges. After spending a half-day on the mountains I decided to go down a little gulch, which increased in dimensions until it became a tremendous hollow between two imposing hills which bordered the creek and its bottom became quite a little woodland valley, and had an old Indian trail meandering down it. This trail extended into the bottom of the main creek. I was walking in the Indian path rapidly around the point of a steep spur that was formed by the junction of the gulch and river, when to my surprise I found myself within ten or twenty paces of two grizzly bears. I had come around the point close to them and halted instinctively. At the same instant (although neither of them saw me) one of them raised up his back and rather swelled up apparently to more than a foot higher and delivered a short, deep, coarse growl. He evidently had not seen me, but as the hunters have it, "he had winded me." They began to stir and look about and grow more angry until I backed around the jutting promontory out of sight of them and left them by another direction. I well knew that if I should wound one or both of them, which was all that I could hope to do, that they would turn on me and drive me up a tree, where I might have the exquisite pleasure of perching to keep them company for a day or two. I thought that if I had to set in a tree with two grizzly bears guarding me until some of the party found me in that rugged county, it would be like a rat in a trap and the trap forgotten. And it is well known that these animals will go off a distance out of reach of sure gunshot range, and watch for a victim up a tree, with great patience. I believed myself out of the hearing of my comrades and knew that there was too much vacant country about there for them to ever find me if I was missing at camp. So while these monarchs of the mountains were rearing upon their hind legs and turning around like an awkward man in a cotillion at a ball, looking for the object of their displeasure, I was leaving the unholy place by climbing the adjacent mountain.

These two beauties were soon out of my sight, for I prosecuted my course directly up the mountain nearly to the top, thinking that if such friendly specimens as I had just seen were occupying the valleys that day, I should choose the highlands for my leisure.

I was high enough when I reached a backbone near the top to have the best view possible in such a wilderness. I could see all the surrounding country, which appeared to be one grand illimitable mass of imposing peaks, ridges, spurs, and crags, stretching away to the very horizon. All, all of it appeared to exist without a purpose unless perhaps to exaggerate chaos and confusion—at once baffling all reason and ignoring all known human systems and orders. "A mighty maze without a plan," and to us poor mortals a topless, bottomless, and boundless myth, yet composed of halfway, real materials.

The whole scenery was thickly clothed with pine, fir, and many species of resinous and galipot kinds. I noticed in the distance some smoke arising out of the very bottom of a ravine. I looked a little longer and saw from its rapid increase and the flicker of flames that the mountain had been fired. I knew that these mountains would burn easy and rapidly, for I had seen them burn around Georgia Gulch and on Blue River, where a single tree would burn with an explosive vehemence that would shoot a flame far beyond its top, whilst it would roar like a storm. This fire took hold upon these green pine trees with a wonderful grasp and spread like it would over a surface of turpentine, and by the aid of the wind, set into commotion by it, the fire would reach up a mountain from its foot to its summit in the twinkling of an eye. A neighboring mountain, whose materials were warmed up to combustion, would in its turn go off and explode a solid sheet of flame from its base to the top and far beyond into forked termini, reaching into the clouds for more materials. Now a few moments had passed since this mighty expanse of green-land billows lay fixed in calm and silent repose beneath a cloudless sky, contrasting their indifferent dark frowns with the sunny rays of heaven, whilst the light and wholesome mountain air leaped from peak to peak and from crag to crag, scattering its health and cheerfulness everywhere. But what a change in so short a time. Another and another flame, one after another, begins at the foot of a mountain, and creates its own steady breeze to press it against the doomed mountainside, until strength sufficient is gained, when a sudden conflagration roars up to the summit with fearful ferocity, killing and crisping everything in its course as black as night.

The wind now seemed to have been awakened to capricious activity and began veering its course hither and thither, starting new fires to sweep the mountains in new directions, which was done with as much skill and businesslike intention as often results from a well-worked fire engine in skillful hands—as it sweeps the burning buildings around and about it.

The wind thus shifted its direction, constantly carrying in its course a solid flame, apparently unbroken for a mile or more in extent. Again and again the breeze would seem to lean steadily against mountain after mountain until ferocity enough was stirred to sweep savagely away the materials in its course with impassioned anger, and only check long enough to take a hold on another to traverse with similar quick results. Vulcan and Jove thus continued their powers for destruction and continued to destroy until late in the night. The distant roar, like distant thunder, at intervals broke the silence of night to tell the story of its sleepless energies and perseverance.

While I was standing on this mountain, or rather perched upon a sharp, naked, projecting spur, at the beginning of this grand conflagration, I contemplated it as something pretty. But when it began to stir up the imagination to that pitch which probably suggested Dante's Inferno and to lawlessly increase to a terrific recklessness, I became confounded, alarmed—crawled off of my perch and started in the opposite direction. But my slow progress up the mountain, compared with the speed of the fire, decided me to proceed around it on its side nearly the same route that I had so lately come. I knew that if the wind should turn in my direction, the flames of fire would reach the top of that mountain while I was considering what direction to go. I now wondered why I had sat so long quietly without thinking of the possibility of my own mountain being quickly visited like the others. The more I thought of it, the more I dreaded it, and the faster I proceeded. A sudden roar, which sounded like it might be at the bottom of my mountain, started me at my best speed, which I kept up until I was on the opposite side of its summit. I was now determined to go down the mountain to any watercourse at its foot, where all the fires seemed to begin, notwithstanding the presence of grizzly bear. I found the Bald River, which is little more than an ordinary creek, and followed it until I came to the camp a little before dark, and found the "boys" setting fire to the trees immediately around it, in order to get the benefit of a slow fire instead of that conflagration. We now came to the conclusion that the Indians had discovered us and set the woods on fire to run the game off, or to burn it up, together with ourselves. It would surely be hard to conceive how any animals would survive or escape such conflagrations as swept these mountains on this occasion, and such as was still going on, for the roar could be still heard, and in some instances, the sudden illuminations in the distant skies made by the quick shooting and darting of the flames into midheaven, as seen through the darkness of the night, offered a weird and melancholy scene. I loved a green mountain wilderness, but a charred, crisp one, like black death, bespeaks the handiwork of Satan, and therefore loses its charm, if it ever had one.

We struck camp on the following morning and beat a hasty retreat for Georgia Gulch. When nearing the gulch we came across four men who had gotten lost in the hills and ran out of food and ammunition, and therefore came near starving. Three of them agreed that the fourth had saved all of them by a lucky throw with a stone. They claimed to have corralled in a little nook against the side of a mountain a small number of bison, among which was a calf, and all of the animals escaped by dashing past them, except the calf which received the stone about the head (like Goliath did) and fell. The calf was secured and slaughtered and they did eat; so they said. But from the way they ate the provisions which we gave them, one would not be likely to believe that they had lately eaten a buffalo calf.

While in the northwestern portions of the Rocky Mountains, I have frequently observed that river and creek bottoms are found lower, near the foot of the mountains bordering them, than directly on the bank of the watercourse. But so is the bottom of the Mississippi and other rivers. But the difference is, as it appeared on the mountain streams, in the section mentioned, that the bottom land is covered with a stout turf, and next to the mountain foot this turf will wave like water when disturbed. I was once on a mountain overlooking Blue River with a few others besides myself. I descended the steep hill to within a few paces of the foot when I was warned by some of those who were lingering behind to "look out." I stopped and soon discovered a huge boulder coming down the hill at a fearful velocity. It passed a little distance from me, and as I looked to see how far it would roll out upon the level, green, grassy river bottom, I was surprised to observe that as soon as it struck the level it rolled into the ground without check or impediment. After its disappearance through the grassy turf the surface of the ground would distinctly heave with repeated and separate undulations for as much as twenty paces in extent from the spot where the stone entered the treacherous ground.[4]

I walked out upon the grass and discovered that by standing in one place for a few moments the water would collect around my feet and form a little lake where I stood. Then I would move to another spot and the water would disappear from the first position and settle around my feet again where I stood, at the second position. And so of any position I might take. The ground would sink under my weight like "rotten" ice under the feet of a skater. I rode unawares onto a treacherous surface, like one just mentioned, and the horse became so frightened that I was compelled to dismount quickly in order to get it to move in any direction. Thinking that I would soon get over the wavy ground, I hurried ahead, leading the horse while he blundered, stopped, and started by spells, and when still he would refuse to start until the water had collected about his feet and

---

[4] This condition results in the formation of peat-bogs or quaking-bogs in other regions of the nation. "When soil parent material is nearly impervious to water or is so located topographically that water stands continually at or slightly above the surface, the plant growth, as it perishes seasonally, builds up a body of organic material known as peat." United States Department of Agriculture, *Soils and Men, Yearbook of Agriculture, 1938,* 975.

Fairplay, Colorado.

A Chinese mining operation at Fairplay.
Library, State Historical Society of Colorado

mine to a dangerous extent. Thus we blundered, myself and the horse, for three hundred yards—one frightened as much as the other. It did seem so long that I thought surely that all "terra firma" was left behind, and when we did reach solid land, the great change again confused the horse so that he continued to stumble and blunder for some minutes, as though he still expected every step to lower him.

There are many such deceptive localities as this in the mountains. Quite a considerable space of the kind lies near the sink of the Humboldt River.[5] Now, for speculation as to its cause. My part of it shall be short, for I can conceive of no cause unless the water had sought the lowest places at the foot of the mountain and formed little lakes or ponds, and the leaves, grass, and trash blown by the wind had settled and floated on the surface of the water until it became sufficient to decay and produce grass to such an extent as to finally form a turf. This sod certainly floats upon water, although to look at it only, it appears like any other grassy land. If that explanation will not do, we will have a more scientific spectator to attend to the matter. There is only one thing about it which is certain to my mind, to wit: The shaky ground is there as above stated, howsoever it may have been formed.

While passing up Swan River on one occasion I observed a beaver house situated upon some of this treacherous ground. It seemed to be the headquarters of all the beavers in that section. I did not venture to go to it on account of the loose ground, but could distinctly see it and a part of its formation. It resembled in shape the old-fashioned potato burrow of our fathers, and stood about seven or eight feet in height and had doors or pigeonholes leading into it at the ground.

There were cottonwood trees in the vicinity, of two feet in diameter, gnawed down by these industrious little animals. The prints of their teeth all around the deftly girdled tree showed the marks of many weary nibbles. I cannot tell nor even guess the distance this beaver nest reached into the ground. When we first came in view of

---

[5] The Sink of the Humboldt River, in which the river terminates, is about ten miles from Lovelock, Nevada, on the Pershing-Churchill county line. Federal Writers' Project, *Nevada: A Guide to the Silver State*, 127, 138.

this ingenious beaver den, it was surrounded by a band of white wolves which retreated on our approach.[6] They were the prettiest wolves I ever saw. They crossed the river and began to climb one of the highest, steepest peaks that I ever saw in Utah Territory. One of our party, after remarking its shapely proportions and its towering pointed height, ended his comment by saying, "You have to look twice to see to the top of it."

The wolves, which were climbing this peak with difficulty, might easily have been taken for remarkable white sheep by the inexperienced explorer. The question was asked, as we were leaving the place, if all of "old Brigham Young's dogs were that white"; if they were, they eclipsed the morals of his saints in pure outwardness.

Wild geese, ducks, and mountain trout were found here, but not in profusion.

Some of our old party were located at the little town below the mouth of Georgia Gulch, called Parkville.[7] We made this our headquarters. The town was not yet two years old, but including the cabinites along the gulch and its tributaries, there was probably a thousand men upon an average, while thousands probably came and left, keeping up a constant flow to and from the place. A sawmill had taken the place of the whipsaw; a theater was established; plenty of billiard saloons, with ardent spirits, mostly made of drugs. The different games known to professionals were constantly exercised for winnings, great and small—eucher, seven-up, cribbage, faro, monte, roulette, jourqueseft, rondo, keno, tan, diana, and all other games known to the profession were brought into requisition by the necessity of gain and frolic.

[6] The only specie of wolves known in the mountains of Colorado were the southern Rocky Mountain wolf. Wolves vary greatly in color, but those in the Rocky Mountains are largely gray. Their backs have black-tipped hairs but the color fades to a whitish gray on the underbody. Some lighter species might have appeared white to Conner but odds were great against his seeing "a band of white wolves." Warren, *Mammals of Colorado*, 91–92.

[7] Parkville was located about five miles east of Breckenridge at the juncture of Georgia Gulch and Swan River, in Summit County, Colorado. The community at one time in the 1860's was reported to have over 1,800 voters, but today only a few protruding timbers from tailings and obscure graves mark the site. Ransome, *Geology and Ore Deposits of the Breckenridge District, Colorado*, 17; Hollister, *Mines of Colorado*, map.

The American Ditch Company brought water to the gulch with which to run sluices by a ditch some ten miles in length, measuring it around with its numerous meanderings.[8] The ditch would sometimes spring a leak somewhere in its course around a mountain and finally break and wash away the side of the mountain before it was discovered.

An old lady came into the gulch and set up the first "deadfall" (the mountain parlance for grog shop) in connection with a hotel. She brought her daughter with her, whom she addressed by the affectionate sobriquet of "Sis." Sis was the first young lady to arrive in Georgia Gulch, and the fact that she waited upon customers gave the establishment a heavy run of business. Miners would come from neighboring mines quite a distance to get to buy a drink from Sis. The common remark of the miners, when meeting friends, was first, "Boys, there is a gal in the gulch." "When did she come?" "Oh, I don't know, but she's there." "Hurrah! Hurrah for Georgia Gulch; come, let us all go see her." And off they would go to see Sis, with as much curiosity as boys who go to see the monkey. Pretty soon, however, a number of the female sex found their way over Snowy Range and into the gulch, and some with families of little children. The large flume that carried off the "tailings" and muddy, sand-clogged water from the mining operations of several hundred men ran down through the main street of the town and extended a half-mile below, where it emptied its contents. Steps were built up over the flume at the street crossings. One of the "first families" who had a young hopeful had turned the boy out to grass as usual. The little fellow was leaning over looking into the swift, muddy water in the flume when he concluded to put his hand in it. He was taken in as soon as he touched the water, and carried off so rapidly that a quick active race by one of the bystanders was required to catch him within the space of a hundred yards. The miner came back and gave the boy to his mother after the little fellow was well drenched in the muddy slough and came out looking like a half-drowned gopher.

[8] During the summers, water was in short supply along the tributary gulches of Swan River. To relieve the shortage, ditches were dug to tap the waters of Blue River as early as 1860. Hollister, *Mines of Colorado*, 334.

Some "rough" across the street called out to the miner, "Halloo there, where did you catch that beaver?" "O, I caught it in the flume here." "How many traps have you set in the flume?" &c. All this time the poor woman was frightened out of her wits and was industriously wiping the sand out of her little cub's eyes; therefore had only time to look cross at the perpetrators of this heartless levity.

Last and not least came the military. A recruiting officer came also and unfurled the United States flag and planted the staff over the store of Jones and Haskell, two substantial Union men. Through this medium, we received the war news from the great rebellion in the States, which we could not realize. This put the war spirit into the market, and it multiplied and increased to an extent to exceed the most sanguine expectations. Some of the population emigrated to Washington Gulch, southwest of us, which was discovered more than a year before and was as rich, if not richer, in gold than Georgia Gulch.[9] The famous Gregory diggings off toward Denver furnished us for a while almost as many men as our gulch furnished Washington Gulch.[10] We went to Washington Gulch (which is the present site of Leadville), and we had a big account of a snowslide that came down the mountain and completely covered up the miners' cabins. This slide was equal to several acres in extent and brought snow, earth, stones, and trees along in its wild ride. One large tree never fell but took its ride of half-mile or so in a standing position and finally settled on top of a miner's cabin and stood erect until the snow melted in June. There are doubtless many citizens of Lead-

[9] Washington Gulch does not show on detailed maps of Leadville and its environs. Conner perhaps means California Gulch located just south of present-day Leadville, Colorado, which had a population of 5,000 to 6,000 miners in 1861. Hollister, *Mines of Colorado*, 316–18; Emmons, *Geology and Ore Deposits of the Leadville Mining District, Colorado*, plates.

[10] John H. Gregory, accompanied by Wilkes Defrees, made his discovery on Gregory Hill, between Central City and Blackhawk, Gilpin County, Colorado, on May 6, 1859. Before the placer mines at Gregory Gulch were exhausted by 1863, miners followed other leads to California Gulch, Georgia Gulch, Buckskin Joe, and other areas still in production. Caroline Bancroft, "The Elusive Figure of John H. Gregory, Discoverer of the First Gold Lode in Colorado," *Colorado Magazine*, Vol. XX, No. 4 (July, 1943), 121–35; *Henderson, Mining in Colorado*, 121; Hollister, *Mines of Colorado*, 60–63.

ville who have but little idea how and what it cost to settle this region in the beginning. A young man, a native of Kentucky, met an Indian of the Arapaho tribe, who agreed to go with a party and show them much gold if he could be protected against the Utes. The Utes inhabited the mountains and the Arapahoes the plains, and they were enemies. The young man referred to was anxious to go with the Indian and therefore obtained the consent of six other men to accompany him. His name was Sanders. It took great persuasion to get the Arapaho to consent to go with so small a force, and he absolutely refused to go until the whites pledged themselves never to give him up to the Utes. They did pledge the Indian to die with him or defend him. They started on their route toward the subsequently discovered Washington Gulch (and still later, Leadville), and were stopped by the Utes in the little gulch not far from the present Leadville, known as Dead Man's Hollow. The Utes demanded the Arapaho and agreed for the whites to go in peace. In vain did the whites insist that they had promised the Arapaho protection. He was firmly demanded, and his delivery was the only condition upon which they all might depend for safety. The white men adhered to their pledge and a battle was the consequence.[11]

The unburied bones of these seven white man and one Indian gave the name of "Dead Man's Hollow" to this little ravine, which was subsequently named as one of the landmarks by which persons were directed to the then Washington Gulch. The Utes were then at a quasi-peace with the white man, and the chief who conducted

[11] Other sources describe similar incidents but do not place the events at present-day Leadville. Hollister says, "In July [1859] the prospectors had found their way into the South Park. Two or three small parties were set upon by the Indians, and murdered and mutilated in the most approved Indian style. J. L. Shank and J. L. Kennedy were the first victims. Soon thereafter the bodies of six killed and scalped white men, and one dead Indian, were found. They were never identified." Hollister, *Mines of Colorado*, 72. William N. Byers, editor of *Rocky Mountain News*, provides Bancroft with the following account: ". . . so many tarried [at Tarryall], and such was the squabbling over claims that a portion of the population determined to seek for mines elsewhere, and to their delight soon discovered them. But the first party of eight men which left Tarryall was killed by Indians, except one, while passing through a ravine, which took from this circumstance the name of Dead Man's gulch." Bancroft, *History of Nevada, Colorado, and Wyoming*, 383.

this battle afterward stated that at Georgia Gulch those seven whites and one Indian succeeded in killing twenty-nine of his men and wounding many more, before they died. From the description the chief gave of the conduct of those unfortunate men, their pledge to the poor Arapaho was nobly complied with.[12] "They would defend him or die with him!" They did both. Miners went in search of the missing men and found Washington Gulch where the Arapaho was leading them.

This section of the Rocky Mountains is numerously marked by snowslides. Their tracks are plainly visible. The wide and neatly cut openings through the heavy forest timber, sometimes extending from the top to the foot of a mountain, attest the power of heavy snows to carry away a heavy forest.

We moved back to Georgia Gulch and found the unhappy war spirit on the increase and men enlisting liberally under the Stars and Stripes. All miners and tradesmen who had hithertofore associated with friendly feelings were now being gradually estranged from each other. Then the war spirit began to disclose its natural and latent cussedness. Rebel and Federal friends became Rebel and Federal enemies. Abuses became general and from the stronger side, whether the stronger side be Rebel or Federal. Men began to get uneasy, while the audible mutterings of war were creeping into these wild mountain recesses.[13]

[12] Bancroft distinguishes three bands of Utes in Colorado at this time. The White River Utes of northwestern Colorado were led by Navava; the Uncompahgre Utes, south of the White River, were led by Ouray; and the Southern Utes were led by Ignacio. Bancroft, *History of Nevada, Colorado, and Wyoming*, 470.

[13] It was thought at the outbreak of the Civil War that a third of Colorado's population sympathized with the Southern cause. Confederates posted handbills from Denver to the mining regions offering to pay for arms and ammunition. Undoubtedly, it was intended to raise a force to co-operate with Confederate troops from Texas and Arkansas and seize Colorado and New Mexico. William Gilpin, governor of Colorado Territory, acting vigorously, raised the First Colorado Volunteers to full strength by September, 1861. Recruiting offices were opened in the principal communities and mining camps, and this activity created interest in the Civil War. Except for a few incidents and raids, little Confederate activity took place in Colorado during the Civil War. Frank Hall, *History of the State of Colorado*, I, 275–76; Norma L. Flynn, *Early Mining Camps of South Park*, 67; Albert B. Sanford, "Camp Weld, Colorado," *Colorado Magazine*, Vol. XI, No. 2 (March, 1934), 46–50.

This state of things began to impose new and additional burdens upon this hithertofore patient people who had known no war, except that which was had with the Indians, wild animals, and poverty.

Someone brought into the gulch a pair of very young mountain-sheep lambs. A stranger offered one hundred dollars for them, to take to the States with him. The lambs were little, bluish-colored, awkward creatures, and the man who wanted them was a Northerner. Someone standing near remarked that the "blue-bellied Yankees now even wanted blue sheep" and dwelt at some length upon blue lambs in general. This all passed away at the time, but pretty soon a drunken fellow was hunting the offender and on failing to find him, shouted at the top of his voice, "Hurrah for the North." A Georgian, who was sitting in a butcher-shop door, greasing his boots with a lump of tallow, replied by shouting, "Hurrah for the South." Then the Yankee shot at the Rebel and the Rebel shot at the Yankee, and both repeated the pleasantry, which ended by the Yankee being shot directly through the body. This was followed by another "reb" stepping into the street with a double-barrel shotgun and emptying both barrels into the U.S. flag over the recruiting office, riddling it into tatters.

This act was not calculated to heal the breach already made. So a good Union man went in search of the offender with a navy six-shooter in his hand and failed to find the Rebel. The next chapter began on the following morning by the offender looking up the prosecutor and proposing to play a six-shooter game with him, whereupon the prosecutor declined and the matter ended.

This quarrel was taken up and renewed by two other patriots who represented each side of the great rebellion. They mutually agreed to settle it by a duel and thus save any necessity of committing their respective friends. Their friends happened to be lively, sensible fellows, who agreed for them to fight a duel provided that they would shoot each other across a table in a miner's cabin and each hold at the same time, with his left hand, a corner of the same handkerchief. This was agreed to by the combatants, and the seconds began the necessary preparations. Each second loaded carefully his principal's navy six and prepared the table and handkerchief, and even entered into the minute detail of covering the charge in the cylinder of the revolver with tallow to make the pistol shoot slick and to keep it in order, as is the custom in this section to keep the weapons always in proper order. Finally all was pronounced ready for the catastrophe. The two victims stepped forward with unflagging determination depicted on their countenances to make the opponent yield or take the consequences. Each took his stand on opposite sides of the table and opposite to and facing each other, about four feet apart and each holding a corner of the handkerchief now stretched between them with their left hands and the deadly pistols they held in the right hanging down by the side. Now the picture, as they turned their eyes upon each other steadily as though each would read the other's heart through his countenance, was complete.

Two men armed with heavy six-shooters stood by each of the principals, whose duty it was, according to prearrangement, to shoot down the principal who took advantage of the other by shooting before the word was given. All was now deathly silent. "Make ready" brought the two cocked pistols to a level across the table nearly breast to breast. "One—two—three." On the word "three" both fired and both fell. The table was quickly removed and each prostrated man's coat stripped off of him. Dr. S[tewart], a Virginian, knelt on the floor and felt each man's pulse and passed rapid opinions upon them. Then pulling open the shirt to search for the wound, and as there was none, he remarked the fact in surprise, as he hastily examined the other with the same result. This announcement from the doctor encouraged the wounded men enough to induce an effort to get up, which they did, by blundering to their feet, looking like two mortals just out of a painful and confused dream. The doctor said amidst his puzzled stupor that each man had a red spot on his chest, but there was no bullet hole in either of them. Now those who were in the trick burst into uncontrollable laughter which could have been heard for a mile. They had duped both the principals and the doctor by charging the pistols with powder only. It was the force or concussion of the atmosphere that made the two red spots at such near range. Mirth and levity ran high, ignoring with the greatest indifference the petulant oaths, scowls, and threats of the doctor alike with the idiotic grimaces and alternating good and evil shown by the countenances of the principals. The doctor abruptly left, stating as he went that he had a pistol that did have bullets in it. His departure was greeted by boisterous calls to "Come back and get your fee." "Don't be disappointed, we will pay it, &c." But the doctor never halted but left the detested place and its inmates to themselves. As for the two duelists, it can only be said that they were a brace of the funniest and most foolish-looking specimens in that camp. But however, thus ended this famous duel, and seemingly to the satisfaction of all parties. The principals made friends—each declaring that he didn't fall from trepidation but from the force of the powder. For the sake of harmony all this was admitted, and the incident was soon lost in the cloud of others of daily occurrence.

I saw a similar duel fought on the plains once previously to the above incident, or rather, similarly prepared weapons. Uncle John was rather a young man to earn the expressive and characteristic sobriquet of uncle. But he and Mr. Eugene Palmer got up a duel. It arose from Mr. Palmer throwing a cup of hot coffee in Uncle John's face. When their seconds had prepared their pistols and delivered them to the combatants, they turned their attention to their camp duties after bidding the angry ones to "Go shoot it out." One rough fellow, Nick Beery, who was not aware of the pending joke, exclaimed to the duelists, "Go off; away off, on the plains and settle your foolishness, for if you even shoot me accidentally, d——n if I don't kill you both." They went "away off on the plains" and emptied their pistols at each other, without effect. They both, at first, concluded that they couldn't shoot that day from some cause or other. When they came into camp their seconds were prepared for them. The second of Mr. Palmer remarked to the crowd of anxious fellows, who were standing around, that "I told Uncle John privately that Mr. Palmer's pistol had no bullets in it." "You are a liar, you didn't," exclaimed Uncle John. Uncle John's second remarked, "And I told Mr. Palmer in a whisper that Uncle John's pistol had no bullets in it." "Well, now you know you are lying, sure enough," says Mr. Palmer. Now the "big" laugh rated high—too high to catch the distinct oaths hurled in profusion at the two seconds. The two duelists now allied themselves for mutual protection and wanted to shoot everybody in the camp, but the odds were against them and they accepted finally the better part of valor as they plainly had to do, and submitted to the open and bold charges of their folly without flinching. Thus ended this little unpleasantness. "All's well that ends well."

I left Georgia Gulch in August and passed over the range to Jefferson. It was snowing just a little. Although this was unusual, it is common to have frost upon this range in all of the months in the year. It was cold on top but pleasant when I came down the Atlantic side. I noticed while on the top of the ridge a burned spot on a tree ten feet high from the ground, where I had camped long before and built a fire against this tree up on top of the snow. The snow was gone, leaving the fireplace on the side of the tree high up amongst the limbs. I remember Mr. Palmer, who fought the dual with Uncle John, was my camp-mate upon that occasion and a terribly bleak, cold night we had of it, with only two blankets spread on some pine boughs that were supported by the snow. Just before this incident I had remained all night on the top of this mountain range without any blanket or bedding; hence I built a fire the same way against a tree on the snow and stood and sat around it all night.

While upon this subject it might not be amiss to notice the grade of snow in this section during seven months in the year. When I arrived in Georgia Gulch in April, I found the steep mountainsides stripped of its timber. Some stumps were to be seen above the snow, and probably five, ten, and fifteen feet high, depending upon the depth of the snow when they were cut. So in the month of July and from then on, until December, stumps can be seen varying from a foot to fifteen feet in height. It was a common query made by strangers, "What was that tree cut off so high up for?" And they frequently disbelieved it when told that the snow was that high when the tree was cut off. It was the spring alluded to that I saw Mr. James Bennett up a steep mountainside about three hundred yards after firewood. He had obtained quite a long, heavy pole and was on his snowshoes, dragging the pole by the handle of his ax, which he had stuck fast into it. He was coming down a ridge formed by Georgia Gulch and one of its tributary hollows. The snow was deep enough to cover all the stumps between him and the foot of the hill except one. This one had broken up the snow a little, as the snow was settling down around it but not enough to draw any attention. James Bennett and his log got to going too fast for him, and he therefore squatted on his snowshoes and traveled like he was an eight-foot slide runner, increasing his speed each moment. He was depending rather upon the roughness of his pole to regulate his velocity, but it didn't do it. The seat of his pants were nearly touching the surface of the snow as he shot down that hill, holding on to the ax-helve for a balance and ran his snow slats astraddle of the treacherous stump, and he sat against it so suddenly that the stump turned him a complete somersault; and had it not been for the snow crust breaking where he lit, there was no reason why he should not have tumbled on down the mountain for a hundred yards.

Some of his goods went over the ridge toward the tributary, while the ax and snowshoes separated, some of them to go down one side of the ridge and the remainder to go down the other side. But all kept sliding until a landing at the foot of the mountain was made, and for a wonder no serious damage was done. There were, however, several persons prostrated from broken legs caused by becoming frightened at the snowshoes running away with them and consequently jumping out of them and breaking through the crust of the snow on alighting. The body would always have too much momentum to be stopped immediately on breaking into the snow, and therefore broken bones were generally the consequence.

CHAPTER SEVEN

Confederates Gather at Mace's Hole

As before stated, I arrived in the little newly built town of Jefferson about August, 1862, where I established my headquarters. From here I visited the main divide between this little town and Georgia Gulch frequently, and on one occasion I climbed the left-hand peak south of the gap through which the road passes from Jefferson to the gulch. This peak had the appearance of having split open at some period and the side next to South Park having tumbled down the hill, covering the woodland about three foot deep with rocks. The woods does not extend to the top of the cordillera; therefore, the top of the ridge and the summit of the peak are bald. It was a part of the bald portion of this mountain that seemed to have peeled off and fell away into the woods three thousand feet below. It was a fearful sight to go close to this perpendicular wall and look over. It was an achievement that I never knew anyone to accomplish without first tying a rope fast to some bush or tree, to hold as the approach was made to the brink. I spent a day on the bald mountain just described. There is but little difference, if any, in the height of this position and the highest point in the United States territory. I saw an antelope up there. It ran off from me about forty yards and stopped. I didn't attempt to shoot it as I never could get its meat down that stupendous mountain. I shook my hat at it and it turned its hair forward after their fashion when frightened, and became quite white in appearance as it left that region.

I also saw a crescent-shaped lake that bent around the summit of that mountain. It must have been nearly a half-mile in length but narrow—probably not more than ten or fifteen yards in width. The water was very blue and transparent. In descending that range I followed a very steep little hollow. Long before I got down to where the woods began I saw a diminutive chicken not larger than a quail. It was shaped exactly like our poultry chickens except that it was a little flat on the back and less[er] stature perhaps than a quail, and cackled in a fine tone, but just like any other chicken. It sprang from under a rock, half jumping and half flying, and perched on a stone to cackle. I attempted to cut its neck by a pistol shot so as not to spoil it, as it was a curiosity. But every time I missed it would flutter off farther until I lost it altogether. I never saw one like it before or since. Its color was a dark brown and marked dimly, crosswise of the feathers.[1] Before I reached the woods I found a herd of mountain sheep that led me over such sharp ridges that I was fearful of falling and therefore had to coon it, as one sometimes does a log over a creek. I was thus compelled to crawl over one stretch for a distance of three hundred yards. There would be no hope for the safety of anything but a mountain sheep in this locality during a dark night. The only way a man could manage to get out, if he didn't want to fall a half-mile to some place or other, would be to find before dark some spot big enough to locate on, and remain quietly and still until daylight. I quit the sheep and went into the woods below me and thence on to my headquarters. I had rough but not such steep sailing.

Three miles north of Jefferson and near the foot of this main divide a ranch for herding and caring for stock had been established the year before by Messrs. Boyce and Keen, old citizens of Iowa and Missouri.[2] They took in stock at $1.50 per head per month. During the spring of this year I had been to this ranch and captured a young antelope not larger than a jack rabbit.

---

[1] This description fits a white-tailed ptarmigan.

[2] The first individual mentioned at this point is Boanerges R. Boyce, who was one of the "large farmers of the Huerfano and one of the early commissioners of Huerfano County." D. W. Working, "The Hicklins on the Greenhorn," *Colorado Magazine*, Vol. IV, No. 5 (December, 1927), 187.

I had left it with the herder of this ranch, to be taken care of. It had been living about the ranch nearly all summer and was very docile and had become about half grown or more. I went to get it and was surprised that it would follow me with as much confidence as would a dog. When it became well acquainted with me it followed me hunting for a day at a time without leaving me farther than ten or twenty paces. When it became startled it would turn its hair forward and run to me, and sometimes would stand against me, while it industriously watched about and looked for the cause. At the sight of a mountain sheep or the report of my gun, it would leap like its life was at stake until it reached me. On such occasions it would always look after the cause of the trouble, after getting to me. I could toy with its ears or slap its jaws, while it was frightened, without drawing its attention.

I accounted for its failure to become used to the report of a gun: the fact that I shot its mother to capture it. And when it was left to its own resources for safety, it ran for more than a hundred yards and hid in the grass like a rabbit. When I picked it up the poor little lamb cried piteously. I was loath to give up my pet, but the war was going on in the States, and I had made up my mind to attempt to get home by the way of Texas by which a plain of twelve hundred miles or more had to be traversed to reach it. To reach that destination seemed a world of trouble and danger alone, without the bother of taking my antelope. Then I knew that the route was through Comanche country for the most of the way. I gave my antelope to a young man to take it to Missouri.

The last time I ever saw it, it was walking beside a man following behind a wagon loaded with hay in South Park. When I met the party, the little animal recognized me and started to follow me back my way and continued to follow until I drove it off to the wagon. These animals are even more docile and gentle than the deer.

Writers of limited experience in the western territories are the ones who have hitherto give the most voluminous reports to the press. I have just read an account of the habits of the mountain sheep. The author was evidently a passing visitor. He confined these animals unconditionally to the high ranges, crags, and spurs of the

Rocky Mountains, when in reality those places are their places of resort, but they go into many other characters of country to feed.

While at the range of B[oyce] and K[een] as above referred, I have shot them on the level park at the foot of the range while they were feeding on the fresh grasses like other animals. Morning after morning I have seen them, after descending thousands of feet from the rugged crags of Snowy Range, come out upon the comparatively level park at least a half-mile from the foot of the range to feed. And I have seen the herder of the stock at this ranch have very many pretty chases after them, as he pursued a herd of them to the foot of the mountain on a horse or mule.

I once found a herd of them feeding amongst the quaking-asp trees on the level about two miles north of this ranch near the foot of the cordillera. All except one slowly strayed off into the foothills of the cordillera. This one stood for some time looking at me over its shoulder, as it stood with its rear to me, and never moved when I shot and missed it. I had nearly gotten my gun recharged when it fled off on the course of the others.

We would sometimes overhaul them before reaching their crags and gorges and bring down a mutton, and sometimes succeed in "lifting" one off his chosen perch upon an inaccessible crag such as a hawk would probably choose to alight upon, and in such cases there would be no skinning to do. After he was done falling and tumbling a few hundred yards, what was left of him would have to be picked, more after the manner of dressing a fowl than a mutton. Their flesh is dark and unsavory. Their coat is of long bluish hair possibly three or four inches in length, which is densely mixed with fine wool. This wool is not visible until we turn the long hair forward. Altogether their suit or coat of hair and wool seems to be thoroughly waterproof.

But the tremendous horns of these sheep are the greatest animal curiosity in the Rocky Mountains, unless indeed the antlers of the elk are equally monstrous. Their horns circle away from the side of the head, as the sheep grows in age, like those of other sheep. But as the horn winds in nearly a perpendicular circle the arc must be necessarily great on account of the diameter of the horn. I saw one of those horns compared by measurement with a one-gallon water keg, and they were found to be about equal in circumference.

It is wonderful that a sheep of the weight of 150 to 200 pounds can carry such heavy horns so nimbly over the most precarious and dangerous paths, where the least awkward step would precipitate them probably a thousand feet. But they seem not to vary their actions in the least on account of height and can stand over an awful abyss with an indifferent nonchalance truly miraculous. Their horns take up all of the room on top of their heads generally. I have seen some instances in which a little narrow strip of skin probably a quarter- or half-inch in width was visible between the roots of the horns, but the greater number of the oldest, their horns will grow against each other.[3]

The greatest deception that nature has seen fit to practice upon my blindness since I have been able to discern and contemplate anything was perpetrated in the Rocky Mountains by a facetious presentation of distant views. During my whole sojourn of seven consecutive years in the midst of this great chain of mountains, if I ever saw anything located where it really was, at any considerable distance, I do not now remember it. If I started to go to a mountain that I felt sure that I could shoot a ball over from where I stood, my impatience would only be enhanced by an hour's walk toward it without being perceptibly nearer it than the point from where I had started. The small distant object seemed to cast its focal angle so far, without uniting its converging rays into a single line of nothingness, that I almost became a skeptic upon my early lessons on natural philosophy. The exceedingly clear atmosphere aided the observation, of course; but then it did appear that if the atmosphere was perfectly transparent, that an object could be seen at any distance. This bit of philosophy was once forced upon my mind by a ludicrous but practical illustration. I was in company with two others on a prospecting tour in the spring when the mountains were heavily

---

[3] Conner's description of mountain sheep or the bighorn sheep is fairly accurate. But instead of bluish coats they are predominately grayish brown, and the larger and older rams can weigh up to three hundred pounds. Warren, *Mammals of Colorado*, 301–306.

Alexander ("Zan") Hicklin, before 1855.
Library, State Historical Society of Colorado

The Alexander Hicklin home in Rye, Colorado.
Library, State Historical Society of Colorado

clothed with snow and the snow had a pretty solid stout crust on it.

The crust had stability sufficient to bear a man's weight. We were en route to headquarters. After climbing a high, treeless ridge to the top, we stopped to "blow" a little before beginning the descent of the opposite side. The beautiful white snow began a steep grade on our course down the mountain, but gradually lost its precipitous angle as its surface presented a long, smooth, and graceful sweep reaching to and into the woodland plot at the foot of the mountain away below us. We were very fatigued and each of us carried one of the tools necessary for prospecting—a shovel, pick, and sheet-iron pan. We had traveled up and then down, and up again, and down again, alternately and so continuously that we were almost broken down in the knees and therefore we were loath to start down this hill. I soon discovered a new mode of travel. I carried the pan and it was not far to the foot of the mountain.

So, I sat the pan on the snow and took a seat in it and concluded to ride down the hill. My quick, informal start soon convinced me that my speed would accelerate to an unnecessary expedition down that hill, and I therefore began to clip the snow crust with my heels, to check up a little. But the cloud of snow thus raised about my face blinded me as completely as it also served to convince me that I was sailing too fast. I could not see for the flying snow stirred up by my feet, and I began to think about the trees that I might ride over on this flying trip. I made an effort to throw myself out of the hasty vehicle, but failed. This frightened me worse than ever and quickly prompted another more desperate effort that sent me out of my seat to cutting all sorts of pranks and somersaults, extending over a distance that I would have guessed to have been at least a hundred yards, before coming to a final halt. The strangest accident of the whole event was that there was no broken bones. The pan didn't stop until it had reached the center of the woods about a mile from its place of departure. Now, as accustomed to these mountains as I was, I had no reasonable idea of the distance from the top of that ridge to the foot, and believe that if I had continued my unobstructed course for as long as that incline plane held out, that a cannon ball might have been sent in pursuit without ever catching up. I had never before thought of the ease with which I might have lost that pan by accidentally letting it fall. But however, this is a digression of greater dimensions than was at its beginning intended, and therefore I will take a direct route back to my headquarters at Jefferson, in South Park at the eastern foot of the cordillera.

I went up the range near the little town of Hamilton and in the evening about dark a stranger drove up in a little wagon and stated, in answer to inquiries, that he was from the States, and in the course of his detail of news stated that "We have lost one of the best men in the United States, and one whose life was worth the whole Confederacy." "Who was it," queried someone. "Ellsworth—he was killed by a hotelkeeper at Alexandria by the name of Jackson." "Ha, ha, ha," laughed a big good-humored fellow, who continued, "You skeared me, stranger. I was afeard that it was the big ole secesh of all." Thus, little repartees were continuously being drawn out upon both sides, of the great war question, from apparent reluctance, but really from careless indifference.

But things could not remain thus without change. And therefore a gradual earnestness began to present itself, which grew into a bold taking of sides. Everybody was presumed to have a decided choice. There was no escaping, whether there was even an individual expression or an overt act committed or not. Amid this confusion thus engendered, the public mind became unsettled and impatient. Heavy doubts hung all around these old hills. The first regiments of Colorado troops had been raised and sent to New Mexico to fight Sibley, the Confederate general.[4] The second was now being raised for the

---

[4] Colonel Henry Hopkins Sibley, the developer of the Sibley tent and Sibley stove which were widely used by field troops, resigned from the United States army on May 13, 1861. Sibley recruited Confederate forces in Texas and late in 1861 assumed command of Southern troops in the Territory of New Mexico with headquarters at Fort Bliss, Texas. The First Regiment of Colorado Volunteers was organized during the summer and fall of 1861. Led by Colonel John P. Slough, Lieutenant Colonel Samuel F. Tappan, and Major John M. Chivington, the First Colorado Volunteers fought at the Battle of La Glorieta Pass. William A. Keleher, *Turmoil in New Mexico, 1846–1868,* 145, 160–61; William Clarke Whitford, *Colorado Volunteers in the Civil War: The New Mexico Campaign in 1862,* 47, 52, 85–97.

United States service.[5] To offset this preparation, a Rebel regiment was put in course of organization, whose nucleus was located in "Mace's Hole," in the vicinity of the headwaters of the Green Horn Creek, already referred to as flowing out of the mountains across the strip of plain lying between the mountains and the Arkansas River, nearly opposite the town of Pueblo. From Mace's Hole to Georgia Gulch and neighboring settlements, mining camps, and &c., where these Rebel recruits were secretly enlisted, was about the distance of 140 miles, guessed measurement. The foot of the Rocky Mountain range, in which is located Mace's Hole, fronts nearly directly opposite the present site of the town of Pueblo, from which place the vicinity of the Hole can be easily seen. This salubrious and healthy climate is unsurpassed by any other in the world. And the reader will remember that it is in the same section where our party of five spent the previous winter, as a nomadic hunting tribe.

I took my final departure from Jefferson in the South Park and came out of the mountains to the plains by the way of Canon City, where I crossed the Arkansas and followed around the foothills under the shady frowns of the Rocky Mountain front range. I crossed the numerous little streams over which our little party hunted, and upon whose banks we had frequently slept during the previous winter, and finally found myself at Mace's Hole. There were nearly six hundred men encamped within this singularly formed, rock-bound, natural amphitheater for the purpose of organizing a regiment for the Rebel service. But really there was never this number in the hole at once, but this was the headquarters. To describe Mace's Hole is not the task of a moment. I will therefore brief its outlines as to its fitness for a camping ground and place of concealment and quiet.

If we would dig a circular pit with perpendicular walls into the side of a great mountain range down to a level bottom but little elevated above the adjacent plains, and then cut a ditch from the bot-

[5] The Second Regiment of Colorado Volunteers was composed of two companies organized earlier by Colorado Territorial Governor William Gilpin and other forces authorized in February, 1862. Colonel J. H. Leavenworth led the Second Colorado Volunteers which were stationed at Fort Lyon until April, 1863. Then the regiment was sent east, and it fought in Missouri against Confederates led by General Sterling Price. Bancroft, *History of Nevada, Colorado, and Wyoming*, 423–24.

tom of this pit through the foothills for a distance of half a mile to
the plains, through which to drain the pit—then we would have a
similar place to Mace's Hole.

There was so much confusion of acts, sentiment, and doubts here
and subsequently that I lost my notes. I cannot therefore be minute
and absolutely correct about the dimensions of Mace's Hole. But
from my best recollection, this hole was about half a mile or more
in diameter and completely hedged in by a perpendicular wall, varying in height from ten feet near the ditchlike entrance around the
circle, rising gradually higher as it neared the higher ascending mountain, where it was hundreds of feet in height, then gradually descended around the other half-circle to the mouth of the ditch or
entry. This entry was a narrow lane between two walls also, until
it opened on the plains. The ditch was like the "hole"—bounded by
perpendicular walls and possibly from twenty to fifty feet in width.
Such was the place selected by Col. John Heffiner in which to organ-
ize his Confederate regiment.[6] It was within a mile of the military
road leading from Denver, Colorado, to Fort Union, New Mexico,
already described. It was also within about the same distance [from]
the adobe station occupied by Mr. Dotson, an ex-marshal of Great
Salt Lake City in 1856,[7] and the same who was on duty when the
Mormon authorities came into a conflict with the troops of Col.
Albert Sidney Johnston at that time.[8] This adobe building had been

[6] Colonel John Heffiner, to whom Conner often refers, is not mentioned in
the Colorado press during the fall of 1862. Heffiner's name does not appear in
other works concerned with Confederate activity in Colorado, and it is not listed
in the index of the *Official Records of the Union and Confederate Armies*.

[7] Peter K. Dotson was commissioned United States marshal of Utah Territory
in 1855. Two years later he was ordered from the Territory by Heber Kimball but
returned with the United States army in the summer of 1858. After leaving Utah,
Dotson settled at Fountain City, now Pueblo, Colorado, in 1860, and became a
cattle rancher. The editors have changed "Dodson" to "Dotson" in Conner's manuscript. Hubert Howe Bancroft, *History of Utah*, 539; Bancroft, *History of Nevada,
Colorado, and Wyoming*, 634; Leland Hargrave Creer, *Utah and the Nation*, 159.

[8] Albert Sidney Johnston, a veteran of the Black Hawk War, the Texas Revolution, and the Mexican War, was ordered by President James Buchanan in 1857
to lead 2,500 troops into Utah and establish United States authority which had
been questioned by Mormon leaders. Johnston's forces, however, were delayed by
Mormon resistance and winter storms so that they did not enter Salt Lake City,

erected and was still owned by Zan Hicklin, Ole Zan, as he was familiarly called by soldiers and passing citizens.[9] He was well known in Colorado and cut quite a figure in Federal and Rebel affairs before the storm was over. Mr. Hicklin was a man of light complexion, over fifty years of age, and over six feet in height. He was a bachelor who could not read and by his own professions, a California sport.[10] Ole Zan rented his station house and lands to Mr. Dotson for the latter to control and to keep hotel for the soldiery who escorted the United States mail, and to cultivate the soil. Ole Zan moved out and built a little establishment on the road farther south, about half a mile from the station, and hired a few Mexican greasers and turned his attention to herding and raising stock and cattle in particular. He visited Mr. Dotson and family daily. They were the only houses within fifteen miles, and of course they were very intimate. Mr. D[otson] had two interesting daughters and a wife, who constituted his family. But he kept some Mexican laborers to work the first and only cornfield I ever saw in Colorado. The two girls were about the same age, one being an adopted Mormon girl and very pretty. Ole Zan would daily play with the children and call himself

Utah, until June, 1858. When Texas seceded from the Union, Johnston, then commander of the Department of the Pacific, resigned from the United States army. He served as a general in the Confederate army until his death at the battle of Shiloh, April 6, 1862. Billington, *The Far Western Frontier*, 213–17; Creer, *Utah and the Nation*, 115ff.; Clarence C. Bartlett, "Albert Sidney Johnston," *Dictionary of American Biography*, Vol. IX, 135–36.

[9] Alexander Hicklin, or Zan Hicklin, migrated from Missouri to New Mexico and eventually settled in 1859 near Greenhorn, Pueblo County, Colorado. His adobe house, known as the Hicklin Ranch House, became a favorite resting place for travelers. Hicklin, before his death on February 13, 1874, was a substantial farmer and stock-grower, using large numbers of Mexican laborers. Working, "Hicklins on the Greenhorn," *loc. cit.*, 183–88; Sarah J. Moon, "Recollections of Fort Garland and Southern Colorado," *Colorado Magazine*, Vol. XXIV, No. 2 (March, 1947), 73–79.

[10] Only a portion of this statement is correct. It is evident that Hicklin did go to California in 1849 and could not read or write. Alexander Hicklin, however, married Estefana Bent, daughter of Charles Bent, first territorial governor of New Mexico, on October 20, 1856, at Taos, New Mexico. Frank Hall in his *History of Colorado*, II, 257–58, basing his account on manuscript notes furnished by Conner, says that Hicklin was a bachelor. Hall corrects this error on pages 488–89 in the next volume of his work. Working, "Hicklins on the Greenhorn," *loc. cit.*, 183, 185; Moon, "Recollections of Fort Garland and Southern Colorado," *loc. cit.*, 78–79.

Ole Secesh, until the girls learned to call him Ole Secesh. Ole Secesh was the man who pointed out to Heffner the splendid concealment which Mace's Hole offered for the secret equipment of a Rebel regiment. He furnished beef cattle for all these men free of charge for weeks. He would never fail to walk from his own ranch up to Mr. D[otson]'s on the regular days for the soldier escort to pass with the mail. He would call himself Ole Secesh in the presence of the soldiers to disarm suspicion. He never failed to go with the soldiers of the United States when he was asked to guide them anywhere. In short, Ole Secesh was both a consistent rebel and a federal and similar in his characteristics to a bad boy. I once heard a minister of the Gospel describe [a bad boy] by saying that "That boy has got one top, two bottoms, one back, two sides, and a multitude of faces." He [Hicklin] was an uncompromising Rebel sympathizer and succeeded in deceiving the government authorities for a long time, but was caught up with at the end of his services. Hicklin, as I have stated, could not read or I would never write this, for fear of accidents. But however, if he is yet living, he will have to count his age at about eighty years.

Whatever be the number of tops and bottoms that he claimed, this peculiar man certainly had a multitude of faces, and for a long time those numerous faces were good comely faces, or ugly ones, just as he pleased to make them. This was accounted for by the well-known and conceded fact that while Ole Secesh was a good-natured, generous man, he was also a very shrewd one. He was the frankest-spoken man, when soldiers and suspected enemies were listening, that I ever heard speak or talk in common conversation. And just so soon as he was alone, his countenance assumed a stern, crabbed, and thoughtful appearance. He was gruff, rough, and careless of the opinions of others—had a store of versatility, and [was] exceedingly self-reliant. He had all sorts of a character—he would act the fool to perfection one moment, become dignified to the point of repulsion the next. I have seen him arouse himself out of a brooding, discouraged thoughtfulness into a joking, rollicking spirit of amusing wakefulness in a moment.

He was both a Rebel and a Federal, just as occasion required, and was rarely ever mistaken as to what kind of an occasion he was dealing with.

He frequently acted as guide for the new levies of soldiers, arriving, and [was] always ready to pilot them to Fort Garland, which was an outpost not quite forty miles away from his ranch toward New Mexico, around the meanderings of the front range of the Rocky Mountains. Like a good businessman, Ole Secesh, on arriving at Fort Garland, would consult Major [Charles] Whiting, the commandant of the post, and deport himself with such dignity and judgment as to enlist the confidence of anybody.

He wore a tall silk hat, the kind usually called a plug, and stood and walked erect. After enjoying the freedom of the fort he would return to his headquarters through the rugged mountain trail known to but few beside himself, and on arriving he would immediately attend to Heffiner regiment in Mace's Hole, by providing their runners with provisions of beef cattle without money or price.

The United States troops who passed Mr. D[otson]'s station three or four times per week to and fro, to escort the military mail, began to suspect the existence of an organized force of Rebels somewhere in Colorado, and the authorities at Denver began to investigate a little. Although the escort passed within a mile of Mace's Hole four times per week, it was not known in what part of the Territory the Rebel band inhabited. An officer of high rank would now sometimes be seen with the escort at Mr. Dotson's station. Ole Secesh would always be at the station and consult with him about the report of Rebels in the Territory.

He would tell the officers to leave the question to him. Then he would rattle away foolishly with the most extravagant promises and propositions and succeed in making the soldiers think that he was crack-brained on some subjects. He would agree to find their locality and take his "Mexicans," as he called them, and kill or capture every one of "them d——n rebels," and wind up his extraordinary proposals by assuring the soldiers that "Ole Secesh knew how to do it." He never failed to be about the station when the soldiers were expected, whether on their regular days or not, and generally got information for Col. Heffiner's men. After talking foolishly to the soldiers as long as they would stay, he would look after their departure in a ludicrous manner and remark that "It's a wonder how such d——n fools ever found their way from the States out here."

He always informed the officers that he came to the station expressly to meet them, to give them such information as he had. Sometimes he came to report the result of some business which they had previously commissioned him to do. On one occasion he told the officers that a band of Rebels had passed his ranch in the night and stole quite a number of his beef cattle that he intended for the United States troops, and that they were heading toward New Mexico. But Ole Secesh forgot to tell them that the cattle had gone to Mace's Hole. And to look at him so frankly and so plausibly giving his story and at the same time know the facts, it would be calculated to convince one that he did really have a multitude of first-class faces.

No new recruit was ever allowed to come directly to Mace's Hole. They were recruited and sent to a small camp up above Pike's Peak more than fifty miles from Mace's Hole. This small camp was in charge of trusty men, some of whom would accompany the recruit to Mace's Hole as their escort. By this means a traitor could not jeopardize the safety of any but the little recruiting squad.

Now we have shown Ole Secesh up as a traitor, and it is but just to give his character its real value by detailing some of his idiosyncrasies as an offset. After a thorough acquaintance with this peculiar man, a candid mind would be loath to cast one spot upon his name if yet living, or one reflection upon his memory, if dead.

There are many undoubtedly yet living who knew him and knew him as a whole-souled benefactor in his way, while his generosity to all creeds, colors, and conditions stood unimpeached. The name of Zan Hicklin has a kindly reminiscence attached to it in the minds of many who are alive yet. Previously to this station being occupied by Mr. Dotson as a military mail station, Ole Secesh occupied it as his private stock rancho. He had no associates but his Mexican herders, trappers, and what few stragglers that would ask lodging for a night or two, either citizen or soldier. The travel increased on this military road as the mining population of Colorado increased. The persons coming that way were generally en route for Fort Garland, already referred to. This station I presumed to have been considerably over a hundred miles from Denver.[11]

Trappers would sometimes make this ranch their headquarters for months. I knew one by the name of Jones, who lived with Ole Secesh awhile. Not a fictitious Jones either, but a man who called himself Jones in reality, and was a large, fat, heavy-set Jones, who was good natured and gave me a dressed beaver skin by which to remember him.[12]

One evening, while Jones was out hunting, two travelers, en route for Fort Garland, halted and asked if they could get lodgings for the night for themselves and their horses. The proprietor answered that "Them horses looked mighty poor and scrubby for two *nice* men to be riding." "But that's not the question; we want to know whether we can get to stay all night." "Oh, to be sure, d——n it, get down; but I could give you two better horses than them." "We don't want any horses but only want some feed for these." "Yes, yes, they look like they need it." The men dismounted and fed their horses and then took a wash and spent some time in combing their heads and otherwise preparing for supper. Hicklin couldn't read but he was a good judge of human nature and was an unconditional enemy to all that looked like what he called "putting on style." No act of theirs was lost on him, but one would not think that he noticed anything. They finally partook of the supper and smoked. While the two strangers were conversing together without noticing anyone else and while they were enjoying their smoke leisurely, Hicklin beckoned Jones into an adjoining room. Then he cautiously and pretentiously spoke in a whisper, just loud enough for the strangers to hear a part of it. "Jones, I don't think it is worth while to rob these

[11] If this station was in the vicinity of Greenhorn, Colorado, it would have been about 125 miles from Denver.

[12] Conner may be referring to William McGaa, who was known in Colorado Territory as Jack Jones. McGaa, reputedly a son of a lord mayor of London, migrated to Colorado Territory where he married an Indian woman. Authorities assert that McGaa's wife was either Sioux or Arapaho. He engaged in the fur trade, was one of the first three settlers at the mouth of Cherry Creek, and was a member of the Denver Town Company. LeRoy R. Hafen (ed.), "George A. Jackson's Diary, 1858–1859," *Colorado Magazine*, Vol. XII, No. 6 (November, 1935), 210 and 210n.; Nolie Mumey, *History of the Early Settlements of Denver*, 46 and 46n.

fellows. You hardly ever see dandies with any spare cash, and their horses are no account." Jones now muttered inaudibly as if replying. Hicklin then muttered, too low to be heard, when he ascertained that the strangers were listening instead of talking. He came out now into the strangers' room and graciously proposed to show them their bed. All of this had its effect. The two gentlemen wanted to go see how their horses were doing. "No, no," the host was too kind to see the "gentlemen" go to look after their horses and insisted on them re-tiring, while he attended to the horses, and immediately called loudly for one of his Mexicans, whom he sent to look after the horses, with additional orders to come back and report. He then proceeded, "No, gentlemen, don't be uneasy about your horses," &c., with exceeding politeness. The men were confounded and knew not what to do, and Ole Secesh knew how puzzled they were, although he didn't seem to notice their confusion. "Turn in, gentlemen, and have a nap, for I know you both must be very tired."

There was no alternative; the strangers turned in, but didn't have the nap, for they arose during the night, found their horses, and made what they doubtless considered a lucky escape.

On the following morning Ole Zan had a big frolic and a jolly laugh over the apparent trepidation of his two guests. He remarked that he knew that they were too *nice* to have any sense. He now "wondered" where the "two fools had strayed to," and cautioned Jones to be careful when he shot into the next herd of antelope that he came across, for fear of shooting one of these fellows, whom he felt certain would stray off with the first herd they met.

On a similar occasion to this, two men put up with our host, and one of these was also a very nice man, and the other a rough and camplaisant, gruff fellow. The one would ask for what he wanted at the table, and the other would reach and help himself. The one would ask that his horse be well fed, and the other would go and feed his own horse, as though he wouldn't trust anyone to do it for him. In short, one was very polite and gentlemanly and the other was a ruffian. On the following morning, when they were ready to depart, the unsociable, gruff fellow walked up to Hicklin with a prompt, "What's my bill, sir?" "One dollar and a half, sir."

The money was paid without another word. Directly came the polite fellow with a "Please have my horse caught and state my bill, sir." "Yes, sir; your bill is seven dollars, sir. Jose, oh, Jose, go catch the gentleman's horse and fetch him out." "Will you please allow me to ask why you make such a difference between my bill and that of my friend here?" "Yes, sir," was the prompt response. "It is because your friend waited upon himself, and it took everybody about the ranch to wait upon you, and then they didn't do it well."

The fellow paid the bill and the two strangers departed. After they were gone, Ole Secesh told Jones that if he was not about the ranch himself when those fellows returned, "to pay that d—n fool seven dollars back again for him."

Hicklin was continuously playing this sort of prank upon strangers and thereby became widely known throughout the country by many who had never seen him. But it was probable that he who could have had the impudence to saddle his horse and ride off without paying or offering to pay anything would have been the best fellow of all. Ole Secesh would have made him a present the next time they met.

Not long after this incident, two other travelers put up for the night at the station. They came just in time to see Jones ride up to the house with an antelope that he had killed, butchered, and carried before him on a horse wrapped in a white sheet. The sheet was quite bloody. Hicklin took the antelope down and carried it into his kitchen and put it away. Jones went to attend to his horse and left Hicklin and his guests in a quiet conversation, as they were leisurely seated and enjoying a smoke. Those who are acquainted with the early settlements of Colorado know that smoking was an universal luxury in the mountains and on the plains. When Jones returned to join the party, Ole Secesh called him into the kitchen. Jones well knew that the host wanted some fun and obeyed. He began by chiding Jones in *sotto* voice. "Why, Jones, don't you know that the Arapahoes are not fit to eat this time of year? Why didn't you fetch a Ute; you *know* they are fat. Jones mumbled something in a low tone, but he was cut short by the impatient response," But d——n it, you can easily see that; that was an old, sickly buck, and hardly fit for a grizzly to eat." Jones here whispered something about not having time enough and that he thought that this old Indian would do for this time, well fried in lard and well seasoned. "Did you save his skin?" was the next query in a whisper. "Yes, I hung it up to dry on some chaparral." "Why, d——n it, the wolves will get it—go and send one of my Mexicans after it." Jones here walked promptly out of the house to attend to the order, while Hicklin came out and resumed his seat and conversation with his guests.

He had all the talking to do, for his guests had become dumb since he had left them. "Why, gentlemen, you seem to be discouraged and thoughtful. Your trip to Fort Garland is only forty miles from here, and there is not much danger from the Indians this time of the year. Cheer up and prepare to take a snack; supper will be ready in a few moments—come have a wash." Here he presented them with the necessary articles with which to prepare for tea. The strangers had lost all of their vivacity and had ceased to be good cheerful company. But our host made up for all deficiencies by good-humoredly rattling away, only stopping now and then to offer some polite attention to his guests. But supper was ready. "Come, gentlemen; come and have a lunch after your tiresome day's ride. We have but little away out in this mountain country to eat, but we are used to it, you know, and have learned to make out on it. But I know it will go hard with you at first, but you will soon get over it." Here the host passed the coffee &c., for he had no wife and therefore one of his "Mexicans" did the cooking, and he attended the table himself. "Have some of this antelope, sir; it is the finest meat we have at the foot of the mountains this time of year—pass your plate, sir, and try a bit of it."

"Not any—thank you, sir—now." "You have a piece, sir"—to his other guest—"for you have no idea how nice and tender it is, if you have never eaten any—do have this piece and try it."

"No," neither of his guests ever ate much meat anyway and wouldn't take any just then. The host was very sorry that he didn't have something better than antelope for his guests, as they had taken a long and irksome journey and must be hungry. But here he came to himself suddenly and his face lighted up and he remarked: "Oh, I beg your pardon, this is Friday. I like to have forgotten myself, and I presume that you are Catholics." Each one looked at the other. One fellow took the start and said that he was a Catholic. Then the other, feeling that the excuse would miscarry if he was also a Catholic, but still desired its benefits on the present occasion. He therefore admitted that his family were Catholics and that he always respected their custom in this matter while at home and saw no reason to depart from it although he was not a Catholic himself. Here the kind host asked to be excused repeatedly, and of course was gratefully excused.

Just before finishing their supper the host discovered that he had made a mistake. It was not Friday; it was Saturday. Here the guests became confounded again, as Ole Secesh began to intrude the antelope meat upon them earnestly. No, they were now done eating and wouldn't choose any just then. Hicklin now accused himself for the unfortunate mistake and insisted that it was no rue to save his meat, as there was plenty of antelope all [a]long the foot of the mountains. His guests knew that but didn't care for any meat for supper. The host now enjoined the cook to have plenty of antelope for his guests at breakfast and to season it well and try and make amends for the unfortunate accident which had prevented the gentlemen from even tasting this savory meat. But the gentlemen concluded to proceed on their journey after supper and declined to remain all night just for the purpose of having antelope for breakfast. All the importunities and overtures of the host was exhausted in vain. The gentlemen had pressing business and were compelled to move on, and did move on in the night.

Ole Secesh allowed them to depart, fully satisfied that they had seen and been offered cooked Arapaho Indian to eat under the name of antelope. Jones wanted to know why he had not told those men the joke before they left, so that they wouldn't be telling people that his station palmed off cooked Indian on travelers, for antelope. "Oh, I don't care what they tell people; they ain't got any sense anyhow; and then they are only a couple of d——n Yankees; that's plain."

Hicklin was accosted by the commanding officer at Fort Garland to know if he raised any vegetables at his ranch for sale. He replied that he did and could furnish the whole garrison with all it could use.

The officer informed him that he would send during the week for a six-mule wagonload, to which Hicklin replied that he could load his wagon any day and that the vegetables were going to waste by rotting in the patches.

The officer reminded Ole Secesh that it was a distance of forty miles over a rough road and that it would require a heavy escort to secure the safety of the team, and but for the fact that his men were all getting scurvy, he would not risk his team so far from the command.

Hicklin knew all of this and promised to have the vegetables all ready to load so as to save time. The matter was thus settled to th[eir] mutual satisfaction and they parted. In a few days a splendid six-mule government team, accompanied by eight or ten cavalrymen, drew up to the vegetable houses and ungeared the mules and fed them. They had been two days on the road. Ole Secesh was on hand and had the cavalry horses fed and cared for. He ordered a "big" dinner for all the men. He sent all of the soldiers to the house to wash and smoke and to get dinner and rest, while he took his Mexicans and loaded the wagon in a proper way so as not to bruise the vegetables. He packed the wagon bed as full as it would hold and placed corn husks between every layer, and even chinked every crevice with corn husks for the better protection of the edibles, and lastly, had the top of the load thatched neatly with straw over which the soldiers' blankets were spread as a finish. When all was ready the host informed the sergeant that the wagon was ready. The sergeant remarked that his men had all eaten dinner and that they would be off right away on their return trip. And thinking that the host's prompt action was intended to get them away from his premises on short terms, the sergeant began to apologize for imposing such a number upon him at one time. Ole Secesh impatiently replied, "That's no matter—no matter at all. The government has been very kind to Ole Secesh, and I sell all of my cattle to Uncle Sam's soldiers except what I let Capt. Madison have."

Capt. Geo. Madison was a rebel officer of Gen. Sibley's Army of New Mexico in 1861.[13] Capt. Madison was said to have a roving commission to cut the mail lines of the Federals in the territories and in the West generally.

The sergeant was soon on his road home with his vegetables. After they were gone, Old Zan chuckled a little and told Jones that he wouldn't be at Fort Garland when "them vegetables arrived, for his herd of cattle." "Jones," he says, "if any [of] the officers or soldiers should want a guide during the next week to go to Ft. Garland, you must be here to go." "Why?" says Jones. "Well, I have to attend other matters." "Other Madisons?" queried Jones. "Yes, yes, if you want it that way."

The sergeant arrived in due time at the fort and the soldiers all volunteered, in great expectation of good things, to help to unload the wagon. The commandant was sent for to come and see the vegetables which now lay in a pile, and consisted of a huge wagonload of corn and pumpkins. The officers looked at each other in amazement, while the soldiers sniggled. The sergeant was sent for, and the commandant wanted to know if he brought that load of corn and pumpkins here. The sergeant looked confounded and went and looked into the wagon to see if it was unloaded. He then couldn't answer exactly, whether he had brought them or not. The officer informed the sergeant that there was too much joking in the whole matter for the military. The sergeant was not fit for a soldier, if he could be so easily be made sport of by an idiot. He sent to know of Ole Secesh what he meant by sending him corn and pumpkins instead of vegetables. Hicklin sent word back to the officer that he had sent him the only kind of vegetables he had and had done the best he could do for him, and that if he didn't believe it, he could come and look for himself.

Pretty soon after this incident, a young man came by the station,

[13] In August, 1862, an irregular band of Confederates, estimated at thirty-five men, led by Captain George T. Madison, seized the Fort Garland mail train. A five-hundred-dollar reward was offered by the federal officers for their capture, but the Confederates eluded the pursuing Union troops and made their way back to Texas. Denver, *Rocky Mountain News* (August 11, 14, 18, 19, and 23); Central City, Colorado Territory, *The Tri-Weekly Miner's Register* (October 31, 1862).

just before night, and asked how far it was to Fort Garland and whether he could get there before dark. Hicklin told him, "O yes —you can get there before dark or a little after." He pointed toward New Mexico and said, "Do you see that ridge yonder about a mile?" The fellow said he did. "Well, if it is daylight when you get there, you can easily see the fort. As soon as you get upon that ridge you have a pretty, level lawn clean on down to the fort."

The stranger departed, after thanking Hicklin kindly for the information, little dreaming that Fort Garland was at least forty miles away by the shortest goat path through the mountains, which was but little nearer, if any, than the wagon road.

But however, all things are said to have an end, and so did the confidence imposed in our old friend by the government authorities. He was suspected of complicity with the rebel regiment in Mace's Hole, or some organization; for they knew not where it was. But it was plain that the military were agitated, for troops from Fort Lyon on the Arkansas were scouring the country all along the foot of the Rocky Mountains. Some appointees of the regiment had been to Fort Garland on a tour of inspection. They were courteously received by Major Whiting, and shown around, and dined. The Major thought that they were hunters and trappers, as they represented themselves to be. They had no difficulty in taking the measure of all obstacles and departed for Mace's Hole. They reported at Mace's Hole that there was about thirty or forty soldiers in the garrison and most of them were rebel sympathizers and the remainder wanted to desert, and that from all indications, the fort could be easily taken without firing a shot. In the event of taking the post, the regiment in Mace's Hole could easily be armed and equipped fully and supplied with all the necessary war material that it could take on the trip to Texas. The appointees spoke in high terms of the commandant, Major Whiting, and complimented him as an exceedingly courteous, soldierly-looking old gentleman. So the day was appointed and arrangements made for the effort to seize on Fort Garland. A man was appointed to superintend and to take charge of all the livestock and wagons. Mr. Stewart, who was a doctor from Virginia, was to take charge of the artillery, and three persons were appointed to remain behind and blow up the magazine as a finality. The men appointed to seize the sentinel were to go into the fort casually and remain quiet, with concealed six-shooters, until they saw their friends coming.

The calculation was that a sufficient number of men were to be near at hand to overpower the fort within its walls, and to have the matter ended before it was known what had happened. One man had a surrender written out for Major W[hiting] to sign, and ax-men enough were to be ready to cut down his door in case he closed himself in his room. All these preparations were complete and the regiment was only waiting to call in its little recruiting camps and for the appointed day to arrive. Now this humble subscriber was up near Pike's Peak at an out-of-the-way place called a recruiting camp.

But I learned that a young man from Fort Garland had ridden down into the neighborhood of the station, kept at the time by Mr. Dotson, who has been referred to as the only friend and neighbor of Ole Secesh, and found his way by some means into Mace's Hole. He was the only man who had yet come without credentials, and he boldly stated that he wanted to join that institution. An eye was kept upon his movement during the whole day. Near night he mounted his horse and in great levity rode off toward the mouth or beginning of the rock-bound land leading out of the "Hole." He was ordered to halt and he refused, but stated that he was too tired to stay longer and kept going, and was fired at and missed. He now spurred vigorously for the outlet, but was cut off by the sentry at that point, shot and killed. Some of the regiment, it seemed, were dissatisfied at the result which led to bad feeling in the camp. But it so happened that most of the officers were out upon some duty or other, including the Colonel. At any rate he was en route for Mace's Hole from the little camp referred to and met the Colonel and a lieutenant, who gave me the above particulars as they were told to them. They informed me that the troops from Fort Lyon on the Arkansas, to the number of one thousand, were scouring the country and that our regiment had become discouraged by the representations made to some of them in camp during their absence and had scattered to the four winds of earth, and that to ever get them together again was a hopeless undertaking. The colonel remarked that he had spent five thousand dollars on the regiment and that the money and the regiment were both gone, and all upon the account of the presence of traitors and cowards. They passed on after stating that they intended to escape, whether all the rest were taken to the Federal prisons or not.

He arrived at the station and saw Old Secesh, but he didn't know him, nor indeed did he know personally but very few of this Rebel regiment, nor was he seen very often, only by a few. I knew no one at the station, and consequently I hurried on and passed Ole Secesh's headquarters, about half a mile south of the station, and thence along the foot of the Rocky Mountains until I came to Huerfano Creek, a distance of fifteen or twenty miles. I knew the creek by the singular butte, which I described as the one I had camped near during my hunting expedition the winter previously.

A Texan, with whom I was well acquainted, had located a ranch here to raise grain, and claim, and to hold the possessory right to a large tract of land. It was a Spanish grant. He was a handsome, gentlemanly, and well-informed man. He was also an uncompromising secessionist, and ex-Californian from the Territory of New Mexico to the House of Representatives of the United States. Bo Boyce was his name, and he was one of the few men that Ole Secesh would trust.[14] It was his mule that I had been riding and I had left my own with him, so as to have it in good condition for a long trip. But he informed me that Federal troops had placed an espial of a half-dozen soldiers around his house and that when they left they took my mule, as well as some of his own stock.

He also informed me that the main body of troops of the Federals had marched up the "Picket Ware" (a creek since and previously called Las Animas) toward the Rocky Mountain front range, and that they were patrolling this creek to cut off all the stragglers of Heffiner's regiment of Rebels.[15] This creek flows out of the Rocky

[14] B. R. Boyce was never a territorial Representative to Congress from New Mexico. See the *Biographical Dictionary of the American Congress, 1774–1949.*

[15] The Purgatoire, Picket Wire, or Las Animas River is the largest tributary of the Arkansas River flowing from the south. Its sources rise in Las Animas County, Colorado, and it flows through Otero and Bent counties before it joins the Arkansas at Las Animas, Colorado.

Mountains and across the strip of plains south of the present town of Pueblo and empties into the Arkansas at Fort Lyon. On the south side of the creek lay the Raton Mountain, which is a huge spur from the front of the Rocky Mountains, extending into the plain for many miles. This creek flows at the northerly foot of the spur. In going toward New Mexico or Texas this would be crossed. The military road which followed for several hundred miles the meanderings of the mountain range fronting the plains, and the same road that passes Mace's Hole and Mr. D[otson]'s station, also crossed this creek, and also the spur of Raton Mountain on its route to Fort Union, New Mexico. Picket Ware was still forty miles off toward New Mexico and Texas, and upon its bank was the next military mail station. The Federal troops were now busy picking up incipient Rebels everywhere and killing a few once in a while.

But however I was at the house of Mr. B. B[oyce], considering the whole matter over, not knowing what instant a little squad might step in upon me, but I had nothing to do with these schemes. I knew the soldiers would pick me up on suspicion as others, but this was the only house in many miles, and I had to risk it for a night at least. But however this regiment and all of its hopes were frustrated permanently. Each member of that regiment had to take care of himself as best he could. Many were captured, including three captains and the colonel. I saw a copy of the *Rocky Mountain News*, a little paper printed at Denver, in which was detailed the capture of the Colonel and the additional fact that he was ironed too heavily to feed himself. Although this humble subscriber was placed in the Captain's list and not yet captured, this fate of the Colonel sounded queer, read from a newspaper.[16] I didn't feel much guilty, because my object was to get to my home before being forced into any ranks at all. But of course he was presumably as guilty as was any man in Mace's Hole. He felt too badly committed to return to the settlements in the mines, and there was too many hostile Indians to

---

[16] Unfortunately, the extant files of the *Rocky Mountain News* for 1862 are incomplete. The issue containing the story referred to by Conner is missing from the files held by the Library of Congress, the Denver Public Library, and the Colorado Historical Society.

travel alone. It had not been a month since I had been compelled to hide in the brush alone and witness a horde of Indians at the foothills, practicing their ponies in the war drill all the evening until night, and I then had to creep out of my concealment and slip off in the dark like a wild animal. I knew that the road to the States in any direction was too far by at least six hundred miles for one man to travel alone, with any degree of safety. It was evident that the Rebel regiment, whose ill-starred growth brought so much speculation as to results and so on, was defunct, without leaving even a skeleton by which to trace its existence. All that could now be done was either to walk up to the Captain's office and settle; or I felt that I was committed hopelessly without being guilty of any offense on earth except any chance to leave the country in any kind of company.

But the government seemed to want everyone who had ever taken up a temporary residence in this valley, and the prospect of imprisonment during an indefinite period of war was not the most beautiful contemplation to be wasting time on.

My Texan friend, who is now dead, advised me to go up the creek into the mountains and that he would supply me with food until the storm blew over. I declined the advice and kindly offer, and concluded to cease hiding out amongst the Indians and wild beasts any longer. The military mail had been captured by Capt. Madison of Gen. Sibley's army in 1862 on this creek, and the rider's saddle &c. were thrown into the creek just above this house where it was still to be seen. At my request Mr. B[o] B[oyce] furnished me with a suit of secondhand clothes, like those worn by his greaser workhands, and I went back near the scene of our Rebel exploits and arrived in the night at the station of Mr. D[otson]. I was dressed in a check shirt, cotton overalls for pants, a dilapidated chip hat of Mexican manufacture, and wore a pair of moccasins. And by the way, this was not an unusual costume for workhands about these mountains. When I came in sight of the station I circled around it to an old dilapidated pen built of poles and filled with corn husks. I excavated an opening under the shucks in which I thrust all of my visible worldly effects: my bodily apparel, a pair of blankets, a tin cup, one canteen, two six-shooters, a Sharps carbine, and a butcher knife. There was no fence around the field or yard. I now, with my light and airy dress on, proceeded to the house and rapped upon the door. Everybody was asleep in the silent, still night, and therefore my warning was distinct and awoke the landlord easily. He wanted to know who was there. I told him that it was a stranger. He asked me if I wanted to stay all night. I answered in the affirmative and he opened the door and held a navy six-shooter in his hand. But after he made a light and saw my poorly clad body, his fears banished right away and he laid his pistol right away. He looked at me from head to foot and then asked if I was lousy. This took me so unexpectedly that I came near saying that I didn't know, but I halted in time to tell him, "Of course not." He was not talkative and put me to bed after he finished looking at me all over, three or four times.

When morning came I was astonished at my own appearance. I was up early and my heart sank within me, to contemplate the late, proud-looking landscape which now looked like gloom tempered with darkness. I knew the change was in my poor frail imagination and would likely stay there until the dark doubts which hung around every step and position were dispelled. My hope of approaching departure for the States seemed to have deserted me entirely. I felt almost an irresistible impulse come over me sometimes to put on my clothes and arms and make a reckless dash for some quarter or other. But then the distance was so great and progress so uncertain that prudence and patience would gain a victory for me and resignation would be the temporary relief. I was called into breakfast by a Mexican whose gutterals I but imperfectly understood. The question uppermost in my mind was [whether] I [was] a good enough dissembler to face the landlord in an experienced manner with impudence enough and with a hard face, to carry out my object. I intended to play the laborer and lackey at all hazards, and as I started to breakfast with a resolute brace-up style that only a regular-laid-out plan could have enforced, I felt defiant and confident. I took my seat at the table and saw but little in my surroundings except that two young girls before referred to exchanged smiles on me. Don't be frightened, my friends, for this is no love story, but I did feel more ridiculous than I ever did before. When breakfast was over I applied to Mr.

D[otson] for work and told my story, better than I thought I could. He wanted to know my price, and I stood him out for the best wages he ever gave. He asked if I could "pull" corn. I professed to be an excellent hand. He agreed to give me a dollar per day to gather corn and I went to work with a Mexican, with whom I had many amusing repartees in gutterals, or Anglo-Mexican language. This was the first time in my existence that I ever hired myself out to work, and I rather liked it for a few days and until my hands began to become lacerated all over by the slivers of the cornstocks. The corn had been watered by means of irrigation, and hence it was very low and some of the ears grew just at the surface of the ground. I worked and passed backward and forward to the cornfield daily and met and ate dinner and sometimes supper and breakfast with the soldiers who were escorting the mail. On some occasions there would be a squad hunting for H[effiner]'s stragglers, who would stop and get dinner. [Page missing in manuscript.]

What to do, or how to get away, was the question. I proceeded to the field on the following day and remained there all day, and told the Mexican that I was sick and didn't want any dinner. On going up the hill from the field, late in the evening, toward the house, I met the two young ladies coming to ride on a load of corn, which was being driven by another Mexican. The adopted daughter didn't get on the wagon, but began again her inquiring glances toward me. I brought the matter to a close by telling her that if she was determined to get me into trouble, that I had but little doubt of her success. She looked stunned for a moment and disclaimed earnestly any such intent and promised not to notice me in anyone's presence again, and she faithfully complied with her promise to the end. But still I felt that it was a bad job, and I was only a little gratified that none of the rest of the family had seemed to notice me. This young girl afterward informed me cautiously that the soldiers had just passed with two prisoners of Colonel H[effiner]'s regiment. This act restored my confidence a little, but my mind was made up to leave on the first opportunity.

And here another little incident enhanced my determination to depart as soon as practicable. That was of the fact that Ole Secesh was suspected of treason, and the officials were going to investigate it. I kept at work all the time. Some soldiers came to the station after him. There was a colonel along who ordered the arrest of Ole Secesh. Another squad of soldiers had driven off twenty head of his cattle and appropriated them to their own use as the property of a Rebel. The adobe house was ordered to be torn down, as it wouldn't burn, but the order was not obeyed for some cause or other. Pretty soon after the order was made, Ole Secesh arrived and was arrested as above stated. The colonel asked him where he had been for a few days. He replied that he had been to Fort Garland to guide some of "our" men thither. "Whom do you call our men?" queried the colonel. "Why, the blue-coat Yanks, who do you s'pose?" Here the colonel had him taken in charge and went into the house himself to talk with Mr. D[otson], who persuaded the Colonel to revoke his order to destroy the house as it was in his own charge and [seeing] that it covered his wife and children and protected them from any possible or sudden Indian affray that might take place at any time. Ole Secesh sent for the colonel to come to where he was in the custody of two soldiers, and on arrival of the officer promptly asked, "What the devil do you want to be cracking your jokes on me for?" "This is no joke," says the officer. "Now, Colonel, don't be jealous, because I have about got all Col. H[effiner]'s men about corralled." "I'll give you all the credit for cleaning out Mace's Hole if the d——n Rebels did steal nearly all my cattle. I think the government will pay me for the cattle, won't they, Colonel?" The Colonel now came to the conclusion that Ole Secesh was an idiot and went away to consult Mr. D[otson] upon the subject. The officer came back and was standing near and Hicklin went up to him and tapped him confidentially on the shoulder and asked him to step aside for a moment. The colonel walked with him a few steps and stopped, when the prisoner turned to him with, "Colonel, you got me into this, and you ought to know how to get me out." "You ought yourself, to know how to get out," answered the colonel. "How?" responded Hicklin, looking the colonel earnestly in the eyes. "Why, take the oath of allegiance to the government of the United States and become a good loyal citizen." "Take what, Colonel—did you say?" "Why, take the oath, the oath to the government." "But you, Colonel, you said something else too, you know." "Well, the oath of allegiance is what I said." "Well—well—what's that, Colonel? I ain't no scholar, you know, Colonel." "I mean, that you will have to swear to be a good and loyal citizen to the Union and then live up to it." "Well—well—Colonel, is that all?" "Certainly, that's enough if you will obey it in good faith." "I'll do it, I'll do it—swear me." The Colonel proceeded to have a long oath administered to him while Ole Secesh stood with his hand up, looking the officer who was administering the oath in the face with desperate earnestness, painful to behold. When it was ended the colonel gave him some good advice to which exceeding attention was paid. Ole Secesh now looked downward and about his feet a moment with quite an expression of sadness depicted in every feature. Suddenly he raised his head and looked at the officer with childish simplicity and animated tone of voice and exclaimed, "Colonel, Colonel, does that let me in?" "In what?" responded the colonel. "Why—into the Union." "Yes, if you live up to it." "Clean in, Colonel?" "Yes, of course." "Oh, my G-o-d, Colonel, I feel like I've got religion."

Hicklin now gave the officer another familiar wink to step aside a moment with him, and when they were at a safe distance he began the introduction of his business by saying to the Colonel that "this is between you and me, Colonel, you know, and it ain't to go no farther, you know, Colonel." The Colonel did know and said, "Of course." The informer proceeded, "Now, Colonel, I knowed that these Rebels had been a stealin' my cattle, and I believe I kin trail 'em with my Mexicans to start at Mace's Hole, where they was camped. You see, Colonel, I broke up Mace's Hole because, you know, I sent my Mexicans to hunt my cattle and they found signs of the Rebels and came and told me and this scared 'em and they left. My Mexicans never tell me lies. They told me that your soldiers took twenty head of my cattle while I was gone to Fort Garland, but I knowed if they did, you would make 'em bring 'em back or the government would pay me for 'em—the government has always been mighty good to me." The Colonel concluded that he would not have time just then to go to Mace's Hole but promised Ole

Secesh that his cattle that had been taken by the soldiers should be paid for and gave him some sort of voucher in writing for the amount of one thousand dollars, upon which Hicklin afterward received the money. Hicklin boasted after this to some intimate friends that he could give H[effiner]'s Rebel regiment enough cattle to feed them for a month and Uncle Sam would pay for them cash up, and no grumbling. He then shouted, "Hurrah for Ole Secesh; if all Dixie's men could work it as well as Ole Secesh, they would whip the fight without any sort of doubt." But before the Colonel and his men left, Hicklin agreed to take his Mexicans and capture every Rebel that attempted to pass that vicinity for Texas, and boldly told the Colonel that he would bet that Ole Secesh could capture more rebels with his Mexicans during the next three weeks than all the soldiers about there. But his greatest trouble was to know what to do with them, as he had not enough house room for them all, and he blandly asked the Colonel in *sotto voice*, if it would be any harm just to "kill 'em" if he got too many to keep, and added that his Mexicans would just as soon "kill 'em" as not. "No," the colonel told him, "don't do that, but bring them to Denver." "I'll do it—I'll do it, Colonel, and if they attempt to escape, you know, and my Mexicans do kill any of 'em, it's not my fault, Colonel." "No," responded the Colonel, "that would be their own fault, if they attempt to escape." "Just so, just so, Colonel, and if me and my Mexicans don't come with a batch inside of four weeks, you may know that they tried to escape and I can't always help what my Mexicans do, you know, when they don't like Rebels much anyhow." Arrangements were now all satisfactory on both sides, and the Colonel took his leave along with his men and left "Ole Secesh" at home in peace. After they were gone he laughed fit to kill himself and remarked that "No wonder they can't whip the South, when they have such d——n fools for colonels as this fellow." Then he ended by, "Why, Jones, he wouldn't make a good trapper—he wouldn't know how to skin a beaver, I'll be cussed if he would." "I didn't quite finish the job," he mused, "for I would have given one of my best cattle if I only could have gotten to show that Yank Mace's Hole, where the rebs had been, but it's all right anyhow, for he's gone off believing that I am a d——ned idiot and I know that he is one, without going anywhere." Here "Ole Secesh" finished his respects for the Colonel's departure with a hearty laugh and a "Hurrah for Ole Secesh."

I was well acquainted with the popular recreancy against Federal soldiers in the early settlement of Colorado. While I was in the vicinity of Hicklin's Station the year before this (1861) on the hunting expedition and encamped on a little stream near Mace's Hole, the first regiment of Colorado Federal troops came along en route for Canby's army in New Mexico.[17] They were unarmed and expected to remain so until they arrived at Fort Union in New Mexico several hundred miles distant over an unsettled country. These reckless fellows took everything they could lay their hands on. They pressed horses and beef cattle into service at every little settlement from Denver to Hicklin Station. They left their ill-gained beef cattle scattered all along the road, and Ole Secesh got his share of them like others, who turned their attention to money-making.

These troops arrived in New Mexico in time to participate in the battles [of] Val Verde and Cooks Canon and others.[18] But after they passed this section of country about Hicklin Station, there were six government wagons loaded with bacon came and went into camp on a little stream called Apishapa Creek. This bacon was intended to follow Canby's troops, but from some cause lay here in camp for a month. Sibley's army of Texans was confronting General Canby, and there was but little idea afloat as to who would hold New Mexico. But suffice it to say for the present purpose that my Texas friend Mr. Bo Boyce on the Huerfano and "Ole Secesh" knew more than all the rest of us. It will be remembered that our little hunting party only consisted of five in the winter of 1861, when this train of wagons

[17] At the outbreak of the Civil War, Union forces were commanded by Colonel E. R. S. Canby, a veteran of the Seminole and Mexican wars. He was replaced as commander of the Department of New Mexico by General James H. Carleton in September, 1862. Keleher, *Turmoil in New Mexico*, 194.

[18] Only one independent company of Colorado troops fought at the battle of Valverde on February 21–22, 1862. The First Regiment of Colorado Volunteers did not reach Canby's command until March 10, 1862, when they arrived at Fort Union, New Mexico. Instead of "Cooks Canon," Conner probably was referring to the decisive action at Apache Canon, also called La Glorieta Pass, March 26–28, 1862. William Clark Whitford, *Colorado Volunteers in the Civil War*, 78, 85ff.

were on this little creek, as before stated, and in reality it was detained until it would be definitely known who would hold New Mexico— Canby or Sibley. The wagon master of this train and the man who controlled its movements was one John Sowers.[19] He passed for the same S[owers] who accompanied the notorious Lopez expedition to Cuba, and was captured and condemned to be shot, and pardoned by the Queen of Spain through the interposition of the United States authorities at the instance of John J. Crittenden of Kentucky.[20] There was no absolute knowledge as to the purpose of Sowers' detention of the train, but there was no doubt that the delay was intended to correspond with General Sibley's success in New Mexico, and he could have had the bacon if he had defeated Canby as Sowers expected. But when Sibley's defeat was ascertained, the train moved on to New Mexico. Sowers was afterward arrested for some other treasonable offense and tried at Denver and acquitted. But report had it that the court reminded him that the United States had twice saved his life, and therefore his allegiance thereto should be unquestionable in the future. There are many details of this little affair that might be beneficial some future day, but too lengthy to detail here.

[19] Narciso Lopez in 1851 succeeded on a third attempt to land an expedition on Cuba, hoping to free the island from Spanish rule. Working closely with Southern expansionists, Lopez enlisted the aid of many Southerners, among whom was John Sowers of Berryville, Kentucky. Samuel Flagg Bemis, *A Diplomatic History of the United States*, 315–16; Anderson C. Quisenberry, *Lopez Expeditions to Cuba, 1850–51*, 128.

[20] John J. Crittenden, perennial United States senator from Kentucky before the Civil War, served at attorney general in Fillmore's administration. His interest in the Lopez case arose from the fact that William L. Crittenden, a nephew, was among those summarily shot in Cuba. About 160 prisoners were sent to Spain for imprisonment at the Spanish colony of Ceuta, located across from Gibraltar. Diplomatic officials of the United States could only request the release of the prisoners. Tensions relaxed when Queen Isabella of Spain pardoned the prisoners when they landed at Ceuta. Robert G. Caldwell, *The Lopez Expeditions to Cuba*, 92, 112–13; Bemis, *Diplomatic History of the United States*, 315–16; E. Merton Coulter, "John Jordan Crittenden," *Dictionary of American Biography*, Vol. IV, 546–49.

CHAPTER EIGHT

A Hasty Departure from Colorado

Time hung heavily upon me about the station. Doubts, impatience, and anxiety began to play unmerciful pranks upon me. I had seen no opportunity to depart. I began to wish that I was again away back in the mountains in the mining districts.

In my reflections I traveled over the whole scenery of previous experiences in the ranges of mountains during calms and thunderstorms. I loved to think of it, so as to loose my senses, as they pictured me to myself in the present situation. One instance in particular engaged my reflections for a day or two whilst I was "pulling" corn. It was during the rainy season of the year before that I was on top of one of the many stupendous mountains about me, when I noticed a dark fog slowly boiling up the different hollows in sight, and believing that a thunderstorm would be the result, I began to ascend the hill. But on reaching a fine view several hundred yards below the top, I halted and interestedly observed the action of the clouds, now increasing rapidly and pressing up the different hollows toward their sources. I stood on this spot until the great and apparently bottomless ravines all around me were filled full of dense clouds. The bright sun shone down upon the scene like it hung over a cloudless ocean and made me imagine that I was standing upon one of the many neighboring islands plainly pictured by the different peaks projecting about the level of dense fog or clouds. It grew to a strange and ominous spectacle as the now baffled senses began to waver and fail to discern whether this great ocean of clouds were moving or whether the mountaintop isles were floating about in them. These living, moving islets stood high enough above the sea at their bases to meet and receive the splendid salutations of the morning's ray from the source of all light and to lend a weird and prophetic existence to all latent animation, imaginary and inspired.

A position upon one of those little islands or peaks above the clouds offers a grand and animated scene to the eye of a thoughtful and responsible mortal mind, and especially when all of the passions and powers of "Jove" have accumulated the combined elements of all nature into one single resolution to bewilder the senses and reveal the powers of the Most High. It is impossible to observe such a display without feeling a plain and palpable sense of its connection with Deity. The sun is pouring down with serene profusion upon those dark, electric clouds. The whole upper world is bright and spotless, while beneath my feet the dark clouds extending toward the four quarters of earth lazily hang, change, roll, like a seething crater, while they are continuously presenting a thousand fleeting rainbows that are ever changing, mixing, and commingling like a golden panorama floating upon the boundless waters. These strangely beautiful contrasts are heightened to the pitch of sublimity as the continuous streams of forked lightning begin a part by playing, darting, and existing everywhere amongst the rainbows, accompanied by every pitch of intonation, from the sharp peals of soprano to the continuous roll of the deep, hoarse, guttural bass, that shakes the earth. Peal after peal is renewed at intervals and reverberating in the adjacent canyons and gorges, to be re-echoed back again and again into the choir of inharmonious elements in regular and continuous succession, confounding and amazing the senses into an awe-stricken condition truly helpless.

What a transition. One hour previously this unparalleled, romantic mountain wilderness lay all calm and silent in its prodigious repose, with its native dark gloom subdued and softened into an air of harmless indifference by the omnipresent smiles felt and seen everywhere to permeate this weird but still beautiful landscape. The stimulating enchantment of the sunny rays and the soft balmy influences of a pure and gentle breeze were generously tendered to the lonely and anxious God-fearing heart to allay its doubts and inspire a confident safety here in a new and unusual situation. But before receiving the full benefits of the late apparent feast of such beautiful contemplations alone and away from mortal interference, the elements quarreled, the war began, and quickly destroyed the law of peace in this landscape so beautiful that God may be said to have created it with a smile, to have substituted those of despotism to encourage rage and reckless impetuosity to the extremest extent. The senses are overpowered and fail to keep pace with the rapid presentation of differing subjects that are continuously thrusting themselves forward to be disposed of in the midst of such confusion of mind, body, and elements. It is impossible for this pen to describe such a scene with any degree of satisfaction. The physical came to the relief of the mental in this instance and indistinctly left the indelible trace upon the mind that deep beneath the din created by the elements was a continuous nervous quivering of the earth in perpetual response to the law and agitated undertones of hoarse thunder, subterranean.

During this whole time not a single drop of rain has fallen on me. But a terrific deluge has fallen below and I could distinctly hear the waters rushing down the gorges and over the falls and innumerable precipitous places in the distant gulches and creeks far beneath my position.

Everything becomes quiet again and without the aid of fire or another thunder gust will likely remain so, but such instances of remarkable rainstorms in the Rocky Mountains are frequent. And in some localities during the rainy season they are daily occurrences and rarely ever fail to bring with them a spice of grandeur, tempered a little with sadness and doubt as to what such great and apparent fruitless efforts can be intended for, away in this habitless and sterile waste. Yet, day by day have I seen the clouds crowding up the hollows, beginning nearly at the same hour each day to appear and increase until the ravines are filled full nearly to the mountaintops, when a little flicker of electricity on the top of the clouds would signal the beginning of the strange and dismal war. But he who takes his position on one of the mountain summits above the timber line can contemplate the "lists" in safety, for there is but little rain or thunder ever found that high up, and he can also enjoy perennial sunshine there if he will skip the nights. However, it is no part of my purpose to comment upon the cause of nature's intent in such matters, but only to mention the facts and leave them to whosoever may take the task on himself to account for them. For all the acts which are accompanied by scrupulous doubts that rest upon the question of their justice or injustice bear prolific fruits of restless impatience, whether they are sanctified by custom or not. And when the conscience eases itself by submitting the doubt to the arbitration of a friendly law indifferent, it is simply committing its own important business to a questionable authority. I therefore apprehend that there is not absolute safety on a mountaintop during a storm, and we also know that the staunchest obedience to mortal reasoning is continuously subjecting us to a loss of anticipated rewards. Then I shall close the subject here by asserting my belief that "God" alone presents us with the only requisite laws for absolute safety on the mountain or at its foot.

As before hinted, this digression was caused by a dreamy uncertainty while at work in the corn at the station. Suspense had become painful. I took a day to myself, borrowed a gun, and went hunting. I proceeded toward the source of the neighboring creek called "Muddy," and near the mountain foothills. I saw but little game and didn't look for any, but was busy with numerous speculations as to how I should get off to the States. The termination of the Rebellion seemed very indefinite, and to be imprisoned for its probable continuance seemed to promise a horrible pastime. It was nearly night and I took up a direct course for the station. I was traveling along a little goat trail when I espied at some distance to my left what appeared to be a confused pile of rags. I started immediately toward it and discovered the knuckles of a man's closed hand projecting from the rags toward me. It proved to be a Mexican, judging from his complexion and the remnants of his apparel, and was nearly a skeleton. The wolves had eaten the most of his flesh away, leaving one hand and both feet sound. His feet were protected by a high, stout pair of moccasins. I left the body and proceeded to the station

161

and informed Mr. Dotson of the discovery, and where to find it. He remarked that he supposed that the carcass would be as well where it was as anywhere in the world—that it was several miles out of the way and that was sufficient.

The Indians or wild animals had probably caught the poor fellow unarmed. A day or two after this circumstance, while I was gathering corn with my Mexican friend, on a bright sunny morning about ten o'clock in October, 1862, I descried a stranger lazily sauntering up the creek that bordered our little fenceless cornfield. He was engaged in carelessly whittling a stick as he walked. I told my friend to continue work a moment without me until I could go and interview the stranger. On approaching near enough to talk to him easily, I told him, "Good morning." He responded to my salutation, while he eyed me closely. I was impatient while he seemed to be extremely cool and indifferent—cutting away on the stick without looking at it. I noticed that he was unarmed and I promptly demanded, "Who are you, anyhow?" "None of your d——n business," was the quiet passionless response. "It is my business, for I believe you are one of these stray rebels of 'Mace's Hole' notoriety." "It is false," he replied. "Such ragamuffins as you are belong to that make-up, I guess."

I became impatient and insisted on having him talk a little sense, to which he replied, "My name is Buckmaster, and the same who was chief of artillery in Gen. Sibley's army at the battles of Valverde and Cooks Canon in New Mexico last year."[1] He continued, "I was captured and imprisoned at Santa Fe from whence I made my escape two weeks ago by bribing the guard, after being sentenced to be shot for robbing the United States mail over here on the Huerfano fifteen or twenty miles distant." We now came to an understanding, but he would not trust me because he said that he only had fifteen men at his camp up in the mountains two or three miles on the Greenhorn. He asked me sharply where my horse was. I assured him that I could soon get a horse, to which he replied that if I would go and get my horse and come alone to Apishapa Canyon about sixty miles away

---

[1] Sibley's artillery was commanded by Major Trevanion T. Teel at the battle of Valverde. Whitford, *Colorado Volunteers in the Civil War*, 62, 65.

toward New Mexico to his camp that I would find him during the next forty-eight hours, and not after. I was not deceived in this fellow, for I knew him by reputation and had heard of his being at large. The reason that he was sentenced to be shot was that he was captured in the garb of a citizen. Yet he was a Confederate officer and commissioned with Captain Madison to cut the United States military mail lines on these long routes, which they did as before stated, and threw the saddle of the carrier into the Huerfano, the next creek south of the Greenhorn, upon which the station is located. He left me after bidding me to stop at the next forty- or fifty-mile station and get David Kelly, who was sojourning there a little after the fashion of my stay at the station of Mr. Dotson. He remarked to me that Mr. David Kelly knew the way from the next station to "Apishapa Canyon," the place of his rendezvous. After he took his departure, I went back to my Mexican friend and fellow laborer and told him that I was sick and would not work more until after dinner. I had formed quite an attachment to my Mexican comrade, to whom I had lately done all of my talking, and regretted to leave him thus, but necessity dictated all my actions now, and I proceeded up the creek to the frail ranch building of Ole Secesh and found him at home. I now addressed him for the first time, although I knew him so well. I walked boldly up and accosted him, at which he seemed to be a little surprised. I asked him if Mr. Bo Boyc[e], who lived fifteen miles away on the Huerfano, had arranged with him to keep a horse in readiness for anyone. He wanted to know what business that was of mine, and after contemplating me steadily for a moment, inquired if I had not been at work at the station for Mr. Dotson for some time past. I answered a little impudently that he must have seen me there daily for some time past. "Yes, I have," he responded vigorously, "but I never heard you say anything before, and now, on taking a good look at you, I believe you to be a d——n wolf in sheep's clothing." He proceeded lively with, "I believe you are one of them d——n rebels of Mace's Hole, who had been stealing my cattle all along, and if you don't get out of this country d——n quick, I'll report you to the military right away."

I now came boldly to the front and told him that I was one of those fellows and had seen him come with cattle for us, on many dark nights, and I now would report him to the government authorities. I saw that Ole Secesh was puzzled to know what to say about it, and I drew a little scrap of paper out of my old clothes and handed it to him. The hieroglyphics on it brought a smile to the surface of Ole Secesh. He studied me a moment and broke the silence finally by the remark, "You d——ned hypocrite." I told him that one of the young ladies at the station had called me a hypocrite too, but still I didn't believe it. Here Ole Secesh would laugh at me heartily, and then swear at me for "deceitfulness" and wind it up again with a laugh. He said that I was the first to foul him, and he wondered what in the name of goodness had gotten the matter with Ole Secesh that he had failed to find me out. He says, "Yes, I have a horse and I wonder why that fool B[o] B[oyce] didn't let me know who it was for." He called loudly in Spanish for José (Joseph) his Mexican, who answered, and he ordered the horse, which was promptly led up to us saddled and ready for traveling. I asked him what he was going to charge me for him. "Oh, if you have any money, I will not charge you over half-price, and if you have none, it is all the same; you must have him anyhow. He is worth over two hundred dollars easy and the finest bay in Colorado, and can travel longer than you can ride." I told Ole Secesh that I would give him what I pleased for the horse and handed him eighty dollars, and he accepted it and immediately offered it back to me, stating that he ought not to charge me anything and that he was fearful that his friend B[o] B[oyce] would not be pleased if he did. We settled that way and I asked him to have the horse fed well while I was gone to the station for dinner and to prepare for my departure. I arrived at the station before twelve o'clock and met my landlord who thought that I had "gotten hungry right early today." I responded that I was sick and repaired to an old adobe outbuilding to wash and comb.

Mr. D[otson] must have thought that I ate a hearty dinner for a sick man. But however, I sought my shuck (or husk) pen as soon as dinner was over and concealed myself behind it long enough to bring to light my old suit lying in the husks. I came by the house and met my host just coming out. He was evidently startled at seeing a stranger armed and equipped for traveling so near him, and coming to the house from the back way. After gazing at me a moment I proffered to shake hands with him and told him good-by. He now wanted to know what the h——l this meant. Out came the ladies to see about it, all of whom were frightened except the one who had called me a hypocrite. She slapped her hands in great glee with the repeated remark, "Didn't I tell you so?" I bade them a hasty good-by and hurried off toward the ranch, where I had left Ole Secesh. Before I was out of sight over the little intervening ridge I heard Mr. D[otson] called after me to stop and get my money for the work. After telling him to give it to the next wayfarer who sought work of him, I passed over the ridge out of sight of this station for the last time.

It had been my temporary abode and a place where my anxieties had wrung from me a many impatient epithet, but now as I left it forever, a kindliness for the place and its inmates imperceptibly stole over me and taught me that I had formed an attachment for these people, the depth of which I had been totally ignorant of until the present moment while taking my final leave of them. I have seen the kindly face of the pretty little lassie who kept my secret so well on very many occasions since, when my straggling reflections wandered that way. It has now been seven or more years since I left that station and its inmates, and still there lingers about Mace's Hole and those old mountain ranges fronting and shadowing Hicklin's Station a train of pleasant reminiscences not easily effaced.

I proceeded down to the house where Ole Secesh still remained. On my arrival I saw Mr. D[otson] coming and waited until he came up. They both now took great interest in me and made me some trifling presents, but valuable for the good will they contained. On bidding them adieu, Ole Secesh assured me that anyone who could keep his own counsel so well as I could need never fear being captured by such fool officers as commanded the soldier scouts of that country. I mounted and took the range of mountains fronting the plains for my guide and left Mr. D[otson] and Ole Secesh, and I have never seen or heard of them since. I see by the map that Hicklin Station still exists. Ole Secesh was an honest man, but could not help being a Rebel to have saved his own life, and he told me, on leaving, that the chances were that I would never see B[oyce] and that he was surely gone. I arrived at the house of Mr. B[o] B[oyce] on the Huerfano about dark and partook of supper with him and received such directions as he could give me, and I bid him farewell (and as yet a final one) about nine o'clock that night, crossed the creek at his house, and took up my journey alone in the dark and tediously prosecuted it all night without road or trail, keeping close to the foot of the Rocky Mountain front in the edge of the skirt of timber and undergrowth that fringes them all the way to New Mexico. I became entangled in many brushy hollows and gorges that long, lonesome night and learned to trust my horse implicitly to get me out before it was ended. The country was totally uninhabited, and my greatest trouble was to restrain the horse, which seemed to have been half frightened all the while by the sudden retreats of wild animals, continuously occurring. Some of them would start with a crash in the underbrush and break limbs that were so large that one would think that cattle were stampeding through the timber. But the numerical force of the wolves of all sizes made them the meanest animals of them all.

For if there is anything that can add to a lonely, silent night in the wilds of the Rocky Mountains to make it more lonesome, it is the half-defiant and half-distressed howl of a wolf, whose dismal notes portend danger and inspire pity at the same time, and are to be most dreaded and avoided if one desires to fight off the sense of loneliness and sorrowful forebodings.

On the following morning I came in sight of the stream upon which was located the next mail station. I had made a forty-mile trip by sunrise. I picketed my horse to grass over a little ridge of the foothills of the mountains out of sight of the station and lay all day on my blanket and looked at the soldiers patrolling the creek as far down as I could see. This creek was then settled and called "Picket Ware," as before stated, but it seems to have been called before and since the Las Animas River.[2] But however, it is a stream that flows out of the Rocky Mountains into the Great Plains toward and into the Arkansas at the present site of Fort Lyon, previously referred to in these notes. This creek is directed in its course by the left-hand foot of the Raton Mountain, as it proceeds from the main front range of the Rocky Mountains, out into the plain toward the Arkansas. It is really a spur of the Rocky Mountains projecting into the plain.

When night came on I saddled my horse and rode down to the creek and came into the military road near the station—crossed the creek and rode up to the front door of the station and sent a Mexican in to inform Mr. J[im] G[ray] who kept the station and (who I knew, only by reputation) that he was wanted.[3] I saw brass buttons shining in the house as the owners would move about, and I drew back a little. Mr. Jim Gray came out and walked rapidly up to me as I sat on my horse. I handed him a fragment of paper, which he took and hurriedly remarked that he knew me and told me to move away from there and around the house up the creek a few hundred yards to a little frail house and tell the Mexican there to provide for myself and ask no questions. He hurriedly assured me that he would see me during the night. I hurried away and found the Mexican, who acted as promptly without any questions as did his master. I ate my humble fare in silence and with quite a relish as I had had neither breakfast nor dinner during the day. I spread my blanket on the ground and used my saddle for a pillow and slept soundly until Mr. Jim Gray awoke me in the latter part of the night. He gave me any amount of correct but unsatisfactory information. He said that B[uckmaste]r had crossed the creek some miles below and entered the Raton Mountain but could not have gone to Apishapa Canyon (which was twenty miles away in the mountains) for it was occupied by Federal soldiers who were on the lookout for stragglers from Mace's Hole. He also informed me that D[avid] K[elly]

[2] On early maps the Purgatoire River above the mouth of Chacuaco Creek was called Las Animas River.

[3] Hall notes that Jim Gray was a brother-in-law of B. R. Boyce and lived forty or fifty miles to the south on the Purgatoire River. Hall, *History of Colorado*, II, 258.

had gone to B[uckmaste]r and that there was no telling where they were. Also that troops had suspected himself of harboring Rebels who were en route to Texas, and had on the previous day put a rope around his neck to compel him to inform on the movements of straggling disloyalists, and were watching him day and night, to get an excuse to shoot him. He also informed me that the orders of the officers to the private soldiers on the previous morning were to shoot and not to capture suspicious-looking strangers, and that if the said strangers were armed, that fact should justify the killing without further trouble. And lastly, that I would have to put up with such food as the Mexican had for breakfast, as the officers and sentinels had charge of his house and he finished by advising me to get off before day under the penalty of being shot by sunup, if I should be found. But he informed me that my name and description was read frequently at his house to the soldiers. He informed me further that there was a little station twelve miles up the creek in the mountains that would answer for headquarters for a while.

[To remain in Colorado meant possible imprisonment. But Jim Gray provided Conner with some hope of freedom and adventure by informing him that Joseph Reddeford Walker, a veteran of the Rocky Mountain fur trade, had recently passed by Gray's place on his way to New Mexico with a party of men. After trailing Walker's party through the mountains, Conner joined them northeast of Taos, New Mexico. For the next five years Conner fought Indians, explored little-known regions of the Southwest, and prospected for gold. These tales are recounted in *Joseph Reddeford Walker and the Arizona Adventure*.]

Bibliography

DOCUMENTS AND BOOKS

Abbott, E. C., and Helena Huntington Smith. *We Pointed Them North: Recollections of a Cowpuncher.* Norman, University of Oklahoma Press, 1955.

Adams, Andy. *The Log of a Cowboy: A Narrative of the Old Trail Days.* Boston and New York, Houghton Mifflin, c.1903.

Allen, Glover M. *Extinct and Vanishing Mammals of the Western Hemisphere with the Marine Species of All the Oceans.* American Committee for International Wild Life Protection *Special Publication No. 11.* Lancaster, Pennsylvania, The Intelligencer Printing Co., 1942.

Anderson, Nels. *Desert Saints: The Mormon Frontier in Utah.* Chicago, University of Chicago Press, 1942.

Archer Sellers G., and Clarence E. Bunch. *The American Grass Book.* Norman, University of Oklahoma Press, 1953.

Bancroft, Hubert Howe. *History of Nevada, Colorado, and Wyoming.* San Francisco, The History Company, 1890.

————. *History of Utah.* San Francisco, The History Company, 1891.

Bandel, Eugene. *Frontier Life in the Army, 1854–1861.* Ed. by Ralph P. Bieber. Glendale, Arthur H. Clark, 1932.

Bemis, Samuel Flagg. *A Diplomatic History of the United States.* Rev. ed. New York, Henry Holt, c.1942.

Bent, Arthur Cleveland. *Life Histories of North America Birds of Prey.* United States National Museum *Bulletin 167.* Washington, Government Printing Office, 1937.

Billington, Ray Allen. *The Far Western Frontier, 1830–1860.* New York, Harper & Brothers, c.1956.

———. *Westward Expansion: A History of the American Frontier.* New York, Macmillan, 1950.

Bourke, John G. *On the Border with Crook.* New York, Charles Scribners Sons, 1891.

Caldwell, Robert G. *The Lopez Expeditions to Cuba.* Princeton, New Jersey, Princeton University Press, 1915.

Carson, Christopher. *Kit Carson's Own Story of His Life.* Ed. by Blanche C. Grant. Taos, New Mexico, 1926.

Carter, Harvey L. (ed.) *The Pike's Peak Region: A Sesquicentennial History.* Colorado Springs, Colorado, Dentan Printing Co., c.1956.

Caughey, John Walton. *Gold Is the Cornerstone.* Berkeley, University of California Press, 1948.

Chittenden, Hiram Martin. *The American Fur Trade of the Far West.* 2 vols. New York, The Press of the Pioneers, Inc., 1935.

Conner, Daniel Ellis. *Joseph Reddeford Walker and the Arizona Adventure.* Ed. by Donald J. Berthrong and Odessa Davenport, Norman, University of Oklahoma Press, 1956.

Cooke, W. W. *The Birds of Colorado.* Fort Collins, Colorado, 1897.

Cordry, T. A. *The Story of the Marking of the Santa Fe Trail.* Topeka, Crane & Company, 1915.

Creer, Leland Hargrave. *Utah and the Nation.* University of Washington Publications in the Social Sciences, Volume 7. Seattle, Washington, University of Washington Press, 1929.

DeVoto, Bernard. *Across the Wide Missouri.* Boston, Houghton Mifflin, c.1947.

Dick, Everett. *The Sod-House Frontier, 1854–1890.* New York, Appleton-Century, 1937.

Duffus, R. L. *The Santa Fe Trail.* New York, Longmans, Green and Company, 1930.

Emmons, Samuel F., J. D. Irving, and G. F. Loughlin. *Geology and Ore Deposits of the Leadville Mining District, Colorado.* United States Geological Survey *Professional Paper No. 148.* Washington, Government Printing Office, 1927.

Estergreen, M. Morgan. *Kit Carson: A Portrait in Courage.* Norman, University of Oklahoma Press, 1962.

Ewers, John C. *The Horse in Blackfoot Indian Culture.* Bureau of

American Ethnology *Bulletin No. 159.* Washington, Government Printing Office, 1955.

Favour, Alpheus H. *Old Bill Williams, Mountain Man.* Norman, University of Oklahoma Press, 1962.

Federal Writers' Project. *Colorado: A Guide to the Highest State.* New York, Hastings House, 1941.

————. *Ghost Towns of Colorado.* New York, Hastings House, c.1947.

————. *Kansas: A Guide to the Sunflower State.* New York, Viking Press, 1939.

————. *Nevada: A Guide to the Silver State.* Portland, Oregon, Binfords & Mont, 1940.

Fenneman, Nevin M. *Physiography of the Western United States.* New York, McGraw-Hill, 1931.

Ferguson, Philip Gooch. *Diary of Philip Gooch Ferguson, 1847–1848.* In Bieber, Ralph P., (ed.). *Marching with the Army of the West.* Glendale, Arthur H. Clark, 1936.

Flynn, Norma L. *Early Mining Camps of South Park.* N.p., n.d.

Foster-Harris. *The Look of the Old West.* New York, The Viking Press, 1955.

Frederick, J. V. *Ben Holladay, The Stagecoach King.* Glendale, Arthur H. Clark, 1940.

Frémont, John Charles. *A Report on an Exploration of the Country Lying between the Missouri River and the Rocky Mountains, on the line of the Kansas and Great Platte Rivers.* Washington, Printed by the order of the United States Senate, 1843.

————. *Report of the Exploring Expedition to the Rocky Mountains in the Year 1842, and to Oregon and North California in the Years 1843–'44.* Washington, Gales and Seaton, printers, 1845.

Fritz, Percy Stanley. *Colorado, The Centennial State.* New York, Prentice-Hall, 1941.

Gannett, Henry. *A Gazetteer of Colorado.* United States Geological Survey *Bulletin No. 291.* Washington, Government Printing Office, 1906.

Garretson, Martin S. *The American Bison.* New York, New York Zoological Society, c.1938.

Gates, Paul Wallace. *Fifty Million Acres: Conflicts over Kansas Land Policy, 1854–1890.* Ithaca, New York, Cornell University Press, c.1954.

Goodwin, Grenville. *The Social Organization of the Western Apache.* Chicago, University of Chicago Press, c.1942.

Gregg, Josiah. *Commerce of the Prairies.* Ed. by Max L. Moorhead. Norman, University of Oklahoma Press, 1954.

Gregg, Kate L., ed. *The Road to Santa Fe.* Albuquerque, University of New Mexico, Press, 1952.

Grinnell, George Bird. *The Cheyenne Indians; Their History and Way of Life.* 2 vols. New Haven, Yale University Press, 1923.

Hafen, LeRoy R., ed. *Colorado Gold Rush; Contemporary Letters and Reports, 1858–1859.* Glendale, Arthur H. Clark, 1941.

————. *The Overland Mail, 1849–1869.* Cleveland, Arthur H. Clark, 1926.

————. *Overland Routes to the Gold Fields, 1859, from Contemporary Diaries.* Glendale, Arthur H. Clark, 1942.

————. *Pike's Peak Gold Rush Guidebooks of 1859.* Glendale, Arthur H. Clark, 1941.

Hall, E. Raymond. *Handbook of Mammals of Kansas.* Lawrence, Kansas, Museum of Natural History, University of Kansas, 1955.

Hall, Frank. *History of the State of Colorado.* 4 vols. Chicago, Blakely Printing Co., 1889.

Handbook of Colorado for Citizen and Traveler. Denver, Colorado, J. A. Blake and F. C. Willett, 1873.

Harrington, H. D. *Manual of the Plants of Coloralo.* Denver, Colorado, Sage Books, 1954.

Henderson, Charles W. *Mining in Colorado: A History of Discovery, Development, and Production.* United States Geological Survey *Professional Paper No. 138.* Washington, Government Office, 1926.

Herms, William B. *Medical Entomology.* 3rd ed. New York. Macmillan, c.1939.

Hodge, Frederick Webb. *Handbook of American Indians North of Mexico.* 2 vols. Bureau of American Ethnology *Bulletin No. 30.* Washington, Government Printing Office, 1907, 1910.

Hollister, Ovando J. *Boldly They Rode: A History of the First Colorado Regiment of Volunteers.* Lakewood, Colorado, The Golden Press, 1949.

————. *The Mines of Colorado.* Springfield, Massachusetts, Samuel Bowles & Co., 1867.

Hollon, W. Eugene. *The Lost Pathfinder: Zebulon Montgomery Pike.* Norman, University of Oklahoma Press, 1949.

Hoopes, Alban W. *Indian Affairs and Their Administration with Special Reference to the Far West, 1849–1860.* Philadelphia, University of Pennsylvania Press, 1932.

Howbert, Irving. *Memories of a Lifetime in the Pike's Peak Region.* New York, G. P. Putnam's Sons, 1925.

Hyde George E. *Red Cloud's Folk: A History of the Oglala Sioux Indians.* Norman, University of Oklahoma Press, 1937.

Kappler, Charles J. *Indian Affairs: Laws and Treaties.* 3 vols. Washington, Government Printing Office, 1904.

Keleher, William A. *Turmoil in New Mexico, 1846–1868.* Santa Fe, New Mexico, Rydal Press, c.1952.

Klauber, Laurence M. *Rattlesnakes; Their Habits, Life History, and Influence on Mankind.* 2 vols. Berkeley, University of California Press, 1956.

Kraenzel, Carl Frederick. *The Great Plains in Transition.* Norman, University of Oklahoma Press, 1955.

Lavender, David. *Bent's Fort.* Garden City, New York, Doubleday, 1954.

Leavenworth City Directory and Business Mirror for 1859–60. St. Louis, Sutherland and McEvoy, c.1859.

Leonard, Zenas. *Narrative of the Adventures of Zenas Leonard.* Norman, University of Oklahoma Press, 1959.

Lowie, Robert H. *Indians of the Plains.* New York, McGraw-Hill, 1954.

Malone, Dumas, and Allen Johnson (eds.). *Dictionary of American Biography.* 22 vols. New York, Scribners, 1928–37.

Mangum, Charles S., Jr. *The Legal Status of the Negro.* Chapel Hill, University of North Carolina Press, 1940.

Marshall, Thomas Maitland. *Early Records of Gilpin County, Colorado, 1859–1861.* Boulder, Colorado, University of Colorado, 1920.

Mathews, Mitford M. *A Dictionary of Americanisms on Historical principles.* 2 vols. Chicago, University of Chicago Press, c.1951.

Monaghan, Jay. *Civil War on the Western Border, 1854–1865.* Boston, Little, Brown, c.1955.

Morgan, Dale L. *Jedediah Smith anl the Opening of the West.* San Francisco, California Historical Society, 1954.

Mumey, Nolie. *History of the Early Settlements of Denver.* Glendale, Arthur H. Clark, 1942.

Murray, Pauli, ed. and comp. *States' Laws on Race and Color.* N.p., 1950.

Nevins, Allan. *Frémont: Pathfinder of the West.* New York, Appleton-Century, 1939.

Nye, W. S. *Carbine & Lance.* Norman, University of Oklahoma Press, 1943.

Parsons, William B. *The New Gold Mines of Western Kansas.* In Hafen, LeRoy R. (ed.). *Pike's Peak Guidebooks of 1859.* Glendale, Arthur H. Clark, 1941.

Powell, John Wesley. *Report on the Lands of the Arid Region of the United States, With a More Detailed Account of the Lands of Utah.* 2nd ed. Washington, Government Printing Office, 1879.

Quisenberry, Anderson C. *Lopez Expedition to Cuba, 1850–51.* Louisville, Kentucky, John P. Morton & Co., 1906.

Ramaley, Francis. *Colorado Plant Life.* Boulder, Colorado, University of Colorado, 1927.

Randall, James G. *The Civil War and Reconstruction.* New York, D. C. Heath, c.1937.

Ransome, Frederick Leslie. *Geology and Ore Deposits of the Breckenridge District, Colorado.* United States Geological Survey *Professional Paper No. 75.* Washington, Government Printing Office, 1911.

Reports of the Commissioners of Indian Affairs for the Years 1859–1861. Washington, 1860–1861.

Richardson, Rupert Norvall. *The Comanche Barrier to South Plains Settlement.* Glendale, Arthur H. Clark, 1933.

Roe, Frank Gilbert. *The North American Buffalo.* Toronto, University of Toronto Press, 1951.

Rogers, Lore A. *Fundamentals of Dairy Science,* 2nd ed. New York, Reinhold, 1935.

Root, George A. ed. "Reminiscences of William Darnell," *Collections of the Kansas State Historical Society, 1926–1928.* Volume XVII. Topeka Kansas, Kansas State Printing Plant, 1928.

Russell, Osburne. *Journal of a Trapper, or Nine Years in the Rocky Mountains, 1834–1844.* Portland, Oregon Historical Society, 1955.

Ruxton, George Frederick. *Adventures in Mexico and the Rocky Mountains.* London, J. Murray, 1847.

———. *Life in the Far West.* Ed. by LeRoy R. Hafen. Norman, University of Oklahoma Press, 1951.

Rydberg, P. A. *Flora of Colorado.* The Agricultural Experiment Station of the Colorado Agricultural College *Bulletin 100*. Fort Collins, Colorado, Colorado Agricultural College, 1906.

Sabin, Edwin L. *Kit Carson Days, 1809–1868*. New York, The Press of the Pioneers, Inc., 1935.

Sage, Rufus B. *Rufus B. Sage: His Letters and Papers*. 2 vols. Ed. by LeRoy R. Hafen. Glendale, Arthur H. Clark, 1956.

———. *Scenes in the Rocky Mountains*. Glendale, Arthur H. Clark, 1952.

Schmidt, Karl P. *A Check List of North American Amphibians and Reptiles*. 6th ed. Chicago, University of Chicago Press, 1953.

Shannon, Fred A. *The Farmer's Last Frontier*. New York, Farrar & Rinehart, *c.*1945.

Smith, Edward Conrad. *The Borderland in the Civil War*. New York, Macmillan, 1927.

Spencer, Elma Dill Russell. *Green Russell and Gold*. Austin, University of Texas Press, *c.*1966.

Stanley, F. *Fort Union*. N.p., *c.*1953.

United States Department of Agriculture. *Climate and Man, Yearbook of Agriculture, 1941*. Washington, Government Printing Office, 1941.

———. *Soils and Men, Yearbook of Agriculture, 1938*. Washington, Government Printing Office, 1938.

Vestal, Stanley [Walter F. Campbell]. *Joe Meek, The Merry Mountain Man*. Caldwell, Idaho, Caxton, 1952.

Villard, Henry. *The Past and Present of the Pike's Peak Gold Regions*. Princeton, New Jersey, Princeton University Press, 1932.

Warren, Edward Royal. *The Mammals of Colorado: Their Habits and Distribution*. Norman, University of Oklahoma Press, 1942.

Watson, Douglas S. *West Wind—The Life Story of Joseph Reddeford Walker*. Los Angeles, private printing for his friends by P. H. Booth, 1934.

Weaver, J. E., and F. W. Albertson. *Grasslands of the Great Plains*. Lincoln, Nebraska, Johnsen Publishing Co., *c.*1956.

Webb, James Josiah. *Adventures in the Santa Fe Trade, 1844–47*. Ed. by Ralph P. Bieber. Glendale, Arthur H. Clark, 1931.

Webb, Walter Prescott. *The Great Plains*. New York, Ginn and Co. *c.*1931.

Weber, William A. *Handbook of Plants of the Colorado Front Range*. Boulder, Colorado, University of Colorado Press, 1953.

Whitford, William Clark. *Colorado Volunteers in the Civil War: The New Mexico Campaign in 1862.* Denver, Colorado, State Historical and Natural History Society, 1906.

Willison, George F. *Here They Dug the Gold.* New York, Brentano's, c.1931.

Wolle, Muriel Sibell. *Stampede to Timberline.* Boulder, Colorado, Muriel S. Wolle, 1949.

Wright, Muriel. *A Guide to the Indian Tribes of Oklahoma.* Norman, University of Oklahoma Press, 1951.

Young, Otis E. *The First Military Escort on the Santa Fe Trail, 1829.* Glendale, Arthur H. Clark, 1952.

MAPS

"Map of the Military Department of the Missouri." Drawn by Alfred S. Page. National Archives, Record Group 77, Q–125, M–249.

"Map of the Public Surveys in Colorado Territory to Accompany the Report of the Survey General, 1866." National Archives, Record Group 49, Colorado No. 15, M–252.

"Map of the Public Surveys in Colorado Territory to Accompany the Report of the Surveyor General, 1868." National Archives, Record Group 49, Colorado No. 16, M–251.

"Map of the States of Kansas and Texas and Indian Country, with Parts of the Territories of Colorado and New Mexico, 1867." National Archives, Record Group 77, U. S. 318 No. 5, M–253.

"Nell's Topographical Map of the State of Colorado." E. Besly & Co., Publishers, 1889.

"Pike's Peak Timber Reserve Colorado." National Archives, Record Group 49, Colorado No. 2, M–250.

NEWSPAPERS

The Leavenworth Journal, Leavenworth, Kansas.
The Leavenworth Times, Leavenworth, Kansas.
The Rocky Mountain News, Denver, Colorado.
The Western Mountaineer, Golden, Colorado.

ARTICLES

Albertson, F. W. "Ecology of Mixed Prairie in West Central Kansas," *Ecological Monographs,* Vol. VII, No. 4 (October, 1937), 487.

Bancroft, Caroline. "The Elusive Figure of John H. Gregory, Discoverer of the First Gold Lode in Colorado," *Colorado Magazine*, Vol. XX, No. 4 (July, 1943), 121–35.

Bender, A. B. "Government Explorations in the Territory of New Mexico, 1846–1859," *New Mexico Historical Review*, Vol. IX, No. 1 (January, 1934), 1–32.

Colorado Writers' Program. "The Names of Colorado Towns," *Colorado Magazine*, Vol. XVII, No. 1 (January, 1940), 28–36.

———. "Place Names in Colorado (B)," *Colorado Magazine*, Vol. XVII, No. 3 (May, 1940), 81–94.

———. "Place Names in Colorado (C)," *Colorado Magazine*, Vol. XVII, No. 4 (July, 1940), 125–43.

———. "Place Names in Colorado (G)" *Colorado Magazine*, Vol. XVIII, No. 1 (January, 1941), 29.

———. "Place Names in Colorado (I, J. and K)," *Colorado Magazine*, Vol. XVIII, No. 5 (September, 1941), 186–97.

———. "Place Names in Colorado (L)," *Colorado Magazine*, Vol. XVIII, No. 6 (November, 1941), 227–38.

Davidson, Roy A. "Some Early Manuscript Records of Park County, Colorado, 1859–1863," *Colorado Magazine*, Vol. XVIII, No. 5 (September, 1941), 168–73.

Dawson, Thomas F. (ed.). "The Old Time Prospector," *Colorado Magazine*, Vol. I, No. 2 (January, 1924), 60–64.

Hafen, LeRoy R. "Claims and Jurisdictions Over the Territory of Colorado Prior to 1861," *Colorado Magazine*, Vol. IX, No. 3 (May, 1932), 95–102.

———. "Colorado Cities—Their Founding and the Origin of Their Names," *Colorado Magazine*, Vol. IX, No. 5 (September, 1932), 170–83.

———. "The Counties of Colorado: A History of Their Creation and the Origin of Their Names," *Colorado Magazine*, Vol. VII, No. 2 (March, 1931), 48–60.

———. (ed.). "George A. Jackson's Diary, 1858–1859," *Colorado Magazine*, Vol. XII, No. 6 (November, 1935), 201–14.

———. "Ghost Towns—Tarryall and Hamilton," *Colorado Magazine*, Vol. X, No. 4 (July, 1933), 137–43.

———. "The Voorhees Diary of the Lawrence Party's Trip to Pike's Peak, 1858," *Colorado Magazine*, Vol. XII, No. 2 (March, 1935), 41–54.

————. "When Was Bent's Fort Built?" *Colorado Magazine*, Vol. XXXI, No. 2 (April, 1954), 105–19).

Howe, E. W. "A Bit of Weston, Missouri History," *Missouri Historical Review*, Vol. XLVII, Nos. 1 and 2 (October, 1952 and January, 1953), 29–36.

McKimens, William. "Letters from Auraria, 1858–59," *Colorado Magazine*, Vol. XIII, No. 5 (September, 1936), 167–71.

Moon, Sarah J. "Recollections of Fort Garland and Southern Colorado," *Colorado Magazine*, Vol. XXIV, No. 2 (March, 1947), 73–79.

Morris, Ralph C. "The Notion of a Great American Desert East of the Rockies," *Mississippi Valley Historical Review*, Vol. XIII, No. 2 (September, 1926), 190–200.

Parsons, William B. "Report on the Gold Mines of Colorado, 1858," *Colorado Magazine*, Vol. VIII, No. 6 (November, 1936), 215–18.

Pierce, James H. "The First Prospecting of Colorado—Who Did It and What Led to It," *The Trail*, Vol. VII, No. 5 (October, 1914), 5–11.

————. "With the Green Russell Party," *The Trail*, Vol. XIII, No. 12 (May, 1921), 5–14.

"R. J. Pierce and Jacob T. Masterson, Members of the Famous Russell Prospecting Party of 1858," *Colorado Magazine*, Vol. XXVII, No. 2 (April, 1950), 102–107.

Rister, Carl Coke. "The Significance of the Destruction of the Buffalo in the Southwest," *Southwest Historical Quarterly*, Vol. XXXIII, No. 1 (July, 1929), 34–49.

Sanford, Albert B. "Camp Weld, Colorado," *Colorado Magazine*, Vol. XI, No. 2 (March, 1934), 46–50.

————. "The Cherokee Trail and the First Discovery of Gold on Cherry Creek," *Colorado Magazine*, Vol. VIII, No. 1 (January, 1931), 30–34.

Shaw, Dorothy Price, and Janet Shaw Le Compte. "Huerfano Butte," *Colorado Magazine*, Vol. XXVII, No. 2 (April, 1950), 81–88.

Stone, Wilbur F. "Early Pueblo and the Men Who Made It," *Colorado Magazine*, Vol. VI, No. 6 (November, 1929), 199–210.

Willard, James F. "Spreading the News of the Early Discoveries of Gold in Colorado," *Colorado Magazine*, Vol. VI, No. 3 (May, 1929), 98–104.

Working, D. W. "The Hicklins on the Greenhorn," *Colorado Magazine*, Vol. IV, No. 5 (December, 1927), 187.

Bibliography

Wright, Muriel H. (ed.). "The Journal of John Lowery Brown, of the Cherokee Nation en route to California in 1850," *Chronicles of Oklahoma*, Vol. XII, No. 2 (June, 1934), 177–213.

Index

Agama, cornuta (agama coronatum):
58 & n.
Allen, Jack: 68 & n.
Allison and Booth(e): 36 & n.
American Ditch Company: 117 & n.
American Fur Company: 75 & n.
American Gulch: 100 & n.
Antelope: 44, 58, 85, 89 & n., 127–28;
in Hicklin prank, 141–43
Apaches: 39n., 87n.
Apishapa Canyon: 162–63, 167
Apishapa River (Apishapa Creek): 88 &
n., 156
Arapahoes: 17n., 21 & n., 24 & n., 26,
27 & n., 58n., 61, 90, 119–20; in
Hicklin prank, 141, 143
Arkansas River: ix, 20 & n., 21 & n., 23,
24 & n., 28, 33n., 34 ff. & n., 40 ff.,
62, 67n., 68, 84, 85, 109, 133, 148n.,
149, 167
Ash Creek: 32 & n.

Bald River: 109 & n., 113
Bardstown, Kentucky: vii, 3n.
Beck, John: viii, 6n., 7n.
Bennett, James: 124–25
Bent, Estefana (Mrs. Alexander Hicklin): 135n.
Bent, William: 57 & n., 62n.
Bent's Fort (New Bent's Fort): 33 & n.,
57n., 62n.; see also Fort Lyon

Big Bend: 20, 21
Big Timbers: 57n., 58 & n.
Black Hawk War: 35n., 134n.
Blacktail deer: 78 & n.
Black tongue: 74 & n.
Blue River: ix, 73, 74 & n., 75 & n., 77
& n., 78, 81, 107, 111, 114
Boyce, Boanerges R. (Bo Boyce) B. R.
Boyce): 127n., 148 & n., 149–50,
156, 163–66, 167n.
Boyce and Keen (ranchers): 127 & n.,
129
Bradbury, John: 51n.
Breckenridge, Colorado: ix, 77n., 80n.
Breckenridge, Henry M.: 51n.
Brulé Sioux: 35n.
Buchanan, President James: 134n.
Buckmaster (captured Confederate):
162–63, 167–68
Buckskin Joe (mining community): ix,
93 & n., 94
Buffaloes: 43, 44 & n., 45–49 & n., 58,
70n., 105
Buffalo grass: 32 & n., 70n.
Bull Run, Battle of: 94 & n.

Cacti: 32 & n.
California Gulch: ix, 92 & n., 118 & n.;
see also Leadville, Colorado
Canby, Colonel E. R. S.: 156 & n., 157
Canon City, Colorado: 90–91 & n., 133

181

Cantrell, John: 3n.
Carpenter, C. C.: 3n.
Carrington, John Hawkins: 55, 56
Carson, Kit: 75 & n.
Cerro Gordo, Battle of: 35n.
Chacuaco Creek: 167n.
Cherokee Indians: *viii*
Cherokee-Russell Expedition of 1858: *viii*
Cherry Creek: *viii*, 3, 6 & n., 7 & n., 8
Cheyennes: 17n., 24n., 27n., 58n., 62n.
Chintzes (chinch bugs): 29 & n.
Chivington, Major John M.: 132n.
Choctaws: 19
Civil War: *ix*, 57n., 86; news of, 118; enlistments in, 120; Colorado in, 120 & n., 132 & n., 133 & n., 156n.; sides taken in, 132; Hicklin activities in, 134–38
Claim jumping: 76 & n.
Clear Creek: *vii*
Colorado: *viii*, 120n.; in Civil War, 120n., 132n., 133n., 156n.
Colorado City, Colorado: 68 & n.; *see also* Colorado Springs, Colorado
Colorado gold rush: *x*, 3n.; *see also* gold discoveries
Colorado Springs, Colorado: 67n.
Colorado Territory: 74
Comanches: 21, 24 & n., 27n., 37, 61
Confederates: *ix*, 132n., 145n.; at Mace's Hole, 133–34, 136; recruiting methods of, 138; *see also* Rebels
Conner, Daniel Ellis: *vii*, *ix*, 3n., 13n., 16n., 21n., 24n., 31n., 32n., 36n., 37n., 44n., 53n., 57n., 58n., 59n., 60n., 63n., 65n., 98n.; in Joseph Reddeford Walker party, *ix*, 75, 168; en route to Pikes Peak, 10–69; on Indian character, 19–20; in Miner's District, 74–84, 92; on hunting expedition, 84–90; at Georgia Gulch, 108–24; at Jefferson, Colorado, 127–32; at Mace's Hole, 133–46; at Pikes Peak recruiting camp, 147; at R. B. Boyce ranch, 148–49; as ranch hand,
151–58, 162–65; leaves Colorado, 165–68
Cooke, B. A.: 24, 55, 77
Cooks Canon: 156 & n., 162
Council Grove, Kansas: 13, 14 & n., 15 & n., 16, 35 & n., 57
Cow Creek: 20 & n.
Crittenden, John J.: 157 & n.

"Dead Man's Hollow," incident at: 119 & n.
Deer: 58, 88 & n., 89 & n.
Defrees, Wilkes: 118n.
Delaware Indians: 13n., 17
Denver, Colorado: *xiii*, *ix*, 4, 8, 86, 134, 139 & n., 155–57
Diamond Spring: 15 & n., 17n.
Dotson, Peter K.: 134 & n., 135, 138, 150–53, 162, 165–66
Dotson's station: 134–39 & n., 149–51, 165
Duels: 121–24

Eagles: 59 & n., 60
Easter, John: *viii*
Elk: 70, 71 & n.

Fairplay, Colorado: *ix*, 70n., 93 & n., 94, 98
Fall Leaf (Delaware Indian): *viii*
Farnham, Thomas: 51n.
Federals: 120, 121, 145, 148; investigation of Rebel activity by, 137; Rebels captured by, 149; *see also* Union troops
First Regiment of Colorado Volunteers: 132n., 156n.
Fontaine-qui-bouille (Fountain, Fontaine qui Bouille Creek): 67 & n., 68 & n., 69, 84
Fort Bliss, Texas: 132n.
Fort Garland: 7n., 87 & n., 137, 139, 142, 144–46, 153
Fort Laramie: *viii*, 6n., 35n; Treaty of, 24n.
Fort Lyon: 56, 57 & n., 62 & n., 146–

47, 149; *see also* Bent's Fort (New Bent's Fort)

Fort Pierre: 35n.

Fort Union: 87 & n., 134, 149, 156

Fort William: *see* Old Bent's Fort

Fort Wise: 57 & n.; *see also* Fort Lyon and Bent's Fort (New Bent's Fort)

Fountain City, Colorado: 68n., 134n.; *see also* Pueblo, Colorado

Fowler, Jacob: 68n.

Fox Indians: 17n.

Frémont, John C.: 75 & n., 76n.

French, Adnah: 8 & n.

Fur trade: 57n., 139n., 168

Georgia Gulch: 83 & n., 98 & n., 99, 100 & n., 107, 108 & n., 109, 111, 113, 116n., 117, 120, 124, 133

Gilliland, F. G.: 103, 104 & n., 105

Gold discoveries: near Pikes Peak, *vii*; at Clear Creek, *vii*; on Ralston's Creek, *viii*, 6n.; on Cherry Creek, *viii*, 3, 4n., 6–8; in South Park, *ix*, 70n.; on Cripple Creek, *ix*; in Rocky Mountains, 6n.; Tarryall diggings, 72n.; Gold Run, 80 & n.; in Georgia Gulch, 83 & n., 100 & n., 108 & n.; in Humbug Gulch, 83 & n.; at California Gulch, 92n., 118n.; at American Gulch, 100; on Green River tributary, 103; on Gregory Hill, 118 & n.

Gold Run: 80 & n.

Gooseberries: 101 & n., 103

Gray, Jim: 167 & n., 168

Gray, Thomas: 29 & n.

"Great American Desert": 51 & n.; *see also* Great Plains

Great Bend: 33

Great Plains: 6, 32, 51 & n., 54n., 84, 167; soil of, 34 & n., 51, 52; buffalo on, 43, 44 & n., 45; climate of, 52 & n.

Great Salt Lake Valley: 6

Greenhorn River: 86 & n., 87, 88, 133, 135n., 162–63

Green River: 75 & n., 103 & n.

Gregory, John H.: 118n.

Gregory diggings: *ix*, 118

Grizzly bear: 80, 101–102 & n., 103–105, 110, 111, 113

Hamilton, Colorado (mining camp): 70n., 71 & n., 72, 92, 94, 98, 132

Hamilton, E.: 71n.

Hanover College, Hanover, Indiana: *vii*, 3n.

Harney, General William Selby: 35 & n.

Heffner, Colonel John: 134 & n., 136–37, 148, 152–53, 155

Henry, William, and Garrett, Alexander (grocers): 10 & n.

Hicklin, Alexander (Zan) (Old Zan) (Ole Secesh): 134, 135 & n., 136, 148, 156–57, 163–66; Civil War activities of, 134–38, 146, 153–54, 154–56; idiosyncrasies of, 138–46

Hicklin ranch house: 135n.

Hicklin's station: 156

Higginbottom, Joseph ("Buckskin Joe"): 93n.

Highfield, Mr. (Georgia gold miner): 83 & n.

Holladay, Ben: 5n.

Huerfano Butte: 89 & n.

Huerfano Creek (Huerfano River): 87, 88 & n., 89, 148, 156, 163–64, 167

Humboldt River: 115 & n.

Humbug Gulch: 83 & n.

Independence, Missouri: 14n.

Indians: *viii*, 13 & n., 16 & n., 17 & n., 22, 27 & n., 28 & n., 30–31, 33, 43ff., 55, 56, 70n., 81, 90, 121, 162, 168; character of, 19, 20, 25; gibberish of, 31 & n.; travel of, 47–48 & n.

Jackson County, Missouri: 14 & n., 28

Jackson diggings: *ix*

James, Dr. Edwin: 51n.

Jefferson, Colorado: 98 & n., 124, 126–27, 132–33

Johnston, Albert Sidney: 134–35 & n.

Jones, Jack (William McGaa): 139 & n., 140–45
Jones and Haskell (storekeepers): 118
Joseph Reddeford Walker and the Arizona Adventure: ix, x, 168

Kansas City, Missouri: 21
Kansas River: 35n.
Kaw, or Kansa Indians: 16n., 35–36 & n.
Kelly, David: 163, 167
Kicking Bird, Chief: 37n.
King, Elmore Y.: 3n.
Kiowas: 17n., 21, 24 & n., 27n., 37 & n., 61
Kitchen, C. W.: 91n.
Kitchen and Company, Leavenworth, Kansas: 91

La Glorieta Pass, Battle of: 132n., 156n.
Las Animas River: 148n., 167 & n.; *see also* Purgatoire River and Picket Ware River
Lawrence, Kansas: *viii,* 7n., 13 & n.
Leadville, Colorado: *ix,* 92 & n., 118 & n., 119 & n.; *see also* California Gulch
Leavenworth, Kansas: *vii,* 3–7, 10, 24, 71n.
Leavenworth City: *see* Leavenworth, Kansas
Lincoln, Abraham: 14 & n., 57, 58 & n.
Lion, Rocky Mountain: 77 & n., 79n., 106
Little Blue River: 35n.
Little Cottonwood Creek: 20 & n.
Little Thunder (Sioux): 35n.
Long, Major Stephen H.: 51n., 65n.
Long's Peak: 65 & n.
Long Toms: 100 & n.
Lopez expedition to Cuba: 157 & n.
Lost Spring: 16, 17 & n., 20 & n.
Lyon, Brigadier General Nathaniel P.: 57n.

Mace, Juan: 86n.
Mace's Hole, Colorado: 85–86 & n., 87,

136, 146–47, 149, 153–56, 162–63, 167; Rebel regiment at, 133–34, 136–38, 148; description of, 133–34; recruiting methods for, 138; regiment disbanded, 147–48, 150
Madison, Captain George T.: 144–45 & n., 150, 163
Mangas Coloradas: *x*
Manitou Springs, Colorado: 68n., 85n.
Mexicans (laborers): 137–38, 154
Mexican War: 35n., 134n.
Military road: 87 & n., 134, 149
Miner's District: 74, 76, 77, 79, 81, 83, 90–91
Minié guns: 57 & n.
Mormons: 6 & n., 134–35 & n.
Mosquito Range: 71n.; *see also* Snowy Range
Mountain Meadows, Utah: 76n.
Mountain sheep: 128–30 & n.
Muddy Creek: 86 & n., 87

N. B., Mr. (wagon master): 21 & n.
Navaho Indians: 27n.
New Mexico: 84, 87, 90, 132, 156–57, 166
Nuttall, Thomas: 51n.

Old Bent's Fort: 57n., 62, 63n., 76n.
"Old Tahoson" (Indian chief): 37 & n.
"Old Mack" (saloon and hotel keeper): 95–98

Panther: 79 & n.
Parkville, Colorado: 116 & n.
Pawnee Fork: 32 & n., 33 & n.
Pawnee Rock: 32 & n., 33–34
Pawnees: 27n.
Peacock, George: 36n.
Peat, peat bogs: 114 & n., 115
Pheasants: 103 & n.
Picket Ware River: 148 & n., 149, 166–67 & n.: *see also* Purgatoire River and Las Animas River
Pike, Zebulon Montgomery: *vii,* 41, 51n., 67n., 70n.
Pikes Peak: *vii, viii,* 4 & n., 5, 6 & n.,

11, 35ff., 62, 63 & n., 65, 67 & n., 68–69, 84, 85 & n., 138
Placer mining: 70n.
Platte River: 3
Plumb Buttes: 20 & n.
Prairie dogs: 44, 45, 54 & n.
Ptarmigan: 103n., 127n.
Pueblo, Colorado: 34n., 67 & n., 68 & n., 84–86, 133, 134n., 149
Purcell, James: 70n.
Purgatoire River: 58n., 167n., *see also* Las Animas River

Rader, David: 101
Ralston's Creek: *viii*, 6n.
Rampart Range: 70n.
Raton Mountain: 149, 167
Rattlesnakes: 44, 58, 60 & n.
Rebels: 120–21, 148–49, 153–55, 163, 167–68; Mace's Hole regiment of, 133, 148; enlistment of, 133; Fort Garland seizure planned by, 146–47; regiment disbanded, 147–48, 150; *see also* Confederates
Reynolds, Jim: 93n.
Richards, John: 3n.
Ridgely, Missouri: *vii*, 3, 4 & n.
Rister, Carl Coke: 44n.
Rocky Mountain News: 149 & n.
Rocky Mountains: *vii*, 4, 6 & n., 7n., 8, 20, 23ff., 26, 28 & n., 31ff., 34ff., 35ff., 62, 63, 65, 67 & n., 75, 77, 78, 83, 84, 86, 98, 129–30, 148–49, 166–67; Mace's Hole in, 133; storm in, 158–61
Russell, Major: 5 & n.
Russell, William Greeneberry (Green Russell): *viii*, 4n., 7 & n., 28
Russell Gulch: *ix*

Sac Indians: 17n.
Sage, Rufus B.: *vii*
St. Charles River: 85 & n.
Salt Lake City, Utah: 134, 135n.
Santa Fe, New Mexico: 21, 162
Santa Fe Trail: 14n., 17n., 20n., 21n., 36n.

Satanta (Kiowa Chief): 36n., 37n.
Second Regiment of Colorado Volunteers: 133 & n.
Seminole War: 35n.
Shiloh, Battle of: 135n.
Shoshonis: 27n.
Sibley, Colonel Henry Hopkins: 132 & n., 145, 150, 156–57, 162 & n.
Silver fox: 109 & n.
Silver ore: 92n.
Sioux: 24 & n.
Slough, Colonel John P.: 132n.
Smith, Josiah: 68n.
Snowy Range: 70 & n., 71–74, 83, 92, 98, 117, 129
Soda Springs: 68 & n., 60 & n., 85 & n.; *see also* Manitou Springs, Colorado
Southern Cheyennes: *see* Cheyennes
South Park, Colorado: *ix*, 7n., 69, 70n., 71 & n., 83n., 91, 126, 128, 132–33
South Platte River: *viii*, 24n., 65n., 70n.
Sowers, John: 157 & n.
Spanish Peaks: 65 & n.
Squirrels: 87, 88 & n.
Stampedes, cattle: 40 & n.
Stevens, W. H.: 92n.
Sumner, Colonel E. V.: *viii*, 87n.
Swan River: 77 & n., 83, 109, 115, 116 & n.
Swans: 109 & n.
Sweeny, Oliver: 102

Taos, New Mexico: 7 & n., 87n., 168
Tappan, Lieutenant Colonel Samuel F.: 132n.
Tarryall, Colorado: *ix*, 70n., 72n., 93n.
Tarryall Creek: 71n.
Teel, Major Trevanion T.: 162n.
"Tepee Buttes": 34n.
Texas: 90, 128, 132n., 155, 168
Texas Revolution: 134n.
Travois, description of: 27 & n.

Union troops: *ix*, 145n.; *see also* Federals
Utah Territory: 74 & n., 116, 134n.
Ute Pass: 70n.

Utes: 27n., 68n., 70 & n., 82 & n., 87n.,
   119, 120 & n., 141 ff.

Val Verde (Valverde), Battle of: 156
   & n., 162 & n.
Vazquez: *see* Clear Creek

Waddell, Major: 5 & n.
Walker, Joseph Reddeford: *ix*, 75 & n.,
   76 & n.; joined by Daniel Ellis
   Conner, *ix*, 168
Walnut Creek: 20n., 21 & n., 32 & n.,
   35, 36 & n.; incident on, 36–37 & n.
Washington Gulch: 118 & n., 119, 120;
   see also California Gulch

Weston, Missouri: 6 & n.
Whiting, Major Charles: 87, 137,
   146–47
Whortleberries: 103 & n.
Wilson's Creek, Battle of: 57n.
Wind River Mountains: 75n.
Wise, Governor Henry A.: 57n.
Wolves: 44 & n., 53 & n., 58; white,
   116 & n.

Young, Brigham: 6n., 116
Young, Valorious (Valarious) W.:
   8 & n.
"Young Tahoson" (Indian chief):
   37 & n.